D1228370

Do Not Neglect
Hospitality

Do Not Neglect
Hospitality

The Catholic Worker
and the Homeless

Harry Murray

Temple University Press
Philadelphia

Temple University Press, Philadelphia 19122
Copyright © 1990 by Temple University. All rights reserved
Published 1990
Printed in the United States of America

The paper used in this publication meets the minimum
requirements of American National Standard for Information
Sciences—Permanence of Paper for Printed Library Materials,
ANSI Z39.48-1984 ⊗

Library of Congress Cataloging-in-Publication Data
Murray, Harry, 1951–
Do not neglect hospitality : the Catholic worker and the homeless / Harry Murray.
p.   cm.
Includes bibliographical references.
ISBN 0-87722-726-8 (alk. paper)
1. Church work with the homeless—United States.   2. Hospitality—
Religious aspects—Catholic Church.   3. Catholic Church—United
States—Charities.   I. Title.
BX2347.8.H63M87   1990
261.8'325'0973—dc20   90-32825
                                                                  CIP

Contents

Acknowledgments   *vii*

1   Hospitality as Social Relationship   *3*

2   Hospitality in Cross-Cultural Perspective   *25*

3   Catholic Worker Hospitality   *49*

4   The Flagship: St. Joseph's in New York City   *88*

5   In for the Long Haul: St. Joseph's in Rochester   *127*

6   A House of Penitents: The Mustard Seed in Worcester   *161*

7   Personalist Hospitality versus Professional Service   *211*

8   Societal Implications of the Catholic Worker   *253*

Notes   *261*

Bibliography   *269*

Index   *279*

Acknowledgments

Professor Lou Kriesberg once told me that "ninety percent of creativity is bad memory." There is probably little in this book that truly originated with me. The bibliography acknowledges those who taught me by their writings; this section acknowledges those who taught me by their lives.

The members of my dissertation committee provided both intellectual guidance and examples of commitment to social justice. Bob Bogdan, the chair, taught me a style of social research that I have found to be far more human and valid than the quantitative approach. Long before he joined the committee, Jerry Berrigan introduced me to the political side of the Catholic Worker movement and provided inspiration for my first stumbling efforts at civil disobedience. Barry Glassner helped to make my approach to qualitative methods more philosophically rigorous and introduced me to Edmund Husserl and Alfred Schutz. Lou Kriesberg introduced me to exchange and conflict theories. David Edelstein shared his knowledge of the labor movement. Manfred Stanley steered me in some very fruitful directions, especially with his suggestion to explore the anthropological literature on hospitality.

Special thanks goes to Phillip Runkel, the archivist at the Catholic Worker Archives at Memorial Library, Marquette University, for his generous assistance and advice. His knowledge of, and commitment to, the Worker is impressive.

I am grateful for several institutional sources of support: the Charlotte W. Newcombe Foundation and the Woodrow Wilson National Fellowship Foundation for the Doctoral Dissertation Fellowship awarded to me in 1984; Syracuse University for the fellowships awarded me in 1981 and 1983; and Nazareth College for the summer grant awarded me in 1989.

Michael Ames of Temple University Press and two anonymous reviewers helped me to improve (and shorten) the manuscript considerably.

It is impossible, partially for reasons of confidentiality, to thank all of the men and women with whom I lived at the Catholic Worker houses in this study. They treated me with a hospitality that cannot be adequately repaid. They are, almost without exception, persons struggling to live honestly, faithfully, and lovingly. A number have become friends. Some might justly be called saints. I would especially like to remember Alice Erwin, who died a few years ago. She was a great lady.

I can mention some of the recent Workers at St. Joseph's House in Rochester since they were not there at the time of my study. Marilyn Pray, Kathleen Ross, Carolyn Hagstrom, Mike Ruggiero, John Hart, Mike Affleck, Mary Rose McCarthy and many others have continued the work of the house and I have been privileged to work with them since my return to Rochester in 1986.

I would also like to thank the members of the Syracuse Catholic Worker community, who introduced me to Catholic Worker life and whose friendship I will always cherish—Bill Cuddy, Paul Collier, Ron Jaworski, Dick and Mary Keough, Barbara Major, Ray McVey, Henry Nicollela, Mike Sullivan, Ed Whiteside, and many others. Mike and Henry have been a daily presence in the lives of the Syracuse homeless for nearly two decades. Their work has an importance that far transcends my own.

Many others contributed support over the years. Joe DeFrancisco, a fellow graduate student, deserves more than a word of thanks for the support and ideas he gave me—but that's all he will get here. My coworkers at Nazareth College, Lynn Slowik and Kay Valentine, have given me a great deal of encouragement.

My parents, Harry and Betty Murray, and my in-laws, Dick and Helen Simmons, have provided every type of support imaginable. Finally, I would like to thank my wife, Marianne Simmons, and my sons, Thomas and Colin, for their love. It means more than I can say.

Do Not Neglect Hospitality

1

Hospitality as Social Relationship

Several months ago a Catholic Worker friend was invited to speak at the Cornell University School of Hotel Administration about his fifteen years of experience with the homeless. The class that he addressed, entitled "Housing and Feeding the Homeless," was designed to "train selected students on how best to feed and shelter the estimated 2 million Americans who are homeless" (Kaff 1988). According to James Eyster, one of the teachers, "we believe that the skills we teach for the hospitality industry, which caters to the tastes of the affluent and comfortable, should be made available to people less fortunate than ourselves" (in Kaff 1988). Upon returning, my friend wondered whether in a few years he would be found unqualified to feed and shelter the homeless because he hadn't had the "necessary" technical training.

The Hotel School, where I ate a number of excellent meals while a student at Cornell, is not alone in its newfound concern with the homeless. Numerous professionals, including lawyers, doctors, nurses, psychiatrists, architects, and various human-service practitioners, have discovered the problem of homelessness over the past few years and have moved to apply their technical skills to the problem. The skills they bring to the issue vary widely, from designing better buildings for shelters (including live-in boxes) to creating new mental-health outreach programs. They do, however, share at least one assumption—that homelessness can be addressed best by a rational approach of setting goals, designing techniques to achieve those goals, and training people in those techniques so that they can go out and solve the problem.

This assumption is so basic as to go practically unnoticed. Since the time of Max Weber, sociologists have recognized that progressive rationalization is one of the key societal trends in the course of

Western history (Weber 1978; Stanley 1978; Bendix 1962). Within the last century, one of the most prominent aspects of that trend has been the proliferation of professions. Witnessing the success of the medical profession, numerous fields have moved to professionalize—to establish licensing, training programs, and so forth. Although the manifest rationale for such professionalization is that the problem that the field addresses requires technical expertise, many scholars have argued that a primary motivating factor is the search for power and status (Conrad and Schneider 1978; Szasz 1974; Freidson 1970; Starr 1982). Professionalization generally increases the power of practitioners and organizations in the field. Once professionalization has been achieved, the field then moves to expand its power by moving into new areas.

Thus, the movement of the various professions into the arena of homelessness prevention and cure in the wake of the "discovery" of the problem in the 1980s can be explained not only in terms of a manifest desire to help but also in terms of a latent desire to expand professional power by moving into a new area. The professions that succeed in becoming recognized as essential to the solution of homelessness will be able to expand their training programs into a new area.

For over half a century, the Catholic Worker movement has advocated and practiced a different approach to the problem of homelessness—that of personalist hospitality. Helping the homeless is not a task reserved for those with professional training. Rather, it is something that anyone can do—simply by practicing the ancient tradition of hospitality—of welcoming the stranger into one's house and providing him or her with food, shelter, and companionship. For this task one needs no special training; it lies well within the competence of any member of a human community. Indeed, training hinders the practice of hospitality, since it gives the trainee predefined categories into which to fit one's clients, and such a categorization process destroys the openness toward the stranger that is a requisite of hospitality in the traditional sense.

The Catholic Worker approach, while providing an important corrective to professional approaches to the problem of homelessness, has broader implications. It is, in essence, an attack on the application of rationalization to human problems. It declares that some areas of life should not be subject to rationalization—that, although the accomplishment of some tasks might be marginally improved by conceiving of the task in rational terms and applying the most effective techniques, these gains are outweighed by the loss of humanity, of the human touch. In the terms of Martin Buber, rationalization of human relationships transforms the I–Thou relation into an I–It relation, making it nearly impossible to perceive the other in the fullness of his or her personality. It is an argument that humans, and human interactions in particular, are not entirely subject to rationalization and the rule of technique—that, in Marcel's (1950) words, there is an element of mystery to the person that can't be rationalized. It is thus an argument against the application of techniques to the "helping relationship." As such, Catholic Worker philosophy merges nicely with the analysis of the dehumanizing effects of the technocratic approach in human-service organizations described in the literature on "street-level bureaucracy" (Lipsky 1980) and "people-processing organizations" (Hasenfeld 1977).

It is also a cry for reempowerment of the untrained person. As professions proliferate, the scope of activities that a nonprofessional feels competent to perform narrows. One feels incompetent to help someone who is having emotional problems unless one is a trained psychiatrist or counselor. One can't raise one's children competently without a degree in child development. And on and on. What the Catholic Worker position implicitly argues is that any member of society is capable of performing many of the tasks now claimed by various professions simply by virtue of being socialized. It is an attempt to reclaim basic areas of human social interaction for the nonspecialist.

Before I go any further in discussing the implications of Worker hospitality, however, it seems wise to acquaint the reader with both the Catholic Worker movement and my own experience with it before I began to study it as a sociologist.

The Catholic Worker movement

The Catholic Worker began as a monthly newspaper of the same name, founded in 1933 by Dorothy Day and Peter Maurin. Their purpose was to present a Catholic answer to the Communist *Daily Worker* by disseminating Catholic social thought, especially as embodied in the papal encyclicals and the European philosophical movement known as personalism. The paper sold for a penny a copy and provided extensive coverage of union activities, accounts of life in urban slums, and reports on Southern lynchings and other social issues, as well as more theological and philosophical articles. Socially, it advocated positions of pacifism, syndicalism, voluntary poverty, anarchism, and agrarianism. Theologically, under Dorothy Day it was conservatively Catholic, emphasizing such traditional concepts as the Mystical Body of Christ and the Works of Mercy. The paper quickly gained a national circulation among Catholics, rising from 2,500 in May 1933 (the first issue) to 35,000 in May 1934 and 110,000 in May 1935 (Roberts 1984, 179).

From the start, the publishers shared Dorothy's New York City apartment with homeless guests (whom Peter often dragged in with him) and fed those who came to the door. These efforts soon evolved into a breadline and "House of Hospitality." Catholic Worker houses and farms, based loosely on the New York model, sprang up throughout the United States. The popularity of the movement grew until World War II, when its pacifist stance alienated many supporters. Popularity resurged during the Vietnam era, when the Worker became a focal point of Catholic resistance to the war. Dorothy Day died in 1980 (Peter died in 1949), the *Catholic Worker* still sells for a penny a copy, and Worker houses now exist in over sixty cities.

Catholic Worker houses usually adopt three major activities: hospitality (the provision of free food, clothing, and shelter, usually in skid-row areas); direct nonviolent protest against social injustice; and publication of newspapers and newsletters. The hospitality involves actually sharing one's own home with the poor: full-time volunteers live in the houses and, in the "richer" houses, may receive a $10 or $20 per week stipend. The houses receive no institutional funding (from either the government, private foundations, or the Catholic church) and have no paid staff.

The movement has played a crucial role in the development of the Catholic left in the United States and in the recent concern of the Catholic bishops with social issues. The Worker has profoundly influenced the work of Daniel and Philip Berrigan, Cesar Chavez, and Thomas Merton, and they in turn have contributed their thought to the *Catholic Worker* paper. Michael Harrington's influential book *The Other America* (1963), often credited with catalyzing the War on Poverty, drew heavily on his two years at the Worker house in New York City.

My Experience with the Worker

I first encountered the Catholic Worker in 1972, during my senior year at the College of the Holy Cross in Worcester, Massachusetts, in the course of making a retreat based on the *Spiritual Exercises* of

St. Ignatius. Two of my six fellow retreatants were young exstudents who had returned to Worcester to begin a Catholic Worker house. They were hoping after this retreat to rent a small storefront from which they could begin feeding children and offering clothes to people. I felt the idea was a bit bizarre—a strange way to spend one's life when there were so many important things to do. So when I graduated I went on to do one of those important things—earning a master's degree in city planning from Cornell. However, the idea of the Catholic Worker wouldn't go away. I began reading some of the literature, and some years later, in 1976, I met an old friend who was also becoming interested in the Worker, and we decided to visit the New York City house together.

I walked through the Bowery area, past abandoned warehouses and tenements, past bedraggled men lying in the gutter or leaning on the side of buildings drinking wine, until I got to St. Joseph's House on First Street. I arrived a little after the morning soupline had begun—I had missed connections with my friend Jim, so I had gone on alone. The house was a rather rundown five-story row house marked by a hand-painted sign, "The Catholic Worker." I had called the night before to ask if they needed help for the day and had been told, "Sure, come on down." However, when I got there, the line was already in progress and a big man who seemed to be in charge told me they didn't need any more help.

When I returned a bit later, Jim was sitting on a chair by the wall. There were about a dozen people in the room, which had several long tables, a stove, sink, and refrigerator in the back, and a clutter of stuff in front, which I was told was someone's TV repair workshop. (I would not decipher this until years later, as recounted in Chapter Four.) Everything in the room was old and worn, including many of the inhabitants.

An older man gave Jim a copy of the New Testament and asked him to read it to him. Jim read a couple of passages picked out by the old man. We took off our coats, laid them on the chairs, and started to walk around to talk to people. Except for the man who wanted us to read the Bible, we had been practically ignored. A young woman then came up and said, "Don't lay your coats there. You'll never see them again. Put them in here." She locked them in a small green cabinet by the kitchen area, talked to us a few minutes, and returned to her work of preparing the next meal.

There seemed to be no one in charge of entertaining bemused middle-class visitors. People came up, introduced themselves, and went on about their business. By the end of the day, both of us were utterly bewildered as to who was actually running the place. Some of the people were "obviously" clients, but it was rather unclear as to who was "staff." When I asked the people who were sitting around who they were, they replied, "We're Catholic Workers helping those people over there." The response became bewildering, for when I talked to "those people over there" they too replied, "We're Catholic Workers helping those people over there," and would point to the group I had just come from. It appeared that everyone identified themselves as Catholic Workers and others as clients. Everyone seemed free to create his or her own role, and everyone seemed happy with it.

Cockroaches abounded. At one point Jim moved to crush a particularly large one crawling across the floor. A young woman quickly came over and said, "Don't hurt them. They don't eat much."

After awhile, someone asked if we wanted to do something. We said sure and were sent up to the second floor to fold *Catholic Worker* newspapers. We were told that the paper is published nine times a year, with a circulation of 80,000. The Workers fold and paste mailing labels on the 80,000 copies by hand. In a room with several long tables pulled together, half a dozen people, old and young, clean and filthy, were folding papers in half for labeling, bundling, and mailing. I sat down next to a large, foul-smelling fifty-year-old woman. As we folded she kept up a running monologue about how she got an electric shock every time she made love. A young man across the table asked me, "How long can you keep listening to that crap?" After an hour or so of this we returned downstairs and helped chop onions for the evening meal.

At a Worker's suggestion we visited Maryhouse, where Dorothy Day lived, two blocks away. We were greeted at the door and shown into the chapel—a small, simply furnished room with a wooden altar—and told that Dorothy Day was sick and in her room. After a brief stay, we returned to St. Joseph House for a supper of liver and broccoli, shared with about fifty people. I was told that the morning soupline was for all who came, but that only some people were allowed in for supper.

After cleaning up from supper, a small group of about eight or nine gathered around one of the long tables for vespers, the evening prayer of the Catholic Church. I asked one man what had brought him to the Catholic Worker, expecting to hear a reply about high ideals. He said that he had been a Jesuit seminarian and had gone to the Worker farm at Tivoli after suffering a nervous breakdown. He had recovered there and was now helping out. Jim and I left after vespers to catch a subway home.

We decided that we needed a beer after the experience, so we stopped at a Greenwich Village bar. Our joint impression was one of craziness and anarchy such as we had never experienced before. Many of the people there had been apparently "mentally ill" (at least from our middle-class perspective). Jim reflected, "Those sad, sad people. I couldn't take it there." We debated about who actually ran the place—after an eight-hour visit, we had no idea who was actually "in charge." Things seemed to have been accomplished without anyone exercising authority.

A few months later, I decided to visit Unity Kitchen, a Syracuse Catholic Worker house, the closest to my home in Ithaca. I wrote them and got a letter back from one of the codirectors, which read in part:

> We are not really a Catholic Worker house. Both Unity Kitchen and Unity Acres were inspired by the Worker movement and St. Joseph's House in NYC but there is no effort on our part to spread the economic-social philosophy associated with the Worker. We all subscribe to personalist, non-institutional style hospitality to those in need. All Kitchen staff live together in a house located a few blocks from the Kitchen. Please feel free to come by anytime.

I visited the Kitchen one afternoon in March 1977, only to find the door locked and a dozen or so ragged-looking men standing outside. One of them tried to panhandle me, and I debated whether I really wanted to go through with it, but I knocked on the door and was let in. I was introduced to Henry and Peter, the codirectors, who were about my age and had been at the house for eight and six years, respectively. After receiving a brief tour of the ancient, four-story, former venetian-blind factory, I was given a ladle and allowed to dish out soup to the hundred or so guests who shuffled past me after picking up sandwiches and coffee.

After the soupline, I was invited to supper at Simon House, the staff residence. During supper, Peter asked me, "As long as you want to find out about the place, why don't you work the dorm tonight?" Horace, one of the "auxiliary staff," laughed and exclaimed, "Are you kiddin'? Those guys will eat him alive."

Spurred on by that challenge, I drove back to the Kitchen at 8:00 P.M. and was met by Andy, who volunteered there once a week.

We prepared coffee and donuts, then lugged them up to the second-floor dormitory and opened the side door so that the men could come in. There were about thirty beds but we accepted any man who came to the door, so when the beds were filled latecomers slept on chairs or on the floor. No one was turned away before the doors were locked at 11:00 P.M. unless he had been barred for fighting or drinking in the building. I worked until 11:00 P.M., when someone came on to replace me.

I began to work the "early shift" one night a week with Andy and started to get to know some of the guests. Bearpaw, a tall, gentle old man, claimed to have been a lumberjack in his youth. John was a Vietnam veteran who spoke in what seemed to be poetry and had a burning rage within. One passerby reported that he had "punched a truck" one morning as he came out of the dorm after his duffle bag had been stolen. Mark was a lanky young man who perched himself on a chair like a bird and bounced up and down. He told me he had been committed to a mental hospital in the Midwest. When I asked him what for, he grinned and said "unnatural behavior." However, my most vivid memory was of the night when one of the men admired Andy's sweater and complained about the poor quality of clothes in the clothing room. Andy pulled off his sweater and gave it to the man, saying, "Here, do you want it?" I left thinking, "The sweater off his back! This is real Christianity!"

A few months later I learned that three of the regular "staff" were leaving, and I decided to quit my job and join the Kitchen staff. The very next night that I worked I received my first black eye while breaking up a fight between two young guests, one of whom had smuggled a bottle of wine into the dormitory. Henry told me, "I guess you're a real Worker now."

Moving into Simon House gave me a much more complete view of the Kitchen. In addition to operating the free dormitory, we held lunch and supper souplines (except in the summer, when we had only the 4:00 P.M. meal) and generally served between 60 and 120 persons. A few women came in for the soupline, occasionally accompanied by children, but the vast majority of the guests were men. They ranged in age from eighteen to eighty-four; most were either black or white, although there was a sizable number of Native Americans as well. Most were alcoholic or had a history of mental hospitalization.

Meal guests would begin to congregate around the door half an hour before we opened up. One of us would "take the door," opening it at 4:00 P.M., and then stand by it throughout the soupline to keep out those who were barred and to keep them from attacking those who were coming in the door. We refused food to no one. Those who were barred for breaking one of the two rules of the Kitchen—no fighting and no drinking—were given a "bag lunch" to go. People were served "cafeteria style," going along the counter and getting coffee or tea, sandwiches and soup, then carrying it to a table. We had no trays, so it often required a balancing act to get everything to the table intact, particularly if someone was "three sheets to the wind."

The typical day was busy, especially since there were only three full-time Workers. In the morning, one of us would go to City Police Court to see if any of the "Kitchen men" had been arrested and, if the crime had been nonviolent, to plead his case before the judge and possibly get him released to our custody. The morning was usually spent picking up donations or doing repair work. Except for our one day off a week, we had to work both souplines. After a break for supper, one or two of us would return to open the dormitory. Many nights, the dorm was staffed by volunteers, but two of us had to serve as "backups" every night in case volunteers didn't show up. Spare time was taken up in visiting men we knew in hospitals and prisons, in moving people who could not afford a mover, in doing various favors for our guests, and occasionally even in some public relations speaking to various groups, although most of this was handled by Ann, a middle-aged woman who coordinated volunteers and donations.

We asked no questions of our guests. One of our cardinal rules was not to pry into someone's personal history unless she or he volunteered the information. Someone could eat and sleep in the dorm for years without anyone knowing more than his or her first name (and it could be months before we learned even that). Thus, guests were free to tell their story or to remain anonymous. They did not have to interact with the staff on a personal level unless they chose to.

As a consequence, the spirit of the Kitchen was one of acceptance. As one helper told me, the Kitchen was the one place in the city where someone could go without having to justify his or her presence. It was also a place where everyone who came got some help—without interrogation or questionnaires. As one guest told me, "At agencies, you go and wait in line and then they tell you they can't help you. Here, at least you know you'll always get an onion." (Thanks to the donation of about half a dozen fifty-pound bags every week by an onion distributor, we never refused onions to anyone

who asked. And for many, the fact that they were given something—
and were not simply turned away—was more important than what
they were given.)

Although there was an ethic of acceptance, there was not strict
equality. There were three categories of persons at the Kitchen—
staff, guests, and a middle category known as auxiliary staff, consisting of guests or former guests who worked at the Kitchen. There
was no standard role for auxiliary staff; rather, each person carved
out a niche for himself or herself. One man cleaned the dorm every
day but exercised no authority over guests. Others did exercise some
authority over guests and even worked the dorm at night. Some auxiliary staff lived in the Kitchen dorm; others slept downstairs in the
dining room, away from the rest of the guests; still others had their
own rooms or apartments in the neighborhood.

It did not take me long to discover that there was a great deal of
internal conflict. Ann and Peter felt that the Kitchen should begin
to exclude people, should "grow smaller to serve the hidden Christ,"
and should be more selective in terms of who we allowed to join us
as staff. They argued that the lines had grown too long, the dorm too
crowded, the atmosphere too violent. Henry insisted that the Kitchen
continue to feed and shelter whoever came to the door—that this
was the call of the Gospel. I sided with Henry. The argument had
been going on for years but came to a head while I was there.

In 1978 Henry left to run the Chicago Catholic Worker house (St.
Francis's), citing "irreconcilable differences" about what is a Christian way to run the Kitchen. Fortuitously, a young exseminarian
named Ron joined the staff at this time. He sided with me on the
ideological issues and we continued the battle for a year before deciding that we could not prevail against the seniority of Ann and Peter.
We both left the Kitchen shortly thereafter.

The Kitchen changed substantially. Even while Henry was there,
we stopped going to court every day, simply for lack of person-power.
When Ron and I announced that we were leaving, the decision was
made to close the dormitory. (I later heard that the decision had been
described as being "led by the Holy Spirit." I was at the meeting and
had heard only a discussion of lack of workers.) A week or two before we actually left, the Kitchen abandoned its "cafeteria style" of
serving meals and began a sit-down style in which guests were served
by waiters. Shortly after we left, the Kitchen began to require that
guests make reservations for meals and limited the number served
to one hundred. The rest of the people were simply turned away. At

first they allowed people to "fill in" if someone with a reservation hadn't shown up; later, however, they decreed that no one without a reservation would be served even if there were extra places.

A year or two later an even more drastic change was made. A list was published of twenty-four persons who would be served at the Kitchen. They had been "chosen by the Holy Spirit," or so the rumor went. All others were turned away. Ann and Peter publicized their action and called for other churches to "take up the slack." The dinner changed from soup and sandwiches to full-course meals with candles on the table. Even for the twenty-four, however, it was limited to six days a week rather than seven as in the old days. As one rather angry former Kitchen director put it, "I guess the true Christian ideal is to serve surf-and-turf to one person once a month." As Dorothy Day once wrote, "So we take whoever comes to us as sent by God and do not believe in picking and choosing. If we start eliminating then there is no end to it" (1970, 23).

With each of these changes, the Kitchen lost old-time supporters and volunteers. On the day they decided not to "fill in" the spaces of reservations who hadn't appeared, one of the volunteers quit on the spot and invited the excluded guests to his home for a cookout. Another, after asking why they had chosen twenty-four and being told, "That's a Biblical number," responded, "Well, five thousand is a Biblical number too." Nonetheless, new volunteers came, and the Kitchen continues as of this writing. Indeed, although I disagree with Ann and Peter's policies, I do admire their perseverance. My couple of years as a Worker pale beside the length of time they have been doing hospitality.

Old-time Kitchen workers and volunteers moved on to other activities, such as Pax Christi, Jail Ministry, HELP (a business that employees exoffenders), the Catholic Worker on Wheels, and numerous other projects. Henry and Mike (a former Kitchen worker who had also gone to Chicago) opened the Oxford Inn, a free shelter for homeless men under the auspices of Catholic Charities. Although never calling the Inn a Catholic Worker house (since it used government money), they have managed to run it in the style of the old Kitchen dorm since December 1979. (Only recently has the funding agency put pressure on them to do "intake forms.") Many ex-Kitchen workers, myself included, flocked to do volunteer work there. (See Murray 1986 for a description of the Inn.)

The whole experience left me embittered for a number of years. However, it also left me with a sociological puzzle. All of us had come to the Kitchen presumably inspired by the Catholic Worker ideal of hospitality. (We certainly received no material reward for it, unless you consider $10 a week and a room in a decrepit, cockroach-ridden house "material reward.") Yet we had widely different notions of what hospitality was as a daily practice. It was this experience that inspired me to return to graduate school in sociology and begin a study that would give me some clue as to how people in other Catholic Worker houses conceived of and "did" hospitality. My quest for understanding led me not only to do participant observation at three other Worker houses, but also to examine the practice of hospitality and its importance in our own and other cultures.

The Role of Hospitality in Society

Two thousand years ago, the Letter to the Hebrews exhorted, "Do not neglect to show hospitality to strangers, for thereby some have entertained angels unawares" (Heb. 13:2). A hundred years later, Tertullian listed hospitality as one of the three marks of the church. An ancient Jewish proverb reflects a similar attitude: "Hospitality to strangers is greater than reverence for the name of God."

When I used the Syracuse University library computer to search for books about hospitality, I found thirteen that had the word in the title. All dealt with the hotel industry. That fact in itself says volumes about the status of hospitality in our society. Hospitality is no longer a virtue; it is an industry. Or so it would seem.

On the face of it, hospitality in the traditional sense seems so atrophied that it should be treated simply as an anachronism. One could argue with Robert Goodin (1985, 35) that hospitality no longer plays any important role in contemporary Western culture. Hospitality is no longer important, Goodin argues, because travel is no longer very dangerous. Further, one might argue, current norms relegate non-commercial hospitality to the periphery. A "normal" traveler pays for his or her "hospitality" at the local hotel or motel with a credit card. A traveler who pays in cash is perhaps slightly unusual, but still acceptable. But a traveler who has no way to pay for hospitality is assumed to be deviant, undoubtedly poor, and probably dangerous. As one Catholic Worker noted, if one of the apostles whom Jesus had commanded to "take neither scrip nor purse" wound up in a modern American city, he would wind up sleeping on a park bench or, at best, in a crowded city shelter. The custom of hospitality is outmoded, a quaint holdout from primitive society perhaps, but of no functional value in contemporary America.

Such an analysis, however, seriously underestimates the role of hospitality in our society. Many social services perform hospitality to a greater or lesser extent. Halfway houses come to mind immediately, as do Travelers' Aid and the Red Cross. However, hospitals of all descriptions perform hospitality in some sense, since they provide food and shelter in addition to other services. Mental hospitals in particular often provide shelter to those who would not otherwise have it. Viewing these institutions from the perspective of a model of hospitality raises crucial questions. What is the difference between a halfway house with a live-in staff and one with rotating eight-hour shifts? Does the fact that in the former the staff shares their home with the clients while in the latter they do not have any effect on the quality of the operation? Why is the hospitality function of the hospital and mental institution subordinated to the therapeutic function, and should there be more of a balance between the two? When institutions deal with "hopeless cases," why do they conceive of their function as "warehousing," to create a "back-ward" system for "storing" such persons, rather than conceiving of their function as providing hospitality? It is only when we have a model of hospitality that we can begin properly to analyze such questions.

Moreover, there are numerous social movements that have norms of hospitality quite at variance with those of mainstream America. These range from the anarchistic openness of the countercultural crash pads (Berger 1981) to the gentle yet structured means for handling visitors of the Bruderhof communities (Zablocki 1971). A comparison of hospitality practices of different social movements may provide an enlightening dimension to social-movement theory, particularly in terms of how hospitality relates to recruitment.

Hospitality has also been at least one response to the problem of refugees. One needs only look at how the village of Le Chambon, led by the nonviolent pastor André Trocme, sheltered Jewish refugees from the Nazis to realize that hospitality still performs functions crucial for the survival of human dignity (Hallie 1979). One may also look at how individuals provided refuge to Jews in Berlin during the Nazi reign (Gross 1982) to come to the same conclusions. Looking at the United States, one has the examples of the Underground Railroad and the recent efforts of church groups to help resettle Southeast Asian refugees. Finally, one must view the current Sanctuary movement, in which churches are harboring Salvadoran and Guatemalan refugees who face deportation if caught by the Immigration and Naturalization Service, as a prime example of hospitality to refugees (MacEoin 1985; Bau 1986; Golden and McConnell 1986). Such responses to refugees can be better understood through a model of hospitality.

Finally, personal hospitality in the traditional sense is not dead in the United States. During the six months in which I began writing this book, I came across two examples that totally revised my rather negative attitude toward hospitality in our society.

The first occurred just after the birth of my son. Thomas was born five weeks premature and had to be fed by the gavage method, which involved placing a tube down his throat into his stomach. We were told that he would have to remain in the hospital indefinitely so that the nurses could feed him. Through our midwife, we were put in touch with a nurse who knew gavage. She offered to let us come and stay in her house with the baby while she gavaged him and taught us the technique. We eagerly accepted and for over a week lived in an upstairs room in her house while she, in addition to taking care of her own two children, gavaged Thomas every three hours around the clock until we were confident that we could do the procedure ourselves. She and her husband were gracious hosts, sharing their meals with us and refusing to even consider payment for all their efforts. The experience was particularly enlightening for me because these gentle, gracious people were members of the Moral Majority, a group I had been trained to consider hopelessly authoritarian and inconsiderate.

The other example was brought to my attention through my involvement with the Sanctuary movement. We were contacted by a young couple that was looking for help for a teenage Guatemalan refugee. The boy had arrived in their city with only a few dollars in his pocket. He told them he had had only enough money to take the bus as far as that city. He then walked to a church, found it closed, and began knocking on doors. Theirs was the first door he came to. They took him in and gave him hospitality while they called around to find who could help him on a long-term basis. He lived with them for almost two weeks while we, the persons who had publicly declared our willingness to give sanctuary, figured out what to do for him. They had had no knowledge of the Central American issue; however, even after they learned that what they were doing was illegal, they continued to shelter the boy simply because he was a human being in need of hospitality.

The notion of hospitality can also be useful for sociological and political theory. Hospitality has direct relevance to the question of the relationship between rights and group membership (Durkheim 1958; Walzer 1983). Hospitality is the preeminent social form in which rights are specifically created for nonmembers of the group. Hence, no theory of rights and membership can ignore the practice of hospitality.

In recent years, particularly under the influence of Henri Nouwen, a number of theologians have become interested in the topic and have employed hospitality as a metaphor for a variety of other forms of human activity: spirituality, education, the family, and healing (Nouwen 1975); morality (Ogletree 1985); ecumenism (Thiesen 1976); and seminary education (Nouwen 1972).

In short, the model of hospitality upon which the Catholic Workers have based their houses is a form of social relationship that has wide relevance even in modern Western society. Before considering examples of its even greater importance in nonindustrial societies, I must try to specify more precisely what I mean by hospitality.

The Concept of Hospitality

Although its form differs greatly between cultures, hospitality can be defined as a relationship of two social roles—host and guest. Further, it is a relationship that is both voluntary and noncommercial. This definition excludes two social practices that have been referred to at times as "hospitality."

The first of these is commercial hospitality. As I use the term, hospitality is never sold. Reciprocity may be involved; for instance, hospitality may be reciprocated when the host travels to the guest's home, or the guest may present a gift to the host. Money, however, changes the essential character of the interaction. Commercial hospitality is to true hospitality what prostitution is to sexual love. I say this not in a derogatory sense but rather in an analytical sense, following Simmel's (1971, 121–26) analysis of prostitution and of the way in which money changes the essential character of a social relation. Perhaps the clearest demonstration of the effects of money on hospitality is Tec's (1986) comparison of paid and unpaid rescuers of Jews in Nazi-occupied Poland.

Also excluded are cases in which hospitality is forced upon the host by threat of physical violence; for example, the traditional military practice of billeting soldiers in the homes of conquered peoples. Even when the term is used in this context, there is usually an implicit recognition that this is not true hospitality. Thus, when the CIA advised its Contra terrorists to "give a declaration of gratitude for the 'hospitality' of the population," their quotation marks implicitly acknowledged their cynical misuse of the term (Central Intelligence Agency 1985, 55). Similarly, I will not treat the *recet,* the medieval obligation to receive one's feudal lord as a guest in one's home (Duby 1988, 24–25), as hospitality.

Hospitality can best be described in terms of the rights and obligations of host and guest, where those roles are assumed voluntarily and without monetary payment. The host generally has an obligation to receive the guest into his or her home and to treat the guest with respect, cordiality, and generosity. Hospitality is always done in a friendly, caring spirit—otherwise, one is not "hospitable." Although the role of the "gracious host" is often a formal requirement of the norm of hospitality, most cultures appear to distinguish between a host whose hospitality is genuine and one whose hospitality is a front. The Norse sagas, in particular, emphasize the theme of the treacherous host.

Implicit in this aspect of the host's role is the obligation to be receptive in the additional sense of being open to hear the guest's story. The host's role is to learn from the guest rather than to attempt to change the guest. Both Henri Nouwen and Parker Palmer contrast hospitality with the attempt to change the other. "Hospitality, therefore, means primarily the creation of a free space where the stranger can enter and become a friend instead of an enemy. Hospitality is not to change people, but to offer them space where change can take place" (Nouwen 1975, 51). "Hospitality means letting the stranger remain a stranger while offering acceptance nonetheless. . . . It means meeting the stranger's needs while allowing him or her simply to be, without attempting to make the stranger over into a modified version of ourselves" (Palmer 1985, 68).

The host must also allow the guest to remain in some sense a stranger, must accept that she or he will not fully understand the mystery of this other person. This perception of the guest as mysterious is reflected in the identification of guests with the divine or supernatural in many preindustrial cultures. There is also an implicit commitment on the part of the host to protect the guest. The host's home is a place of refuge for the guest. This obligation is particularly prominent in tribal and Islamic hospitality; however, it also plays an important role in Catholic Worker hospitality.

A special social role is created for the guest, who assumes the rights but usually not the duties of a household member. The duties of the guest are often somewhat limited—confined to expressing gratitude, telling stories, or giving a promise of future reciprocation. The guest is often expected to be a bearer of gifts, although these gifts may be quite intangible and unexpected (Koenig 1985, 6). The social role of the guest may, and sometimes does, change if she or he becomes an extended guest. If a guest stays for more than a few days in some societies, she or he is then required to assume the duties of a household member.

The ideal type of the guest is the stranger whose other social identities are unknown to the host except insofar as there are visible clues or the guest chooses to tell his or her story. Moreover, the guest is a particular type of stranger—one who comes today and goes tomorrow, who is not a member of the host's group and has no aspirations to join or even to remain for an extended period.[1]

Hospitality is not always restricted to the unknown stranger, however. The guest may have statuses that are known by the host, in which case hospitality tends to merge into other forms of social relationship: if the guest is poor, hospitality blends into charity; if a trading partner, into business relations; if a relative, into kinship duty; if a representative of another society, into diplomacy; and so forth. Perhaps the most intriguing aspect of the relationship between host and guest is the imbalance of obligations and rights. The powerful host, it would seem, has almost all the obligations; the vulnerable guest, almost all the rights.

Because the roles of host and guest are temporary, hospitality is distinguished from other forms of social relations by its intermediate time frame. It requires a certain investment of time, not precisely specified, but neither too much nor too little. At the lower end of the time continuum (an action that takes only a few seconds or minutes), one must speak of gift-giving rather than hospitality. It is only as the time stretches into hours or days that one begins dealing with hospitality proper. However, at some indeterminate point of duration, in most cultures one would no longer speak of hospitality. A guest who remains for weeks, months, or years usually must be adopted into the group.

The fact that the roles are temporary implies that they are reversible—one's host may later become one's guest, and vice versa. This reversibility lends a certain equality to the relationship. Indeed, in Latin and Greek, the same word is used for guest and for host (Koenig 1985, 7–9; Koenig 1987, 470–71).

The role of host is almost universally only a partial role. A host must simultaneously play other roles (e.g., householder, house-keeper, spouse, parent, laborer) because she or he is still located within his or her own society. Since the guest is uprooted from his or her society, the guest role may be the sole status by which she or he relates to others.

Intriguingly, the roles of host and guest are rarely divided into subtypes, other than the moral distinction between the good or bad guest (or host) and the distinction between poor and rich guests that prevails in some cultures. Since hospitality is an unspecialized task, it does not require intricate subdivisions of the statuses of host and guest (as compared with more specialized practices that have evolved out of it, such as diplomacy, with its intricate collection of statuses and titles).

Hospitality and Rehabilitation

The distinctiveness of hospitality as a form of social relationship can be illustrated by contrasting it with Parsons's well-known model of the physician–patient (rehabilitative) relationship. The contrast can be seen most clearly by contrasting the social role of guest with patient, and of host with physician.

According to Parsons (1951, 439–47) the role of sick person entails four expectations: (1) the person is exempt from normal social-role responsibilities, (2) the person must be taken care of, (3) the person must want to "get well" and rejoin society, and (4) the person must seek technically competent help. The sick role, thus, is designed for a person who must step out of his or her normal social role through no fault of his or her own as long as the person wishes to return to the normal social role by getting the proper technical assistance. In contrast, the ideal-typical guest (1) is also exempt from normal social-role responsibilities, (2) must be taken care of (although to a lesser extent than the sick person), (3) must not want to enter the society of the host, and (4) has no need of "competent technical help." The guest role, then, is for a person who is not of the society of the host but is merely "passing through." Both sick role and guest role lie at the fringes of society; however, the former is for a temporarily incapacitated member of the society, while the latter is for a temporarily present nonmember.

The contrast between the role of the physician and the role of the host also reveals sharp differences. Both stand as mediators between their society and their patient or guest. However, the physician mediates between society and one of its members, while the host mediates between society and a nonmember.

According to Parsons (1951, 58–67, 454–65) the role of physician entails expectations that the physician (1) treat all who need his or her services, (2) will have achieved his or her position through training, (3) deal with only specific problems, (4) remain affectively neutral, and (5) be oriented toward society rather than motivated by self-interest.[2] The host similarly is expected to receive those who need hospitality and not operate out of pure self-interest. However, the role of the host is not as specific as that of the physician since the host may be called upon to respond to a wide variety of needs. Furthermore, the host is expected to display positive emotions toward the guest. Finally, one needs no training to be a host.

The contrasts between the roles of host and healer, and of guest and patient, point to profound differences between hospitality and medicine as models of human relations. This contrast is far from trivial. The medical model currently is not confined to the medical profession, narrowly defined, but rather dominates the field of social services (e.g., Conrad and Schneider 1978). Since most social services have a hospitality component in some sense, the hospitality model provides an alternative approach to conceptualizing human services.

Hospitality and Rationalization

The contrast between hospitality and Parsons's model of the physician–patient relationship is of special significance if one treats Parsons's model as a paradigm of the type of relationships that are demanded by the increasing rationalization of modern society.

Since Max Weber's prophetic warning of the closing of the "iron cage" of industrialism and rationalization, there have been innumerable analyses of the human effects of rationalization and such related trends as industrialization, technicalization, secularization, bureaucratization, and professionalization (e.g., Weber 1978, 1985; Ellul 1964; Martin 1978; Stanley 1978). Most have concluded that, although such trends have produced many benefits, they also pose a grave threat to the very human-ness of human beings. In the area of human relationships, this threat is particularly evident in the trends toward bureaucratization and professionalization.

Although some theorists have emphasized the conflict between bureaucracy and professionalism, others have noted that the two are in many ways complementary because both are forms of rational organization of human activities (Larson 1977, 178–80, 190–99). In particular, both bureaucracy and professionalism emphasize efficiency and technique in human relationships. Because of this emphasis, they share three common approaches to human relations, approaches that place them in stark contrast to the model of hospitality.

In the first place, both assert the need for specialized training, including, where the object of activity is a human, training in how to interact with other persons. Human relations within the bureaucracy or profession, then, become techniques that can be taught and that are designed to achieve particular objectives.

Second, both emphasize the need for impersonality. Neither the bureaucrat not the professional is supposed to allow emotions, prejudices, or personal reactions to a client to interfere with applying the proper interpersonal techniques to manipulate the client. In Parsons's terms, they are to be affectively neutral or, what may be even worse, "supportive" in an impersonal sort of way.

Third, both bureaucracy and professionalism tend to objectify the person, in the sense that they abstract certain qualities from the client in order to place him or her into a category that can be acted upon. Efficient treatment does not allow one to be receptive to the "whole person" of the client; only those traits that are deemed "relevant" to the task at hand can be attended to. "One can think of technique only in terms of categories. Technique has no place for the individual; the personal means nothing to it. . . . Technical procedures, therefore, abstract from the individual and seek traits common to masses of men and mass phenomena" (Ellul 1964, 286).

These three approaches run counter to the approach of hospitality. In most cultures, hospitality is not an activity that requires special training—anyone can be a host (even if one's home is a steam grate). The notion of an impersonal host contradicts the very meaning of "hospitable." Finally, the attitude of receptivity to the story the guest brings is rather difficult to maintain if one's task is to classify the other for bureaucratic or professional processing—if one is trained to abstract certain elements from the story as the only "relevant" information a client offers. (This conflict is illustrated by Scott's [1981, 77–79] analysis of service agencies' use of the term "the presenting problem," an indication that what the client says is wrong is only a facade, behind which the agency will find the "real problem.")

Thus, the more bureaucratized or professionalized an activity becomes, the less hospitable it becomes. This tendency is shown quite clearly in Roy Lubove's (1977) account of the professionalization of social work between 1880 and 1930. The movements out of which social work grew—"friendly visiting" and the settlement houses—both emphasized certain elements of hospitality. The early settlement-house movement, particularly as represented by Jane Addams, emphasized both personal contact with the poor and a hospitable openness to foreign cultures and values (Addams 1910). Although the primary emphases of settlement houses were education and social reform, they did at times practice hospitality in its literal sense of taking in the poor as guests (Addams 1910, 111, 118, 122; Trolander 1975, 18). Friendly Visiting Societies utilized a sort of hospitality in reverse, sending middle-class volunteers into the homes of the poor to give them moral uplift. Although Friendly Visiting was paternalistic and assumed the superiority of middle-class culture, it did emphasize personal contact between untrained volunteers and the poor (Lubove 1977, 1–21).

Emphasis on efficiency and the need to assert a specialized skill led social workers to reject "mere neighborliness" in favor of "social diagnosis," training, "disinterested service," and paid positions. Lubove summarizes some of the criticisms of the original settlement-house movement as follows:

> The settlement . . . was handicapped by its belief in residence as the key to neighborhood or social understanding. The assumption that one learned by absorption or immersion did not satisfy the student's desire for a ready-made helping technique such as charity organization and casework offered, and alienated those who wished to help the poor but not necessarily live with them. (Lubove 1977, 147)

By the 1930s, social work had largely become established as a profession, emphasizing special skills, training, and disinterestedness. The hospitality implicit in its origins had been effectively rooted out, characterized as "mere neighborliness," insufficient for the problems of modern society.

Hospitality is thus a form of social relationship, a definition of the situation, that stands in conflict with modern rationalized, bureaucratic, professionalized relationships. As such, it might be one way of attempting to recapture the capacity for truly human relationships, a capacity that so many of us fear is being lost. In order to investigate this question more fully, it is necessary to see how hospitality has been embodied in nonindustrial societies.

2

Hospitality in Cross-Cultural Perspective

Although hospitality appears to be an insignificant practice in Western industrial society, it has played a crucial role in many non-Western and preindustrial societies. This chapter will examine that role in several preindustrial societies, with special emphasis on the early Christian hospitality that the Catholic Worker movement cites as its main model. The chapter is not meant to be a systematic historical or cross-cultural analysis; I merely hope to provide enough detail on the practice of hospitality in some cultures to flesh out the more theoretical arguments of the previous chapter.[1]

Hospitality in Myth

Even a cursory examination of various traditions of mythology reveals a number of common themes concerning hospitality.[2] One of the most frequent themes is the divinity of the guest.

In both Greek and Norse mythology, the supreme god was associated with the stranger, and hence with hospitality. Odin "frequently appears as the one-eyed stranger, arriving when least expected" (Davidson 1964, 141). Zeus was the protector of the stranger: "Zeus is the avenger of all suppliants and strangers, Zeus patron of strangers, who accompanies venerable strangers" (Hocart 1955, 78). "As the eternal father of men, he was believed to be kindly at the call of the poorest and most forsaken. The homeless beggar looked to him as a merciful guardian who punished the heartless, and delighted to reward pity and sympathy" (Murray 1962, 38). In India, the guest was "compounded of all the gods" (Hocart 1955, 81). In the Fiji Islands, guests were considered "heavenly ancestors" (Hocart 1955, 82).

In a number of myths, the moral imperative of hospitality is re-vealed in strikingly similar ways. In a Greco-Roman myth, Jove and Mercury traveled in human form into Phrygia. There, presenting themselves as weary travelers, they were repeatedly refused hospi-tality until they came to the door of an elderly couple, Philemon and Baucis, who invited them in and provided the best meal their poverty could afford. When the wine ran out, it was miraculously re-plenished, revealing the visitors as gods. The visitors then flooded the inhospitable neighbors' houses and transformed the couple's house into a temple. Jove asked them what gift they would like. They asked to be made guardians of the temple and to be allowed to die together in the same hour. The wish was granted, and in the hour of their death they were transformed into two trees that stood side by side (Ovid 1958, 234–38).

The First Book of Kings relates the following story (17:10–15):

> So he [Elijah] arose and went to Zarephath; and when he came to the gate of the city, behold, a widow was there gathering sticks; and he called to her and said, "Bring me a little water in a vessel, that I may drink." And as she was going to bring it, he called to her and said, "Bring me a morsel of bread in your hand." And she said, "As the Lord your God lives, I have nothing baked, only a handful of meal in a jar, and a little oil in a cruise; and now, I am gathering a couple of sticks, that I may go in and prepare it for myself and my son, that we may eat it, and die." And Elijah said to her, "Fear not; go and do as you have said; but first make me a little cake of it and bring it to me, and afterward make for yourself and your son. For thus says the Lord the God of Israel, 'The jar of meal shall not be spent, and the cruise of oil shall not fail, until the day that the Lord sends rain upon the earth.'" And she went and did as Elijah said; and she, and he, and her household ate for many days.

The Cochiti Indians have a myth about Old Salt Woman, who came to Cochiti with her grandson and was refused hospitality at every house. In return, she turned all the children into chaparral jays. Then they went to Santo Domingo, where they were well treated and fed. On leaving, she said, "I am very thankful for being given food to eat," and she left some of her flesh—salt. From there they went to Salt Lake, first telling the Santo Domingans where she would be if they wanted any more of her flesh. This is why Indians must journey to Salt Lake for their salt (Erdoes and Ortiz 1984, 61).

In a Japanese folktale, a maid who gave a beggar a rice ball after the lady of the house had turned him away was given a towel that made her beautiful when she wiped her face with it. When the beggar returned a few days later, the lady of the house, hoping for a similar reward, entertained him and was given a red sash that turned into a snake after he left (Mayer 1984, 88).

Abraham and Sarah were visited one day by three strangers, for whom Sarah prepared a meal. The strangers told them that Sarah would bear a son even in her old age (Gen. 18:1–15).

In return for her hospitality, the prophet Elisha granted the widow of Shunem a son and then raised him from the dead (2 Kings 4: 8–37).

After Jesus' death, he appeared to two disciples on the road to Emmaus. They did not recognize him, however, until they had invited him to their house for a meal. "He was known to them in the breaking of the bread" (Luke 24:13–35).

In all of these stories a supernaturally empowered being appears as the stranger asking for hospitality. Those who give hospitality to the stranger are rewarded; those who refuse it often are punished.

In various cultures, then, the stranger is either a god in disguise or has a special relationship with a god. This theme of the stranger as supernatural is surely related to another common theme of "primitive" peoples—that the stranger has dangerous supernatural powers that must be negated by ritual. Frazer documents rituals for negating the magical power of the stranger in ancient Turkey, the South Pacific, near Mt. Kilimanjaro, Yorubaland, Madagascar, Borneo, Laos, New Guinea, and South America (1911, 101–5). Hamilton-Grierson notes that "as a general rule the savage fears and hates the stranger, and looks upon him, certainly as an enemy, and, it may be, as a being brutish, monstrous, or devilish" (1925, 884). He backs up his claim with numerous examples from the journals of early travelers.

Thus, in nearly all early societies, the stranger is regarded as a being with supernatural powers. The transition from a practice of excluding and killing all strangers to a norm of ritual hospitality appears to be accompanied by a transition from viewing the stranger as a being with malevolent powers to one who is a god or under the protection of a god, with the capacity to reward as well as punish. The identification of the guest with a god may be as much a reflection of the guest's vulnerability and need for divine protection (since she or he has no group to provide protection) as it is a reflection of the ancient belief in the guest's supernatural power.

The tales recounted above also concur in the assertion that hospitality is rewarded abundantly, that good hosts receive far more than they give. The stranger thus is both opportunity and danger. Hospitality to the stranger can end in a striking reversal of roles, in which the stranger is revealed as the true host (Koenig 1985).

This is not to say that the myths of all cultures treat hospitality in the same way. Norse myths and legends, for instance, dwell on the theme of the betrayal of the guest by the unscrupulous host as well as on the sanctity of the commitment of the host to protect the guest.

A thorough cross-cultural analysis of the treatment of hospitality in myth would prove extremely valuable. Even this cursory examination, however, reveals some important aspects of hospitality as a definition of the situation: the guest as opportunity and risk, the possibility of role reversal, the abundant reward from the gods given for hospitality to the stranger.

Hospitality in Foraging and Horticultural Societies

Reports of Western missionaries, explorers, and anthropologists reveal that behavior toward strangers in foraging and horticultural societies reflects the mythological views cited earlier. The stranger is a mysterious, often sacred being, to whom there are only two possible responses—killing or lavish hospitality. The killing of strangers seems to be confined to extremely isolated bands in which the stranger is held to be nonhuman. Less isolated groups usually have rituals to receive the stranger into hospitality.[3] Most Western observers have commented on the generosity of hospitality offered in such cultures. The early anthropologist Lewis Henry Morgan called hospitality "one of the most attractive features of Indian society" (1922, 318) and added: "Among the Iroquois hospitality was an established usage. If a man entered an Indian house in any of their villages, whether a villager, a tribesman, or a stranger, it was the duty of the women therein to set food before him" (1909, 838).

Anthropologists have established that hospitality performs several functions necessary for the survival of band and tribal societies. It serves as a means of keeping the peace between groups; Marcel Mauss depicts it as an early alternative to warfare (1967, 79). It also facilitates the spread of information and the establishment of trade, often through the creation of pairs of trading partners who offer hospitality to each other, the classic example of which is the Kula partnership described by Malinowski (1961), although here partners did not stay at the other's home. It enables groups to survive environmental disasters by finding temporary refuge with groups in less affected areas (Bodley 1983, 155). Within groups, it fosters social solidarity by lessening the gap between rich and poor (Sahlins 1972).

Although many social scientists, following Mauss (1967), have treated hospitality as a type of gift exchange, others note that hospitality is not always reciprocal, even given a very rough calculation of give and take (Pryor and Graburn 1980; Pryor 1977; Price 1975; Henry 1951). Pryor and Graburn have argued that the imbalance remains even if one accounts for such intangible rewards as gratitude and prestige in a multiple regression analysis.[4] In short, anthropological research has shown that hospitality plays a crucial role in the survival of foraging and horticultural societies and that such hospitality cannot be assumed to be a balanced form of social exchange.

Greek Hospitality

Hospitality in ancient Greece was an important social institution, flourishing in both personal and corporate forms. Travel was dangerous and strict norms of hospitality were one of the few protections for travelers. The liberality of hospitality in the heroic era is abundantly evident in the numerous encounters between Odysseus and a variety of hosts, most notably Nausicaa.

Personal hospitality was based on the notion of reciprocity, so strongly that Greeks used a single word (*xenos*) to mean either host or guest. One developed relations of hospitality-friendship with specific foreigners, whereby each would stay at the other's home when in his city. Stock (1925, 809) notes that this formal relationship had six attributes. First, it was extrapolitical, extending beyond the boundaries of the state, "and so was a beginning of the brotherhood of man." Second, it was reciprocal. He who was the guest one day expected to be the host on another occasion. Third, the relation was hereditary. One's father's hospitality partners became one's own. Fourth, it was inaugurated and accompanied by exchanges of gifts. Fifth, the relationship was signified by tokens that were broken in half, with each partner retaining a half. Thus, one could send a friend to enjoy one's partner's hospitality by giving him one's half of the token. Sixth, the relationship had the sanction of religion, being protected by Zeus. Stock also notes that the Greek custom enjoined the host to refrain from asking the guest any questions before he had been fed (1925, 810). Thus, hospitality was offered to strangers, usually with the expectation that a hospitality partnership would be established.

Corporate hospitality was an inverted forerunner of modern

diplomatic practice. Rather than sending a consul to represent a state in a foreign land, the state would recruit a citizen of the foreign state to look after its affairs in that country. The *proxeno*, thus, "was a person who undertook to look after the interests of a foreign State in his own" (Stock 1925, 810). Usually unpaid volunteers, these *proxenos* would both represent the foreign country and provide hospitality to emissaries from that country.

Roman Hospitality

The Roman system of hospitality paralleled that of the Greeks, even to the point of including Jupiter Hospitalis as the patron of strangers (Stock 1925, 808–12; Haarhoff 1948, 126). However, it was under the Roman Empire that commercial hospitality began to flourish (White 1968, 18–28). In conjunction with their superb system of roads, the Romans erected hospices to shelter official travelers. Alongside the road system there also sprang up for the first time a great number of inns. Although widely regarded as disreputable places, having more in common with the modern brothel than with the modern hotel, the Roman inns are regarded by at least one historian of "commercial hospitality" (White 1968) as the beginnings of the hotel industry.

Early Christian Hospitality

Since the Catholic Worker places itself within the Christian tradition, the role of hospitality in Christian societies is directly relevant to the study of Worker hospitality. A comprehensive study of this topic is beyond my reach. Fortunately, a good deal of social scientific attention has been paid to hospitality in early Christianity, the ideological source for most later forms of Christian hospitality and an important inspiration for the Workers. Therefore, early Christian hospitality will be covered in far more detail than any other form of traditional hospitality.

A sociological exploration of any topic in early Christianity must be highly speculative because little information is available. The primary data source for all such analysis is the New Testament. More peripheral data include noncanonical early Christian letters and tracts (such as the *Didache*) and information concerning the general social situation in the Hellenic world at the time. Nonetheless, even these rather speculative analyses are valuable in an attempt to ascertain the character of distinctively Christian forms of hospitality.

Early Christian hospitality was multifaceted, involving the reception of guests, commensality, and almsgiving. Before discussing the practice of hospitality in the early church, I will investigate the treatment of hospitality in the synoptic Gospels (Matthew, Mark, and Luke),[5] since the Gospel treatment of the topic may be presumed to have formed the ideological base for the actual practice of hospitality.

Hospitality in the Synoptic Gospels

In reading the synoptic Gospels, I was struck by the sheer number of times that hospitality was mentioned. Hospitality was an integral feature of the society in which Jesus lived, a fact that is reflected in the number of parables that concern or presuppose hospitality; for example, the marriage feast (Matt. 22:1–10; Luke 14:16–24), the friend in the night (Luke 11:5–8), and Lazarus and the rich man (Luke 16:19–31). More specifically, however, four themes emerge that relate hospitality to Jesus' ministry and the call of Christians.

The first is the theme that Jesus is one who regularly accepts hospitality. As an itinerant charismatic, he depends upon hospitality for his survival. Further, he accepts it from all types of people. He heals Simon's mother-in-law and she immediately serves him in her house (Mark 1:29–31 and parallels). He stays with Martha and Mary (Luke 10:38–40) and Zacchaeus the tax collector (Luke 19:5–10). He dines with Pharisees (Luke 11:37–38, 7:44–47) and with "tax collectors and sinners" (Matt. 9:10–13 and parallels).

Jesus gives his hosts advice about hospitality. When Martha complains that she is doing all the work of serving while Mary is listening to him, he responds: "Martha, Martha, you are anxious and troubled about many things; one thing is needful. Mary has chosen the good portion, which shall not be taken away from her" (Luke 10:41). When Simon the Pharisee, in whose house he was dining, complains that Jesus is letting a sinful woman wash his feet, he replies:

> Do you see this woman? I entered your house, you gave me no water for my feet, but she has wet my feet with her tears and wiped them with her hair. You gave me no kiss, but from the time I came in she has not ceased to kiss my feet. You did not anoint my head with oil, but she has anointed my feet with ointment. Therefore, I tell you, her sins, which are many, are forgiven, for she has loved much; but he who is forgiven little, loves little (Luke 7:44–47).

At first sight, these two tales seem contradictory—one slights the technicalities of hospitality, the other criticizes a host for ignoring them. Both affirm, however, that true hospitality must be a reflection of love for the guest.

A second theme is that Jesus gives hospitality. This theme is not nearly as pervasive as the first, since, as a wandering preacher, Jesus is rarely in a position to give hospitality. Perhaps the major example is the feeding of the five thousand (Mark 6 and parallels) and the related feeding of the four thousand of Mark 8. This familiar miracle story emphasizes the personal responsibility of the disciples to provide hospitality: "Now the day began to wear away; and the twelve came and said to him, 'Send the crowd away, to go into the villages and country round about, to lodge and get provisions, for we are in a lonely place.' But he said to them, 'You give them something to eat'" (Luke 9:12–13). And then he multiplied the loaves and fishes.

A third theme is that the disciples should demand hospitality. When Jesus sent the twelve disciples out to preach on their own, he commanded:

> You received without pay, give without pay. Take no gold, nor silver, nor copper in your belts, no bag for your journey, nor two tunics, nor sandals, nor a staff; for the laborer deserves his food. And whatever town or village you enter, find out who is worthy in it, and stay with him until you depart. As you enter the house, salute it. And if the house is worthy, let your peace come upon it; but if it is not worthy, let your peace return to you. And if anyone will not receive you or listen to your words, shake off the dust from your feet as you leave that house or town. Truly, I say to you, it shall be more tolerable on the day of judgment for the land of Sodom and Gomorrah than for that town (Matt. 10:8–15; see also Mark 6:7–11, Luke 9:3–6, and Luke 10:4–12).

The words of condemnation to the inhospitable in the above quotation lead us to the fourth, and perhaps the major, theme. Followers of Jesus are to give hospitality:

> He who receives you receives me, and he who receives me receives him who sent me. He who receives a prophet because he is a prophet shall receive a prophet's reward, and he who receives a righteous man because he is a righteous man shall receive a righteous man's reward. And whoever gives to one of these little ones even a cup of cold water because he is a disciple, truly, I say to you, he shall not lose his reward (Matt. 10:40–42; see also Matt. 18:5, Mark 9:37 and 9:41, and Luke 9:48).

One must, however, not restrict one's hospitality to followers of Jesus. It must include the poor:

> When you give a dinner or a banquet, do not invite your friends or your brothers or your kinsmen or rich neighbors, lest they also invite you in return, and you be repaid. But when you give a feast, invite the poor, the maimed, the lame, the blind, and you will be blessed, because they cannot repay you. You will be repaid at the resurrection of the just (Luke 14:12–14).

But the most crucial passage in the Gospels is the discourse on the Last Judgment in Matthew 25, in which Jesus states that the final judgment will be based on one's hospitality to the poor:

> Then the King will say to those at his right hand, "Come, O blessed of my Father, inherit the kingdom prepared for you from the foundation of the world; for I was hungry and you gave me to drink, I was a stranger, and you welcomed me, I was naked and you clothed me, I was sick and you visited me, I was in prison and you came to me." Then the righteous will answer him, "Lord, when did we see thee hungry and feed thee, or thirsty and give thee drink? And when did we see thee a stranger and welcome thee, or naked and clothe thee? And when did we see thee sick or in prison and visit thee?" And the King will answer them, "Truly, I say to you, as you did it to one of the least of these my brethren, you did it to me" (Matt. 25:35–40).

Similarly, those who did not respond to those in need are condemned (Matt. 25:41–46). Two points should be noted on this passage. First, one cannot help but be struck by the parallel with Isaiah 58. Given Jesus' knowledge of scripture, one must believe that he intentionally drew on that passage. Second, as many commentators have noted, it seems significant that the blessed do not recognize Christ in those they served. These two points lead to the conclusion that the passage advocates responding personally to all in need, not just Christians.[6]

In looking at the treatment of hospitality, several points emerge that can be profitably analyzed in the context of modern theories of social exchange. The first is the notion that good acts should not be performed in the hope of receiving a reward from others. Jesus is quite conscious of the nature of social exchange. Specifically, one must be hospitable without consideration of either explicit or implicit social rewards if one is to hope for reward by God.

> If you love those who love you, what credit is that to you? For even sinners love those who love them. And if you do good to those who

do good to you, what credit is that to you? For even sinners do the same. And if you lend to those from whom you hope to receive, what credit is that to you? Even sinners lend to sinners, to receive as much again. But love your enemies and do good, and lend, expecting nothing in return; and your reward will be great, and you will be sons of the Most High; for he is kind to the ungrateful and the selfish (Luke 6:32–35; see also Matt. 5:43–47).

Good deeds, done without thought of reward, store up treasure in heaven (e.g., the story of the Rich Young Man in Matt. 19:16–22 and parallels; also Luke 12:33). This general theme was reflected in Jesus' teaching on hospitality (e.g., Luke 14:12–14). In Blau's (1964) terminology, it could be thought of as a rejection of direct social exchange in favor of indirect "social" exchange in which the third party who rewards one's actions toward another is God. However, it is not at all clear that Jesus is advocating that one be generous in hope of receiving an eternal reward. Certain of the hospitality passages seem to indicate that the eternal reward will be given only if one acts without thought of reward (e.g., Matt. 25).

There is, however, another recurrent theme that stands outside of Blau's scheme. This is the assertion that one must be generous because one has benefited from the generosity of God. It is reflected in the statement given to the disciples before they were sent out on their mission: "You received without pay, give without pay" (Matt. 10:8). Also relevant here is the parable of the Wicked Servant (Matt. 18:23–35), in which the servant is punished because, after his master had forgiven him a large debt, he refused to forgive the debt of a servant who owed him money.

Intertwined with all of this is a belief in the value of the individual person, expressed perhaps most strongly in the parable of the Lost Sheep (Matt. 18:10–14; Luke 15:3–7). In the Lucan version, the parable is told in response to the charge that "This man receives sinners and eats with them."

Although these passages reject the notion of social exchange as a basis for hospitality, there are at least two passages that seem to endorse the notion of social exchange. In his charge to the disciples before their mission, Jesus affirmed that "the laborer deserves his food" (Matt. 10:10). And in the story of the healing of the ten lepers, Jesus became upset that only one of the ten had returned to express gratitude "to God" (Luke 17:11–19).

In sum, hospitality is a recurring theme in the synoptic Gospels. Jesus receives hospitality regularly and gives it on occasion. He commands his disciples to both give and receive hospitality. He rejects the notion that hospitality should be given in order to receive gratitude or other social rewards from either the guest or other persons. Hospitality is to be given because one has benefited from God's generosity. One's reward for hospitality will be given by God only if one is hospitable without thought of reward.

Two Christian practices apparently stemmed from the Gospel treatment of hospitality: commensality (eating together) and hospitality to strangers.

Commensality

Early Christians ate together as part of the ritual of the Eucharist or Lord's Supper. Unlike the modern Eucharist, this celebration involved a meal eaten together at the house of a wealthy member of the local community. In the course of the meal the ritual of the Eucharist, sharing bread and wine as the Lord's body and blood, would be practiced (Theissen 1982, 145–74; Bornkamm 1969, 127–30). The only detailed account of this celebration is contained in Paul's criticism of the Corinthian's conduct of the Lord's Supper (1 Cor. 11:20–34):

> When you meet together, it is not the Lord's supper that you eat. For in eating, each one goes ahead with his own meal, and one is hungry and another is drunk. What! Do you not have houses to eat and drink in? Or do you despise the church of God and humiliate those who have nothing? What shall I say to you? Shall I commend you in this? No, I will not (11:20–22).

After an intensive analysis, which included comparing this description with that of contemporary non-Christian communal meals and banquets, Theissen (1982, 145–74) concludes that the Corinthian meal was one in which the whole community, both rich and poor, gathered in the home of a wealthy church member to celebrate the sacramental Eucharist in conjunction with a communal meal. Food was provided by the rich of the community. He speculates that what Paul was complaining about was that the rich were providing only bread and wine for the poor, but bringing meat and perhaps other choicer items to eat with their peers, thus humiliating the poor and dividing the community. Theissen states:

> The core of the problem was that the wealthier Christians made it plain to all just how much the rest were dependent on them, dependent on the generosity of those who were better off. Differences in menu are a relatively timeless symbol of status and wealth, and those

not so well off came face to face with their own social inferiority at a most basic level. It is made plain to them that they stand on the lower rungs of the social level. (1982, 160).

The fact that Paul waxed so indignant at this practice indicates that this distinction between rich and poor was an aberration from the regular Christian practice. By implication, the normal Christian Eucharist was one in which the rich provided a meal for all in the community, rich and poor—all ate the same food without distinction. Theissen depicts the meaning of the Lord's Supper as follows:

> Bread and wine become something special in the Lord's Supper.
> They must be distinguished from other food. They have a numinous quality. If this is ignored, illness and death threaten. In 1 Cor. 10:17, Paul links a social goal with this notion of numinously charged ele-ments: "Because there is one bread, we who are many are one body." That means, quite realistically: Because all have eaten portions of the same element, they have become a unity in which they have come as close to one another as members of the same body, as if the bodily boundaries between and among people had been transcended. Dog-matically one may speculate in various ways about how bread and wine are transformed into the designated elements, but in any case a transformation of social relationships takes place. From a plurality of people emerges a unity (1982, 165–66).

In the Eucharist, then, all are united into one body, rich and poor. As a sign of this, the rich provide hospitality to the poor, sharing a meal with them without distinction of social class.

Receiving Guests

Counsels to practice hospitality occur in several New Testament letters. Rom. 12:13 states: "Contribute to the needs of the saints; practice hospitality." 1 Pet. 4:9 says in the same vein: "Practice hos-pitality ungrudgingly to one another." Heb. 13:2 is perhaps the most eloquent passage: "Do not neglect to show hospitality to strangers, for thereby some have entertained angels unawares."

In addition to these general moral exhortations, the New Tes-tament lists the practice of hospitality as a specific requirement for certain social types (e.g., bishops in Titus 1:8 and widows in 1 Tim. 5:10). Further, there are numerous accounts of missionaries being received hospitably in various cities (e.g., Rom. 15:28, 16:1; 1 Cor. 16:10; Phil. 2:29).

The admonition to practice hospitality is usually included in a list of good deeds that should be practiced by the Christian, widow, or bishop. When one combines the biblical passages with those of other early Christian writers (e.g., Hermas and Justin, as quoted in Riddle [1938]), one finds that the admonition to practice hospitality is often linked with other admonitions: to help the widow and orphan, to help the imprisoned, to avoid drunkenness, to love one another, to relieve the afflicted, or simply "to do good." Thus, hospitality is usually included in listings of "good works." For example, Hermas praises "bishops and hospitable persons who at all times received God's slaves into their houses gladly and without hypocrisy, and the bishops always ceaselessly sheltered the destitute and the widows by their ministration" (quoted in Riddle 1938, 142).

The first modern scholar to explore the social role of hospitality in early Christianity was Donald Riddle (1938). He observed that hospitality was often considered "a particular task of bishops and widows" (1938, 143), although it was enjoined upon all Christians. He further argued that, in addition to its charitable function, hospitality performed a crucial function in the spread of the Christian kerygma because it provided itinerant charismatic missionaries with food and shelter as they spread the gospel: "But early Christian hospitality was not limited to specialized functions with reference to poor relief, widows, and the persecuted. It is equally important that it operated in the dissemination of the gospel tradition" (1938, 145). Indeed, hospitality was so important that it developed "a virtually technical vocabulary" (Malherbe 1983, 96).

Riddle notes that early Christian churches were "house churches," that is, communities that met for worship in someone's house. Thus, hospitality, even in established churches, was carried on in someone's home, probably most often that of the person in whose house the community met. (For more on house churches, see Filson [1939] and Malherbe [1983].)

Riddle's basic argument was extended several decades later by Gerd Theissen, who distinguished two types of early Christian missionary: the "itinerant charismatic" and the "community organizer" (1982, 27–67). The itinerant charismatic was characteristic of early Palestinian Christianity, a wandering preacher who obeyed the Gospel injunction to take no provisions but to depend entirely on the hospitality of those to whom he gives the Gospel. These preachers, committed to voluntary poverty, were totally supported by the communities to which they preached, in a manner parallel to the itinerant Cynic philosophers (Theissen, 1977). Theissen argues that the original apostles, in contradistinction to the idealized account of Acts, did not reside permanently in Jerusalem but were wandering preachers who perhaps used Jerusalem as a "home base." The community organizers, on the other hand, were epitomized by Paul and Barnabas and were characteristic of a slightly later Christianity. These missionaries, although traveling from place to place as did the charismatics, worked for their living rather than depending on the Christian communities for support. Among this group in particular, the phenomenon arose of sending letters of introduction from persons known by the communities along with the missionary to ensure a hospitable reception.

Intriguingly, the bulk of our information about early Christian hospitality practices comes from debates about issues that arose in the day-to-day practice of hospitality. Thus, one learns about the debate between itinerant charismatics and community organizers only in Paul's defense of his practice of earning his own living, apparently against charges by itinerant charismatics that a true Christian missionary would make no provision for himself, but would depend on hospitality:

> This is my defense to those who would examine me. Do we not have the right to our food and drink? Do we not have the right to be accompanied by a wife, as the other apostles and the brothers of the Lord and Cephas? Or is it only Barnabas and I who have no right to refrain from working for a living? . . . If we have sown spiritual good among you, is it too much if we reap your material benefits? If others share this rightful claim upon you, do not we still more? . . . Do you not know that those who are employed in the temple service get their food from the temple, and those who serve at the altar share in the sacrificial offerings? In the same way, the Lord commanded that those who proclaim the gospel should get their living by the gospel. But I have made no use of any of these rights, nor am I writing this to secure any such provision (1 Cor. 9:3–15).

As Theissen notes (1982, 48), Paul has turned the obligation of missionaries to depend on hospitality into a privilege, twisting even the words of the Lord that he quotes. His defense, then, is that he has renounced a privilege, rather than violated an obligation. The important point is that his failure to depend entirely on hospitality called into question his apostleship.

Another problem is indicated by the Third Letter of John, as analyzed by Malherbe (1983). The letter is one of introduction, to Gaius from "the elder," asking him to give hospitality to Demetrius, apparently a missionary. The letter also complains of another Christian in the area, Diotrephes, who had refused hospitality to missionaries from the elder: "he refuses himself to welcome the brethren, and also stops those who want to welcome them and puts them out of the church" (3 John 1:10).

It is not clear what positions Gaius and Diotrephes held in the community or even whether they belonged to the same church. Malherbe infers that at least one group met in Diotrephes's house for worship, but does not feel that one can conclude that he was a bishop. His power to exclude persons from the church may have arisen simply from the fact that the church met in his home. Nonetheless, his refusal of hospitality to missionaries, which was evidently due to a combination of theological and personal reasons as well as, perhaps, a struggle for power with the elder, was bitterly resented by the elder as a violation of the Christian norm of hospitality.

The final problem with hospitality attested to in the early literature is that of missionaries who abused the hospitality of their hosts. This problem is mentioned most frequently, once in the New Testament and twice in other sources.

In 2 John (10), the elder writes: "If any one comes to you and does not bring this doctrine, do not receive him into the house or give him any greeting," thus advocating that hospitality be refused to false prophets. (This seems a bit ironic considering the fact that his main complaint against Diotrephes in 3 John is his refusal of hospitality to men whom he undoubtedly considered "false prophets.")

Lucian, in his satire "The Death of Peregrinus," tells the apparently apocryphal story of a wandering Cynic philosopher who decides to end his life literally in a blaze of glory—by jumping into a pit of fire after the Olympic games. For Lucian, this act, like the rest of Peregrinus's life, was motivated by a quest for popular acclaim. He paints Peregrinus as a scoundrel, murdering his father and seducing young boys, and as a charlatan. For our purposes, the story is of interest because it tells briefly how Peregrinus ingratiated himself with the Christians, becoming "second to that man they still worship today, the one who was crucified in Palestine because he brought this new cult into being" (Lucian 1962, 368).

Once Peregrinus was thrown in prison for being a Christian, he was constantly ministered to by the Christians:

> The efficiency the Christians show whenever matters of community interest like this happen is unbelievable; they literally spare nothing. And so, because Peregrinus was in jail, money poured in from them;

he picked up a very nice income this way. You see, for one thing, the poor devils have convinced themselves they're all going to be immortal and live forever, which makes most of them take death lightly and voluntarily give themselves up to it. For another, that first lawgiver of theirs persuaded them that they're all brothers the minute they deny the Greek gods (thereby breaking our law) and take to worshiping him, the crucified sophist himself, and to living their lives according to his rules. They scorn all possessions without distinction and treat them as common property; doctrines like this they accept strictly on faith. Consequently, if a professional sharper who knows how to capitalize on a situation gets among them, he makes himself a millionaire overnight, laughing up his sleeve at the simpletons (Lucian 1962, 368–69).

Upon his release, Peregrinus exploited Christian hospitality to ensure an easy life:

So Peregrinus took to the road a second time. For travel expenses he had the Christians—with them as his guardians there was nothing he had to do without—and he kept himself going this way for some time. Then he committed some sort of outrage against them, too—I think he was caught eating the things they're not supposed to—and since they would no longer have anything to do with him, he was hard up (Lucian 1962, 370).

Although a satire, clearly not written by an admirer of the Christians, the story does seem to confirm the picture of hospitality derived from early Christian sources as well as indicating that the problem of "false prophets" was widespread enough to come to outsiders' attention.

The third reference to the problem of giving hospitality to false prophets comes from the *Didache*, a document thought to have originated in the early second century (Richardson 1970, 161–66):

Welcome every apostle on arriving, as if he were the Lord. But he must not stay beyond one day. In case of necessity, however, the next day too. If he stays three days, he is a false prophet. On departing, an apostle must not accept anything save sufficient food to carry him till his next lodging. If he asks for money, he is a false prophet (11:4–6, in Richardson 1970, 176).

The *Didache*, then, presents a different prescription for hospitality than did 2 John. All missionaries are to be received hospitably. Only if their actions prove them false are they to be treated as false prophets. The theologically unsound prophet can be known by his abuse of hospitality.

The document continues by giving more general rules of hospitality, applicable to any stranger:

> Everyone "who comes" to you "in the name of the Lord" must be welcomed. Afterward, when you have tested him, you will find out about him, for you have insight into right and wrong. If it is a traveler who arrives, help him all you can. But he must not stay with you more than two days, or, if necessary, three. If he wants to settle with you and is an artisan, he must work for his living. If, however, he has no trade, use your judgement in taking steps for him to live with you as a Christian without being idle. If he refuses to do this, he is trading on Christ. You must be on your guard against such people (12:1–5, in Richardson 1970, 177).

Finally, the *Didache* speaks of the relationship between hospitality to the preacher and hospitality to the poor:

> Every genuine prophet who wants to settle with you "has a right to his support." Similarly, a genuine teacher himself, just like a "workman, has a right to his support." Hence take all the first fruits of vintage and harvest, and of cattle and sheep, and give these first fruits to the prophets. . . . If, however, you have no prophet, give them to the poor (13:1–5, in Richardson 1970, 177–78).

Hospitality in the Time of the Church Fathers

Another problem of hospitality apparently developed later and is mentioned by Jerome and Ambrose. This was the argument that voluntary poverty and hospitality/almsgiving were not compatible— that if one adopted voluntary poverty, or if one were simply poor, one no longer had the means to give to the poor and therefore was relieved of the responsibility. Ramsey discusses the response of the church fathers to this argument:

> Some people are accustomed, notes Jerome, to plead their own poverty when it comes to offering hospitality, saying that their narrow circumstances prevent them from so doing. Yet the Lord made it particularly easy to observe this word of his [Matt. 10:42], for he said not "hot water" but "cold water," lest a poor person should complain that he had no wood with which to heat the water. Ambrose confronts much the same spirit of resistance: "You insist that you are poor. [However,] your guest does not expect extravagance from you but courtesy, not a splendidly decked-out table but food ready to hand." "If perhaps you say that you have nothing, then be of a giving spirit," Peter Chrysologus tells his congregation in a sermon, "and the

means for giving will not be wanting. Put a stool out for your visitor, set your table, light the lamp. Provide graciously from what you have received" (1982, 236).

By the third and fourth centuries, hospitality had become largely a matter of almsgiving rather than support for missionary activity. The emperor Julian, in the fourth century, attributed the spread of Christianity in large part to its hospitality: "Why do we not notice that what has made godlessness [i.e., Christianity] grow is benevolence toward strangers and care for the graves of the dead and moral character, even if pretended? . . . The impious Galileans support not only their own poor but ours as well" (quoted in Grant 1977, 124–25).

The church fathers advocated hospitality and aid to the poor as a duty of Christians. Basil the Great states:

> That bread which you keep, belongs to the hungry; that coat which you preserve in your wardrobe, to the naked; those shoes which are rotting in your possession, to the shoeless; that gold which you have hidden in the ground, to the needy. Wherefore, as often as you were able to help others, and refused, so often did you do them wrong (quoted in Avila 1983, 50).

A major theme of the Fathers is that the poor are Christ. "Do you really wish to pay homage to Christ's body? Then do not neglect him when he is naked. At the same time that you honor him here [in church] with hangings made of silk, do not ignore him outside when he perishes from cold and nakedness" (Chrysostom, quoted in Walsh and Langan 1977, 131).

Chrysostom even puts words into Christ's mouth:

> It is such a slight thing I beg. . . . Bread, a roof, words of comfort. . . . Show at least a natural compassion when you see me naked, and remember the nakedness I endured for you on the cross. . . . I fasted for you then, and I suffer hunger for you now; I was thirsty when I hung on the cross, and I thirst still in the poor, in both ways to draw you to yourself and to make you humane for your own salvation (quoted in Walsh and Langan 1977, 132).

Chrysostom advocates setting a room aside for the stranger, a "Christ room":

> Make yourself a guest-chamber in your own house: set up a bed there, set up a table there and a candlestick. . . . Have a room to which Christ may come. Say, "This is Christ's cell; this building is set apart for him." Even though it is just a little insignificant room in the

basement, he does not disdain it. Naked and a stranger, Christ goes about—all he wants is shelter. Make it available even though it is as little as this (quoted in Walsh and Langan 1977, 132).

Augustine is quite emphatic that hospitality must be practiced in a context of justice:

A certain exploiter of the property of others says to me, "I am not like that rich man. I give love-feasts, I send food to the prisoners in jail, I clothe the naked, I take in strangers." Do you really think that you are giving? . . . You fool. . . . You must grasp the fact that when you feed a Christian, you feed Christ; when you exploit a Christian, you exploit Christ. . . . If then he shall go into eternal fire, to whom Christ will say, "When naked you did not clothe me"? What place in the eternal fire is reserved for him to whom Christ shall say, "I was clothed and you stripped me bare?" (quoted in Walsh and Langan 1977, 133).

In evaluating the thought of the fourth and fifth century Latin fathers, Ramsey (1982, 251–59) notes that they emphasize the giver rather than the receiver:

Almsgiving in the time and place that we are studying it is characterized less as a work whose motivation is the alleviation of social ills than as a profoundly spiritual exercise. So it is that its thrust is rather heavily donor-centered: it confers benefits on relationship to Christ, makes Christ his debtor, opens heaven to him, and earns him the prayers of the poor. Regularly the value to the giver is emphasized (1982, 252).

The poor are depersonalized in their thought. Even their identification with Christ tended to rob them of their existence as persons:

Rarely, it seems, do the poor themselves take on a personality in the writings of this period. They exist—so it is frequently stated in one way or another—for the sake of the rich, to offer them opportunities for beneficence or to test them. . . . One might suggest that the very concept of the identification of Christ and the poor, at least as some of the Fathers develop it, tended to work against the poor by wallowing them up in him. . . . Augustine replies . . . "Let no one think that the one whose hand is seen is the one who accepts; he accepts who ordered you to give" (1982, 253).

This observation echoes Simmel's (1971, 153–54) comment that performing charity in order to assure one's own salvation depersonalizes the poor recipient.

Ramsey also notes, however, that the Fathers do acknowledge a certain reciprocity between the rich and the poor. By their gratitude and, more importantly, by their prayers, the poor could repay the rich. Indeed, their spiritual repayment was infinitely more valuable than the mere material goods they were given (1982, 257–59).

In sum, hospitality in the early church was closely intertwined with both charity to the poor and the spread of missionary activity. By the fourth century, hospitality had become increasingly a means of aiding the poor. Hospitality was not generally conceived as exchange except in three senses: first, hospitality to missionaries was an exchange for their work in spreading the Gospel; second, hospitality was rewarded indirectly—by God—rather than directly by the guest; third, hospitality and almsgiving could be rewarded directly by the prayers of the guest for the host.

The emphasis on personal hospitality persisted for several centuries. Yet by the fourth century hospitality had become largely a specialized institution presided over by bishops. This century saw the creation of the hospital, the first Christian institution for hospitality. The first hospital was established by the hermit Ephraim in Syria in A.D. 370 to relieve victims of a famine. The rich of the city gave him the resources to create it after he lambasted them in a sermon for their callousness (Bonet-Maury 1925, 804). In Constantinople some three decades later, John Chrysostom established seven specialized hospitals: the *Xenodochium*, an inn for travelers; the *Nosocomium*, for treatment of acute illness or injury; the *Lobotophium*, a shelter for cripples and invalids; the *Orphanotrophium*, a home for orphans; the *Gerontotrophium*, a home for the elderly; the *Ptochotrophium*, a home for the reception of the poor; and the *Pandochium*, a refuge for the destitute (Bonet-Maury 1925, 805). Thus, less than four centuries after the death of Christ, Christian hospitality had been rationalized into a number of specialized functions.

In Western Christianity, hospitality was thus divided into two major functions: hospitals, primarily for the sick and injured, which were administered by the bishops; and hospices for travelers, which were administered by monasteries (Bonet-Maury 1925, 805; Greer 1974). The Benedictines played a particularly important role in the latter and have traditionally acknowledged hospitality as one of their special functions (Winzen 1974; Benedict 1975). Over the centuries, these institutions became increasingly specialized and increasingly aimed toward therapy rather than hospitality per se. (The extent to which this was true for the Benedictines is revealed in Coffin's [1988] analysis.)

Islamic Hospitality

The traditional hospitality of the Semitic tribes was affirmed and elaborated upon by Islam, both in the Koran and in later theological elaborations. Islamic hospitality involves both the sharing of food (Margoliouth 1925, 797) and the granting of protection (Koenig 1987). Sharing food makes the guest a temporary family member and invokes the protection of the host. Three of the Islamic terms most closely associated with hospitality (*djiwar, dakhil,* and *idjara*) have connotations of protection. The word for guest, *dayf,* (like the Greek *xenos*) also means host, indicating an awareness of the interchangeability of such roles.

Islamic hospitality is limited in time: "In the case of the ordinary guest the relationship so established lasts two days and the intervening night, called by the Arabs three days, supposed to be the period during which the food remains in the body" (Margoliouth 1925, 798). A saying attributed to Mohammed runs, "Hospitality is three [days]; all above that is charity." Thus, hospitality is distinguished from charity, even though both may involve the giving of food. Hospitality is offered to a stranger or traveler; charity, to the poor.

The only extant ethnography devoted primarily to the study of hospitality concerns an Islamic tribe, the Swat Pukhtun of Pakistan (Lindholm 1982). Lindholm attributes the tribe's extremely generous hospitality not to their Islamic faith, but rather to an innate need to show generosity, a need that can be fulfilled in their culture only by generosity to a stranger since mutual antagonism is built into all other existing social roles. In sum, Islamic hospitality is a personal responsibility, is distinguished from charity, emphasizes food and protection, and has a limited time-frame.

Medieval Hospitality

Throughout the Middle Ages, hospitality was held up as a sacred duty. In the early Middle Ages, at least, great importance was placed on the host's obligation to protect the guest (Rouche 1987). To some extent, hospitality was enjoined on all. Rouche (1987, 440) cites a Burgundian law that stated that "anyone who refuses to offer a visitor shelter and warmth shall pay a fine of three solidi."[7] Priests had a particular responsibility for hospitality. A twelfth-century decree by Gratian admonished that "a priest should be hospitable" (quoted in Heal 1982, 546). The Fourth Lateran Council insisted in

1215 that every parish offer hospitality. McCall notes: "In some parishes, the traveller or the person in need of succour might be put up in the priest's house; but in others there were by now 'hospitals,' founded and maintained either out of the parish funds or, more frequently, by the bequest or endowment of a private person or persons" (1979, 135).

Nonetheless, most sources agree that the three groups held most responsible for fulfilling the biblical charge of hospitality were the aristocracy, the monks, and the bishops. These groups generally distinguished between two types of hospitality: one for the rich, the other for the poor.

The aristocracy was considered to have a special responsibility for hospitality, since a major religious justification for their wealth was that they share it with the poor and strangers. Heal notes: "A crucial justification for the lavish consumption and display of the late medieval household was that the lord was obliged to provide open hospitality to the stranger as well as the dependent, the rich and the poor alike" (1982, 545). Duby *et al.* indicate, however, that among the French aristocracy the poor "were admitted to receive . . . the crumbs from the lord's table" (1988, 66).

Monasteries and bishops often created separate offices for the two types of hospitality. "Every bishop and every abbot actually set up two hostels, one for the poor and another for the rich, the count-bishops, and other dignitaries traveling on business" (Rouche 1987, 441). The organization of French monasteries also reflected this division, with hospitality for the poor under the almoner and hospitality for rich travelers under the hosteler (Duby *et al.* 1988, 48).

Medieval hospitality was not built solely on Gospel injunctions. Medieval Irish monasteries were renowned for their hospitality and were frequently cited by Peter Maurin (1977). As was the case with Islam, Irish monks drew upon an ancient, preconversion tradition of hospitality. Gerig notes that "in Ireland, hospitality was not only practised as a virtue, but enjoined by law from the earliest times" (1925, 799). Once a guest had eaten, the host was not permitted to attack him or even show disrespect. The host was bound to protect the guest under all circumstances. Primary legal responsibility was given to the kings, who appointed public hospitalers (*brugaids*), who maintained houses of hospitality in return for usufructs of land from the king. The number of houses of hospitality was in the hundreds (Gerig 1925, 801). Irish monks continued this tradition of hospitality, maintaining guest houses for both sexes and washing the feet of newly arrived guests. Tales of Irish saints often stress their hospitality (e.g., Ryan 1972, 318–23).

The other major medieval locus of hospitality was the episcopate. In a fascinating study of the hospitality of the archbishops of Canterbury, Heal (1982) documents that they generally distinguished between providing for the poor and entertaining the rich. Often, the poor were simply given food or alms at the gates of the archbishop's residence (by the almoner), while the influential were entertained more lavishly within. There were exceptions, however. Robert of Winchelsea was renowned for feeding the poor. Heal tentatively suggests that hospitality for the poor became "less a matter of urgency" after the passage of the Poor Laws (1982, 561).

During the Reformation, the hospitality of the archbishops increasingly focused on entertainment of the influential at feasts. This hospitality fostered good relations with influential neighbors and with the monarchs and was used to justify the wealth of the episcopate. Henry VIII cited the archbishop of Canterbury's hospitality as a justification for not confiscating his property (Heal 1982, 544).

The Decline of Hospitality in the West

Most social analysts who have addressed the topic are in agreement that hospitality has been declining in importance in Western society.[8] Laments about the decline of hospitality were frequent by the sixteenth century (Heal 1982, 548), although such laments may be typical of any age. However, by the late 1800s, Sidgwick observed that "hospitality in the progress of civilization has become a luxury rather than a necessity" (quoted in Goodin 1985, 35).

Several theories have been advanced for the decline of hospitality, although none have been fully developed. Lofland (1972) argues that hospitality declined because, as a result of urbanization, the number of strangers increased to the point that one could not treat all of them as special guests. Stark (1983) states that hospitality was religiously motivated and its decline is associated with the passage from what he termed static religion to dynamic religion. Goodin (1985) argues that hospitality declined because travel became less risky.

There is an element of truth to each of these arguments; however, I would add that hospitality declined as a result of increasing societal complexity and specialization. Hospitality is a form of relationship that is essentially unspecialized—nearly anyone can do it and, as was seen in foraging societies, it performs a wide variety of functions. With increasing societal complexity, many of these functions were transferred to more specialized institutions—such as diplomacy, trade, and medicine—and thus became the province of specialists. The norm of hospitality often faded as its functions eroded; however, nothing evolved to replace its most important and subtle function— the establishment of personal bonds among persons of widely different social origins.

The historical examples do give some idea of the range of practices covered by the term hospitality and alert us to the fact that hospitality can have a variety of meanings, forms, and functions. It may be coextensive with charity, as in early Christianity, or specifically contrasted with charity, as in Islam. It can be an explicitly reciprocal affair, as among the ancient Greeks, or it may be essentially nonreciprocal, as in Ireland. It may be a corporate responsibility, a personal responsibility, or both. It may function to facilitate trade, as in Greece, or to facilitate the spread of a religion, as in early Christianity. Perhaps the one thing that was common to all of the above cultures was that hospitality had a strong religious sanction. As we shall see, religious belief also provides a powerful motive for the hospitality of the Catholic Worker movement.

3

Catholic Worker Hospitality

The Catholic Worker is perhaps the most important modern movement to explicitly adopt hospitality as one of its basic tenets. Although the *Catholic Worker* paper was founded in 1933 with much broader purposes, namely to spread the message of the Catholic social encyclicals to the workers and unemployed and to "create a new society within the shell of the old" (Maurin 1977, 83), hospitality quickly became an integral part of the overall Worker program. In the following discussion of the beginnings and philosophy of the Catholic Worker, I shall view the movement through its approach to hospitality. Other aspects of the movement, including its spirituality, peace witness, concern with the labor movement, the work of producing the paper, and its general philosophy, will be covered only insofar as they interact with hospitality. The reader who is interested in a more comprehensive treatment of the movement may refer to a number of excellent sources.[1]

The Beginnings of the Movement

Dorothy Day and Peter Maurin did not found the Worker as an organization designed to carry out certain concrete goals. As Dorothy writes, most of its projects, particularly the Houses of Hospitality, "just happened."

> Our Houses of Hospitality are scarcely the kind of houses that Peter Maurin has envisioned in his plan for a new social order. . . . Our houses grew up around us. Our bread lines came about by accident; our roundtable discussions are unplanned, spontaneous affairs. The smaller the house, the smaller the group, the better. If we could get it down to Christian families, we would be content. Ever to become smaller—that is the aim (Day 1970, 60–61).

49

> When we began the Catholic Worker, we first thought of it as a head-
> quarters for the paper, a place for round-table discussions, for learn-
> ing crafts, for studying ways of building up a new social order. But
> God has made it much more than all this. He has made it a place for
> the poor. They come early in the morning from their beds in cheap
> flophouses, from the benches in the park across the street, from the
> holes and corners of the city (Day 1983, 112).

Although Peter and Dorothy hoped to create a movement aimed
in part at establishing Houses of Hospitality, they did not go about this
task in a culturally orthodox manner. They did not set up an organization for the purpose of creating a series of such houses. Rather,
they went about their mission in personalist fashion—by speaking
of the need for such houses and by beginning a house that would
serve as an example for others. Early issues of the paper made pleas
for the establishment of Houses of Hospitality, showed the need for
hospitality by describing evictions in New York City, cited examples
of persons who provided hospitality, created a counterexample of a
shelter that was not "hospitable" (the municipal shelter), and, most
importantly, recounted their own experiences in establishing a house.
The message contained in the paper was reinforced by the two co-
founders as they traveled across the country several times in the first
few years of the movement. After two years of example-setting, the
movement began to grow. Starting in 1935, groups began setting up
houses in various cities, and by the early 1940s there were over thirty
houses across the country.

Pleas for Houses of Hospitality

The first issue of the *Catholic Worker* made no direct mention of the
notion of Houses of Hospitality. However, the first page of the second
issue (June–July 1933) contained an Easy Essay by Peter Maurin entitled "Houses of Hospitality," which pleaded with Catholic bishops
to create such houses. This issue also contained an article entitled
"Maurin's Program," which briefly explained his three-point program of roundtable discussions, Houses of Hospitality, and agronomic
universities. The section on Houses of Hospitality placed them in the
context of his total program:

> In the Middle Ages it was an obligation of the bishops to provide
> houses of hospitality or hospices for the wayfarer. They are especially
> necessary now, and necessary to my program as half-way houses.
> I am hoping that some one will donate a house, rent free, for six
> months so that a start may be made. A priest will be at the head of

it and men gathered through the round table discussions will be recruited to work in the houses cooperatively and eventually be sent
out to farm colonies or agronomic universities.

Thus, such houses were indeed halfway houses in his program—
providing a place for men who were attracted by the ideas presented in the roundtable discussions to begin to work toward social
change, supplying more seasoned veterans to the agronomic universities. Dorothy Day recalled of his plan that "perhaps I was a bit irked
because women were left out in his description of a house of hospitality" (Day 1963, 22). She quickly corrected this omission—the
first House of Hospitality was for women. The passage is also notable
because it indicates that Maurin intended to set up Houses of Hospitality as part of the Worker movement and not to wait for the bishops
to do it.

The October 1933 issue contained a longer Easy Essay, entitled
"To the Bishops of the U.S.—A Plea for Houses of Hospitality," which
further delineated Maurin's idea for such houses. It follows in its
entirety.

The Duty of Hospitality

People who are in need
   and are not afraid to beg
   give to people not in need
   the occasion to do good for goodness' sake.
Modern society calls the beggar
   bum and panhandler
   and gives him the bum's rush.
But the Greeks used to say
   that people in need are the ambassadors of the gods.
Although you may be called bums and panhandlers
   you are in fact the Ambassadors of God.
As God's Ambassadors
   you should be given food, clothing and shelter
   by those who are able to give it.
Mahometan teachers tell us
   that God commands hospitality.
But the duty of hospitality
   is neither taught nor practiced
   in Christian countries.

The Municipal Lodgings

That is why you who are in need
   are not invited to spend the night
   in the homes of the rich.

There are guest rooms today
  in the homes of the rich
  but they are not for those who need them.
And they are not for those who need them
  because those who need them are
  no longer considered as the Ambassadors of God.
So people no longer
  consider hospitality to the poor
  as a personal duty.
And it does not disturb them a bit
  to send them to the city
  where they are given the hospitality of the "Muni"
  at the expense of the taxpayer.
But the hospitality that the "Muni"
  gives to the down and out
  is no hospitality
  because what comes from the taxpayer's pocketbook
  does not come from his heart.

Back to Hospitality

The Catholic unemployed
  should not be sent to the "Muni."
The Catholic unemployed
  should be given hospitality
  in Catholic houses of hospitality.
Catholic houses of hospitality
  are known in Europe
  under the name of Hospices.
There have been Hospices in Europe
  since the time of Constantine.
Hospices are free guest houses;
  hotels are paying guest houses.
And paying guest houses or hotels
  are as plentiful
  as free guest houses or hospices
  are scarce.
So hospitality like everything else
  has been commercialized.
So hospitality like everything else
  must now be idealized.

Houses of Hospitality

We need Houses of Hospitality
  to give to the rich
  the opportunity to serve the poor.

We need Houses of Hospitality
    to bring the Bishops to the people
    and the people to the Bishops.
We need Houses of Hospitality
    to bring back to institutions
    the technique of institutions.
We need Houses of Hospitality
    to show what idealism looks like
    when it is practiced.
We need Houses of Hospitality
    to bring Social Justice
    through Catholic Action
    exercised in Catholic Institutions.

Hospices

We read in the *Catholic Encyclopedia*
    that during the early ages of Christianity
    the hospice (or the house of hospitality)
was a shelter for the sick, the poor, the orphans, the old, the traveler
    and the needy of every kind.
Originally the hospices (or houses of hospitality)
    were under the supervision of the bishops who designated priests
    to administer the spiritual and temporal affairs of these charitable
        institutions.
The fourteenth statute of the so-called Council of Carthage held
        about 436
    enjoins upon the bishops
    to have hospices (or houses of hospitality)
    in connection with their churches.

Parish Houses of Hospitality

Today we need houses of hospitality
    as much as they needed it then
    if not more so.
We have Parish Houses for the priests
    Parish Houses for educational purposes
    Parish Houses for recreational purposes
    but no Parish Houses of hospitality.
Bossuet says that the poor
    are the first children of the Church
    so the poor should come first.
People with homes should have a room of hospitality
    so as to give shelter to the needy members of the parish.
The remaining needy members of the parish
    should be given shelter in a Parish Home.

Furniture, clothing and food
  should be sent to the needy members of the parish
  at the Parish House of Hospitality.
We need Parish Homes
  as well as Parish Domes.
In the new Cathedral of Liverpool
  there will be a Home as well as a Dome.

Houses of "Catholic Action"

Catholic houses of hospitality
  should be more than free guest houses
  for the Catholic unemployed.
They could be vocational training schools
  including the training for the priesthood
  as Father Corbett proposes.
They could be Catholic reading rooms
  as Father McSorley proposes.
They could be Catholic Instruction Schools
  as Father Cornelius Hayes proposes.
They could be Round-Table Discussion Groups
  as Peter Maurin proposes.
In a word, they could be
  Catholic Action Houses
  where Catholic Thought
  is combined with Catholic Action.

The essay does not suggest that Houses of Hospitality should be started as part of the Catholic Worker movement per se. Rather, they should be an integral part of the parish structure of the institutional Catholic church. This contrasts somewhat with the hope to establish a house expressed in the article from the second issue of the paper. Maurin primarily makes the case that hospitality should be provided to the "Catholic unemployed." Although this emphasis on serving one's own religious group was echoed in the early fundraising literature of at least some of the houses, I know of no attempt to restrict hospitality to this group. The theme of continuity with European traditions of hospitality is one that would be echoed throughout the movement. The notion that individuals should open up their homes to a homeless person is still advocated by the movement. Maurin's designation of the poor as the Ambassadors of God was echoed throughout the early years of the movement, although it has fallen into disuse in recent years. Basically, Maurin's essay outlines an ideology of hospitality that has been advocated by the Worker to the present day.

After the publication of this essay, the *Catholic Worker* published frequent pleas for the creation of Houses of Hospitality. In the same issue, an article detailed the enthusiastic reaction of several unemployed men to Peter's presentation of his ideas on the subject at a meeting of the unemployed held at the Manhattan Lyceum.

The next issue of the paper (November 1933) contained a front-page article pleading for houses "for needy women and girls." Rather than presenting an abstract analysis of the problem, the author (presumably Dorothy) told the story of an unemployed woman who had come into the Worker office after reading a copy of the paper. The article quotes the woman as saying:

> I read Peter Maurin's letter to the Bishops asking for Houses of Hospitality, and I thought of all the Catholic girls and women who are without shelter, and no Catholic institution open to them. The Salvation Army shelters are full of them and they are constantly subject to slurs on their faith. Once I refused to go to Sunday morning nine o'clock service because I wanted to go to Mass, and I was kicked out. That was last year. I'm back at 22nd Street [the Salvation Army Shelter] now, but I have to go next Friday. We are only allowed to stay two weeks. And the Lord only knows where we will go then.
>
> *Where can Catholic women go who through no fault of their own are on the streets and subject to hardships and temptations unspeakable?*

The same issue featured an article that further delineated the notion of hospitality espoused by the *Worker* and outlined a concept of how a House of Hospitality would be organized:

> Hospitality is the keynote of civilization. Its opposite is greed. Our present depression, as has so often been said by those who know, is not so much of an economic or financial, but a moral depression. Let us practice then the moral virtues. Charity is the greatest of all virtues, for what we give to our neighbor we give to God. Can there not be houses where Charity and Hospitality are placed in practical use? . . .
>
> So we arrive at the idea—Catholic Houses of Hospitality! The project has been under discussion for some time by a few, who have been earnestly considering the monastic ideal of service. A plan of action has been drawn up, there is a dim prospect of a house, and, with the grace of God, it seems possible that in the future that [*sic*] there will be a genuine House of Hospitality.
>
> The details of the plan are briefly as follows: Object: The rehabilitation of single Catholic men spiritually, morally, mentally and occupationally along the lines of the Franciscan spirit by a number of those willing to sacrifice themselves permanently or temporarily

without material reward. They will be religious without vows, to teach and work for God, without property, promising never to touch or handle money in any form. The guests will live in the house, and will also work, teach and study; the externes will not live in the house, may be of any age, creed or color, and may use the house in the same way as the guests. Later, when the idea develops, land in the country will be procured, and a small number will be sent out each week for agricultural work, so directing a course towards a future state of self-sustenance. The work of the model house will [be] Spiritual: Instruction in Apologetics, Liturgy, Church History and Music, the development of the house as a center of Catholic Action, assisting priests in parish, educational, social and secretarial work; Educational: instruction in all branches of study with agricultural, vocational and trade instruction, open forums and a newspaper; Occupational: the manual labor of the house (men may work outside for wages or no wages at all); Corporal: the provision of food, clothing and shelter. Food will be given to all who ask, and any surplus to the families living nearby.

The general purpose of the Houses of Hospitality is to form a center of Catholic Action in all fields, to work for, teach and preach social justice, to form a powerhouse of genuine spirituality and earnest educational and vocational work, to dignify and transform manual labor, and to work for the glory and love of God and His Church.

Although the article was unsigned, it did request that interested readers contact "Frater Edward M" through the *Worker*.

In some ways, this scheme bears a strong resemblance to the houses that actually developed. Worker houses generally have some liturgical component, some form of lecture or discussion series, a newspaper or newsletter, and certainly a hospitality component. Worker houses were in the forefront of the pre– and post–Vatican II liturgical reform movement, for example. Even the distinction between guests who live in the house and "externes" seems to anticipate important stratification processes that I observed in Worker houses some half century later. On the other hand, the scheme, with its description of spiritual and educational programs, sounds more like a settlement house than most Worker houses I have known. Worker houses have their spiritual and educational components, but these rarely resemble programs of the sort one would have found at Hull House, for instance.

The paper continued to appeal for the creation of Houses of Hospitality. The December 1933 issue reprinted an article from the National Catholic Welfare Conference News Service entitled "Women: Start a Campaign in Your Organization to Open Shelters." Three issues contained banner headlines (December 1933, February 1934, and October 1934) proclaiming "Houses of Hospitality Real Need Today." Perhaps the most intriguing appeal was a front-page proposal in the February 1934 issue to turn Ellis Island into a national hospice:

> Years ago the place was a hospice for awhile for all those who came seeking the promised land, America. Within its portals they were received if not with open arms, at least with a semblance of hospitality.
>
> Why not, Uncle Sam? Won't you re-welcome to your arms these, your own, who have a greater need than ever before of the haven that you erected for their forbears—a place where families could be kept together, where mothers need not be separated from their children— a National House of Hospitality for your people.

Eviction Stories

A less direct appeal for hospitality was made by citing eviction statistics (June–July 1933, November 1933) and recounting vivid stories of evictions in which Catholic Workers had personally helped the victims move to new quarters, largely through their participation in the Fifteenth Street Neighborhood Council. One story went as follows:

> A Home Relief worker from 22nd Street came to the office to get aid for a woman and child who were being evicted from a decrepit flat in one of the tenements of William Horn. . . . Understanding that the eviction was at three in the afternoon, we sallied forth, but when we got there, the landlord's agent had called off his men, expecting us to do the job of putting the woman out, and thus saving him eighteen dollars.
>
> We refused to move the woman's furniture until it had been brought down by the marshal. We explained to the agent that often a landlord who was unwilling to accept a Home Relief voucher offered to move the family himself, paying five dollars to a neighborhood truckman rather than eighteen to the marshal. This agent, standing sneering and scoffing by the door, refused to do anything.
>
> "You have no sympathy for landlords, have you?" he wanted to know.
>
> We assured him that our sympathy was rather with the weaker party. Alright then, he would call the marshal! The eviction would be the following Monday then, at three o'clock.
>
> Monday came, and the relief worker hastened around to the office, to tell us that the marshal was about to arrive, though it was only one, not three in the afternoon. . . .

Several police and huskies were standing at the door of the tenement to greet what they thought was going to be a delegation of Communists, only to meet instead seven-year-old Teresa, Harry Crimmins and me. They dissolved into thin air. (It is a wonder they wouldn't stay and help us.)

Teresa carried toys, pieces of the baby's crib, parlor ornaments and dishes, and Harry Crimmins and I managed the rest. The Mission Helpers of the Sacred Heart, a community of nuns who run a day nursery and do visiting work in the neighborhood promised to keep an eye on our evicted friend—she is a Protestant—taking charge of her two-year-old child while she works as a dishwasher. . . .

This is only one of the dozen eviction cases we have had in the last month. We have moved Jews, Protestants and Catholics. A German livery stable man loaned us his horse and wagon to move a Jewish neighbor. Jews, Protestants and Catholics have helped us by contributing clothes, furniture and their services (*CW*, November 1933; see also October 1933).

Another story told of an eviction on a larger scale—the destruction (presumably by police) of Hardluck Camp—a group of shacks built and lived in by unemployed men:

There was no protest when Hardluck Camp, built in the vacant lots between Ninth and Tenth Streets and the East River, was torn up that day. The shacks stood bordering dirt lanes—long rows of little cabins made from linoleum, tin, boards and doors salvaged from wrecked houses, and bits of driftwood pulled out of the river. The men got their water from a fire pump over on Ninth Street. They used five gallon cans with wooden handles fitted in them to carry it. . . .

Most of the men were busy packing their odds and ends of clothes and blankets on the tops of broken down baby carriages, getting ready to hike over to Brooklyn where there was another encampment. Some of them didn't know where they were going (*CW*, June–July 1933).

While such stories usually did not contain a direct appeal for the establishment of Houses of Hospitality, the vividness of their descriptions of the plight of the homeless carried a powerful implicit plea, a plea more urgent than that contained in more abstract arguments.

Examples of Hospitality

In addition to pleas for Houses of Hospitality, the early issues of the *Catholic Worker* gave examples of what the Workers considered to be true hospitality. Particularly praised was Father Timothy Dempsey, a priest from St. Louis who opened a soup kitchen that, according to a *New York Times* article reprinted in the December 1933 *Catholic Worker*, served 3,431,268 meals in two years. "Father Tim's methods are a pain to organized charity. He makes no investigations and asks nothing in return. 'When a man's hungry he doesn't need a lecture; he needs food,' is the way he explains it." The June 1935 *Worker* carried a glowing report of a visit (presumably by Dorothy Day) to Father Tim, entitled "St. Louis Priest Gives Example of Real Hospitality." The front-page article not only described his work but repeatedly contrasted it with the work of established charities, thus revealing what Dorothy considered to be true hospitality:

> Father Timothy, as they call him, is the kind of a man they tell stories about. He is supposed to have said: "I can wash forty babies while a social service worker decides what kind of soap to use." And one can see him doing it, too, with the large-hearted efficiency which has built up lodging houses for men and women, a day nursery, a convalescent home, soup kitchen, altogether a bigger outfit to deal with the poor and homeless than the Municipal Lodging House here [in New York City], run by the largest city in the world. At least that's the impression I got of his work. There is a warmth there, a personality which permeates all he does, so that his places are not just shelters, but have a warm, human atmosphere.
>
> The men's houses—there are two of them—have not only cubicles, but dormitories, and there is not the frigidity of charity organizations about them.
>
> "The first duty of the Church is to the poor." "You can't preach the Gospel to men with empty stomachs." These are the things that Father Dempsey knows.
>
> We could give a lot of statistics: The average daily meals for the month of April numbered 2,708; the seven hundred baskets of food given to the poor in the neighborhood the week we were there. But statistics are bare, barren things compared with the man himself. We can tell you he is a big hearty man, sixty-seven years old. That he lives with the poor. He is just as much at home with them on the street as he is in the church. That Tom Mooney, the imprisoned labor leader writes to him, and that he writes back once a month.

The *Worker* also gave some examples from Chicago. The April 1934 issue announced that a home for thirty women had been opened by the Council of Catholic Women. The October 1934 issue contained both a plea for shelters for homeless boys and a description of some efforts in Chicago to shelter such boys. Also chronicled was the work of Dorothy's friend, the Baroness Catherine de Hueck, who had started a community called Friendship House in Toronto. The

November 1934 issue carried a front-page report entitled "Friendship House is New Catholic Front in Toronto—Apostolic Works Against Bolshevism Bring Relief to Distressed." Part of the report discussed hospitality:

> Our doors are wide open to anyone needing a night's sleep; reading *The Catholic Worker* we have been sorry that we had no place for the single foreign girls to find shelter with us for a while. But since last week we will have no need of envying it, for although we have been open officially only five weeks, the needs were so great, the children, study groups and other activities expanding so quickly that we have been obliged to rent the house next door, which Providentially became vacant at that time.

The *Worker* did not limit itself to contemporary examples of hospitality; it also drew on the lives of the saints for inspiration. The April 1934 issue noted the hospitality of the Curé of Ars:

> We have added to St. Joseph and St. Teresa, the patrons of our House of Hospitality, a new guardian and protector—Jean Baptiste Vianney, better known as the Curé of Ars. . . .We were reminded again of his dearly loved parish House of Hospitality for poor and homeless girls, "La Providence." Its work, started in a one-room shack and always distinguished by its poverty during the many years it remained under his direction, became one of his greatest consolations, and its removal from his loving care by the order of his bishop was the last and greatest cross of the saint's life.

The "Muni" as Counterexample

The *Worker* also provided one example of what they did not mean by hospitality—the Municipal Shelter of New York City. The major broadside against the Muni was launched in two articles entitled "Municipal Lodging House No 'House of Hospitality,' " by Herman Hergenhan, appearing in the May and June 1934 issues. The articles described Hergenhan's stay at the Muni after losing his job and exhausting his savings, and they reveal a sensitivity to the effects on self-concept of being labeled deviant decades before labeling theory was advanced in the sociological literature:

> So the broad gates of a twentieth century house of hospitality were flung wide to me. I had joined the ranks of social outcasts in the most modern of democracies. The line of social demarcation was crossed. The scrutiny of a cop had to be undergone after waiting in line for an hour with hundreds of others in the same predicament. We were admitted in batches of fifty. More waiting was announced

by an attendant. Then came the announcement: "Foist-timers step up! Window number one—around the railing!" How reminiscent of tales of prison life! And thus the application of the eighteenth century poor law began to function.

I was quizzed by a bright and shining one—he reminded me forcibly of a regimental drill sergeant. He warned me that if I told a lie in stating my case, I would be sent up the river—as if lying were a characteristic peculiar to unemployed workers. He asked me if I had a mother and what her maiden name is or was. When he knew enough about me and my relationship to this great city to besmear with ink a good-sized sheet of paper, I closed the deal by affixing [m]y signature to a document.

Then he hands me two brass checks with numbers on—for I was now overnight guest number 705 of the City of New York— and indicated that I might "stay here steady," provided I could prove tomorrow by documentary evidence that what I said was true. . . . The bureaucratic machine functioned perfectly. . . .

Line up once more at the lunch counter; grab a tray; keep in step with the man ahead of you; get hold of a tin bowl half-filled with what is technically designated as "Irish Stew" but is more akin to slumgullion in looks and taste; a tin cup of coffee without sugar; three slices of white bread; a spoon partly washed; and another round is completed. Then squeeze your way through a mass of more or less ragged and unwashed humans, balancing your tray, looking for a seat. The food is gobbled down quickly, for the men are very, very hungry, and the command of a flunky to make room for others speeds up the process. There is no "doubling up" for a little more soup or another slice of bread. "No one shall go hungry!"

The guest leaves the table, signs his name once more, attesting the fact that he has eaten one of those much-advertised "square meals," and descends to the basement with a perspiring, cursing mob of men, being shouted at by flunkies who have forgotten that once they were men. The stench from the sterilizing room is enough to make one long for a park bench. When all his clothes are removed, he tacks them with one brass check to recover them in the morning with the other around his neck. The bath which follows is the best feature of the whole enterprise. All are provided with a night gown and a physical examination. The building is heated and the beds are good enough to insure a good night's rest (*CW*, May 1934).

The Muni is filled with endless corruption, special privilege and discrimination. "Give me a nickel once in a while, or a couple of cigaret butts or a late newspaper," says the attendant in the flop, "and I will see that you get a bit of meat in your soup, or see to it that your pockets will not be rifled during the night." . . .

After my first breakfast I had to take a four-mile walk to South Ferry to be once more examined and duly inscribed on the books as a regular soupliner. That I had to wait two hours in line to accomplish this goes without saying. Documentary evidence was required to show that I had lived in the city for two years. I signed my name once more and received a card that proved that I had properly reached the level of pauper and outcast. A total of seventeen hours had been required to reach this status. . . .

It is true that there are a goodly number among those at the Muni with a slum or Bowery outlook, but most of them are down and out for the first time in their lives. Whether habitual loafer and boozer or so-called respectable worker, they all are human, and are entitled to a human standard of existence (*CW*, June 1934).

Establishing the New York City House

The most important step Dorothy took toward beginning a movement of Houses of Hospitality was simply to begin such a house in New York City. This house provided *the* example to those interested in starting such houses, both through the reports of its "progress" contained in the *Catholic Worker* and through the first-hand experiences of the myriad visitors to the house itself, at least some of whom went on to start houses of their own elsewhere.

Hospitality, in its broad sense, was carried on by Dorothy even before the start of the paper, but the establishment of the first House of Hospitality came after the paper:

Our first house of hospitality came into being very shortly after *The Catholic Worker* did—while we were working on the second issue, in fact—in the barbershop we had taken below our Fifteenth Street apartment. A young woman, an unemployed textile worker about to have a baby, took charge of the kitchen and busied herself preparing meals for the homeless men who had already begun drifting in. It wasn't long before we were all eating in shifts (Day 1963, 28).

A later description gives a slightly different story:

Actually, we here at *The Catholic Worker* did not start these soup lines ourselves. Years ago, John Griffin, one of the men from the Bowery who moved in with us, was giving out clothes, and when they ran out he began sitting down the petitioners to a hot cup of coffee, or a bowl of soup—whatever we had. By word of mouth the news spread, and one after another they came, forming lines (during the Depression) which stretched around the block (Day 1970, 92).

Dorothy described the operation of this house as follows:

A pot of stew and a pot of coffee were kept going on the coal range in the kitchen and all who came in were fed. We worked from early morning until midnight (Day 1939, xxxi).

Although Dorothy and her daughter slept in the house,

Homes had to be found for the men—some had been sleeping in Central Park—so we rented an eight-dollar-a-month apartment near Tompkins Square, a rat-ridden place, heatless and filthy, abandoned even by slum dwellers (Day 1939, xxxi–xxxii).

The first New York House of Hospitality to receive detailed coverage in the paper, however, was the Teresa-Joseph Cooperative for Women, an apartment rented by the Workers to shelter ten homeless women. It was first announced on the front page of the December 1933 issue:

Although it cannot be dignified by the name of House of Hospitality, what is virtually a center of hospitality is opening today, December 11, in the parish of the Immaculate Conception Church. . . .

It is not really a "house" that we are opening up, but an apartment in this central neighborhood, steam heated and with a good big bath, six large rooms, five of which can be used as bedrooms, one of them a dormitory holding four beds. The rent is fifty dollars a month. . . .

The winter is on us and we can wait no longer and beds we must have. We will borrow blankets for the time being and use those of the editors. They can roll themselves in coats and newspapers, which are said to be warm, though we are sure they are very noisy. . . .

Christ's first bed was of straw.

The February 1934 issue continued the story:

The women at the Teresa-Joseph Cooperative . . . advise each other as to where to look for work, and they help each other out with carfare, when one has it and another hasn't.

There are ten women now at the apartment and since our last issue the place has been supplied with everything but window curtains and those were things we had not thought of asking for. . . .

For what we really want, be it understood by the readers of THE CATHOLIC WORKER, is a whole house, and a donated one at that where there will be room to house our unemployed women on one side, unemployed men on another, our Catholic library and reading room, our lecture rooms, and the offices of the paper. In other words, what we want is a parish House of Hospitality, and it is a dream which we are working towards, with faith that we will achieve it (CW, February 1934).

The article continued by thanking donors, especially the parishioners of Immaculate Conception. It appears that the Workers were trying to create some identification of the House with the parish in order to adhere to Peter Maurin's ideal of parish Houses of Hospitality, even though the House was clearly the work of the Catholic Worker itself.

The following issue contained another update on the Cooperative:

> During the month about 25 women were cared for, some left to take jobs, three were sent away to a rest house for several weeks. The beds were occupied and yet we never had to turn any girl away. Always, when new ones came in another, providentially, was leaving for a job.
>
> Sometimes during the month some of the girls dropped into the office to discuss their problems with us, stayed for lunch and remained to clear up the dishes. One of them has offered her services in our common kitchen, God be praised, and now the editors' tasks are lightened by this volunteer help (*CW*, March 1934).

These early reports all emphasized the success of the venture and the cooperativeness and helpfulness of the guests, although later memories of Dorothy hinted that all was not sweetness and light (e.g., Day 1963, 31).

Space was again becoming a problem and they began looking for a new house. The April 1935 issue announced that they had taken over an entire house, at 144 Charles Street, which would house the offices of the paper and provide shelter for both men and women. The account told of the hardships of moving into a building with no heat, but emphasized the spirit of cooperation that characterized the move. The Charles Street House, then, marked the first unified House of Hospitality, encompassing all the functions of the Catholic Worker under one roof. The Worker would remain at Charles Street for only a year, however. In April 1936, again finding themselves ridiculously overcrowded, they moved to a larger building at 115 Mott Street, where they remained until 1950.

The "House," in its various incarnations, provided the example on which other Worker houses would be based. Word of this example was spread through the paper, through speaking trips by Dorothy and Peter to other cities, and through the reports of the many people who visited the house in person after reading the paper or hearing Dorothy or Peter speak. No organization was created to manage or even foster the growth of Hospitality Houses throughout the country. Rather, the movement relied almost entirely on the approach of setting an example and letting others choose to respond as they may.

Advice on Hospitality

The December 1936 issue of the *Catholic Worker* announced that fellow workers in Rochester, Pittsburgh, and Chicago were interested in starting Houses of Hospitality and that a house had already been opened in England. The editorial presented Dorothy's advice to those who wished to begin such an endeavor:

> We emphasize again the necessity of smallness. The idea[l], of course, would be that each Christian, conscious of his duty in the lay apostolate, should take in one of the homeless as an honored guest, remembering Christ's words, "Inasmuch as ye have done it unto the least of these, ye have done it unto me."
>
> The poor are more conscious of this obligation than those who are comfortably off. We know of any number of cases where families already overburdened and crowded, have taken in orphaned children, homeless aged, poor who were not members of their families but who were akin to them because they were fellow sufferers in this disordered world.
>
> So first of all let us say that those of our readers who are interested in Houses of Hospitality might first of all try to take some one into their homes.
>
> Several of the women workers of our group here in New York who have jobs have moved down to Mott Street now and taken little slum apartments and are offering a room and bed and board to our overflow. They are exemplifying perfectly the idea of hospitality.
>
> But if family complications make this impossible, then let our friends keep in mind the small beginnings. I might almost say that it is impossible to do this work unless they themselves are ready to live there with their guests, who soon cease to become guests and become fellow workers. It is necessary, because those who have the ideal in mind, who have the will to make the beginnings, must be the ones who are on hand to guide the work. Otherwise it is just another charity organization, and the homeless might as well go to the missions or municipal lodging houses or breadlines which throughout the depression have become well organized almost as a permanent part of our civilization. And that we certainly do not want to perpetuate. . . .
>
> We began with a store, went on to an apartment rented in the neighborhood, from thence we moved to a twelve-room house, and now we have twenty-four rooms here in Mott Street.

It is not enough to feed and shelter those who come. The work of indoctrination must go on. There must be time for conversations, and what better place than over the supper table? There must be meetings, discussion groups, the distribution of literature. There must be some one always on hand to do whatever comes up, whether that emergency is to go out on a picket line, attend a Communist meeting for the purposes of distributing literature, care for the sick or settle disputes. And there are always arguments and differences of opinion in work of this kind, and it is good that it should be so because it makes for clarification of thought, as Peter says, and cultivates the art of human contacts.

Houses of Hospitality will bring workers and scholars together. They will provide a place for industrial workers to discuss Christian principles of organization as set forth in the encyclicals. They will emphasize personal action, personal responsibility as opposed to political action and state responsibility. They will care for the unemployed and teach principles of cooperation and mutual aid. They will be a half-way house towards farming communes and homesteads.

We have a big program but we warn our fellow workers to keep in mind small beginnings. The smaller the group, the more work is done.

And let us remember, "Unless the Lord build the House, they labor in vain that build it."

This editorial contained many of the basic themes of the Worker approach to hospitality, themes that are, for all practical purposes, sociological postulates—that the size of an "organization" affects the style of interaction, that living with another is a move toward equality, that assuming personal responsibility is the way to effect true social change, that a division of labor that separates those "with the vision" from the actual day-to-day work destroys any possibility of achieving one's goals. The Catholic Worker Houses of Hospitality are, in effect, "quasi-experiments" testing the validity of these postulates.

Once Worker houses began to be established in other cities, the *Catholic Worker* paper replaced its appeals for hospitality with letters from the various houses reporting their activities and problems. The movement grew to some thirty houses and farms by 1940, dwindled to under a dozen in the wake of Dorothy Day's pacifist stance during World War II, and began to resurge during the Vietnam War period and following Day's death in 1980. There are now houses in some seventy cities across the country.

Hospitality in Catholic Worker Philosophy

Although there has been little systematic writing on the place of hospitality within the movement's overall philosophy, concern for hospitality permeates Worker thought. This is most evident in the Worker's development of the philosophy of personalism and of the traditional Catholic notion of the Works of Mercy.

Personalism

Peter Maurin brought the term "personalism" into the Catholic Worker vocabulary, adopting it from the European philosophical movement of the same name. Through his and Dorothy Day's interpretation, personalism became *the* Catholic Worker philosophy. Although Worker personalism is not identical to the European brand (e.g., many of the European philosophers were not advocates of nonviolence), an understanding of the latter movement reveals some of the deeper philosophical themes that underlie Worker hospitality.

The European personalist movement flourished in France in the 1930s and 1940s. Its primary voice was the journal *Esprit*, founded by Emmanuel Mounier. Associated with the movement were such figures as Nicolai Berdyaev, Martin Buber, Jacques Ellul, Aaron Gurswitch, Jacques Maritain, Gabriel Marcel, Maurice Merleau-Ponty, and Paul Ricouer.

One of the first modern thinkers to use the term was the German philosopher and sociologist Max Scheler, who wrote his treatise on personalist ethics, *Formalism in Ethics and Non-formal Ethics of Values*, while he was avidly supporting the German war effort during World War I. Scheler argued that the person was the highest conceivable value and defined the person primarily as an actor (one who originates actions). He differed from the later personalists, however, in that he accepted the notion of a collective person (e.g., a corporation or nation could be a person), thus giving the nation-state the same ethical status as the human person.

The French personalists, particularly the Russian émigré Berdyaev, rejected the notion of a collective person. Only a human being could be a person. For Berdyaev, a person must have the capacity to suffer, something a collectivity lacks. However, personalism was not construed as a rigid system. Rather "Personalism is for us at present a sort of general pass-word. We are using it as an inclusive term for various doctrines that in our present historical situation can be made to agree upon the elementary physical and metaphysical conditions of a new civilization" (Mounier 1938, 1–2).

Not surprisingly, the most fundamental concepts of personalism deal with the person. First and foremost, the person is distinct from the individual (Mounier 1938, 71; Berdyaev 1944, 35–37). The individual is a natural phenomenon and, as such, can be a part of a greater whole—a family, a society, a world. The person, however, is a spiritual reality, a universe unto himself or herself. The person can never be a part of anything. The individual may belong to the world of determination, but never the person. The person dwells in freedom. Berdyaev states: "Personality is not the living individual. Personality in man is not determined by heredity, biological and social; it is freedom in man, it is the possibility of victory over the world of determination" (1944, 37).

This notion of the person values the subjective as opposed to the objective. It rejects all objectification of persons, all treating of other persons as though they were things or roles or clients rather than "thous." The personalists follow Kant in proclaiming that one may never use a person as a means. The person is the highest value in existence. Berdyaev states: "The entire world is nothing in comparison with human personality, with the unique person of a man, with his unique fate" (1944, 20).

Every human individual has the potential to be a person; however, the person must be developed, in interaction with other persons. The notion of person is intimately related to the notion of vocation (Berdyaev 1944, 48). Becoming a person means discovering a unified, unifying vocation for oneself (Mounier 1938, 75–77).[2]

Thus, although the person exists in the spiritual realm, in the realm of freedom, the person is undeniably social. She or he emerges only in interaction with other persons, in a community of persons. This fact gives society its purpose—the fostering of the development of persons. Mounier states: "A personalist civilization is one whose structure and spirit are directed towards the development as persons of all the individuals constituting it" (1938, 67).

The personalists rejected the major ideologies of their day—capitalism, communism, and fascism—as antithetical to such a personalist civilization. Some, particularly Berdyaev, were led by their respect for the value of the person to anarchism. Berdyaev arrived at anarchism from his personalist ethics. As the highest value in the universe, the person may never be subjected to anything abstract, including the state. Further, the state is based on the principle of sacrificing innocent persons.

> Is it permissible to execute a single innocent person for the sake of the safety and wellbeing of the state? In the Gospel this question was put in the words of Caiaphas. "It is better for us that one man should die for the people than that the whole nation should perish." It is well known what sentence was decided by these words. The state always repeats the words of Caiaphas; it is the state's confession of faith. Statesmen have always given the answer that in the interests of the safety of the state and the increase of its strength, an innocent man may and should be put to death. And every time that happens a voice is raised in favour of the crucifixion of Christ. The demoniacal stamp which is imprinted upon the state is due to the fact that the state always gives its vote for the execution of Christ: it is its destiny (1944, 144).

The belief in the ultimate value of the person affected the personalists' approach to interpersonal interaction as well as their approach toward society as a whole. Because the person must not be objectified, social interaction must aim toward I–Thou relationships:

> Only when I begin to interest myself in the real presence of men, to recognize this presence over against myself and to understand the person that is thus revealed to me, when I begin to see in every man a "you," a something more than a "third party," and not a thing of indifference, not a mere living being, not a stranger but another myself—then I have posited the first act of a genuine community life without which no institution can have any solid being (Mounier 1938, 96).

The European emphasis on the value of the person permeates Worker personalism and hospitality. For the Worker, hospitality is an affirmation of the inestimable value of the individual person. Once, after explaining how she had been forced to neglect her responsibility for the newspaper to deal with the problems of a guest, Dorothy Day wrote: "When it comes to choosing which is the most important work this morning—one human being is of greater importance than all the papers ever published" (1939, 179). The emphasis on the value of each person also leads to an ideal of equality that serves to diminish such social distinctions as that between the worthy and unworthy poor. "God is on the side even of the unworthy poor, as we know from the story Jesus told of His Father and the prodigal son" (Day 1970, 56). The distinction between guests and hosts is also diminished.

> The editors are generally called the staff. But where does the staff begin and where does it leave off? Joe Motyka and Paul and Charlie, German George, Polish Walter, and Italian Mike are also staff, and as such play an essential part in getting the paper out. Since The Catholic Worker is also a movement, our editors and writers cook, clean, and wash dishes (Day 1963, 131).

The Catholic Worker emphasis on the value of the person occasionally has been expressed using the ancient image of the stranger as God. In the 1930s, Workers often referred to their guests as Ambassadors of Christ or Ambassadors of God. Although this usage has fallen by the wayside, there are still frequent references to the guest as Christ.

> If we hadn't got Christ's own words for it, it would seem raving lunacy to believe that if I offer a bed and food and hospitality to some man or woman or child, I am replaying the part of Lazarus or Martha or Mary, and that my guest is Christ. There is nothing to show it, perhaps. There are no halos already glowing round their heads—at least none that human eyes can see. It is not likely that I shall be vouchsafed the vision of Elizabeth of Hungary, who put the leper in her bed and later, going to tend him, saw no longer the leper's stricken face, but the face of Christ. The part of a Peter Claver, who gave a stricken Negro his bed and slept on the floor at his side, is more likely to be ours. For Peter Claver never saw anything with his bodily eyes except the exhausted black faces of the Negroes; he had only faith in Christ's own words that these people were Christ (Day 1963, 94–95).

Thus, although the homeless are considered to be Christ, they are not expected to be saints or even pleasant.

> It is easy for people to see Jesus in the children of the slums. . . . But these abandoned men are looked upon as hopeless. "No good will come of it." We are contributing to their laziness. We are feeding people who won't work. These are the accusations made. God help us, we give them so little: bread and coffee in the morning, soup and bread at noon. Two scant meals (Day 1983, 112).

However, guests are no more hopeless cases than are "average persons": "It is as hard to see Jesus in the respectable Christian today as in the man on the Bowery" (Day 1983, 114).

This image of the guest as Christ might be regarded as itself an objectification of the person, as Ramsey (1982, 253) argued had occurred in the thought of Eastern church fathers and as Simmel (1971, 153) argued was inherent in the Christian attitude toward the poor. The Worker formulation, however, does not seem to have this effect in practice. The image of the guest as Christ, rather than reflecting a simplistic identification that robs the guest of his or her own personhood, is an indication that the guest has a divine element within himself or herself. It is a symbolic expression of the dignity of the individual person, a reminder that, despite all appearances, one must always be alert for the Christ, for the divine, within the guest.

The writings of Dorothy Day in particular dwell in such vivid detail on the personalities and biographies of the guests that it is difficult to accuse her of objectifying them. Even the obituaries of long-term guests in the *Catholic Worker* reveal an appreciation of unique personalities rather than a type-casting.

Although the Worker has clearly appropriated the European personalists' emphasis on the value of the person, the central concept of Worker personalism is personal responsibility. When asked what they mean by personalism, most contemporary Catholic Workers reply that it means assuming personal responsibility for one's brothers and sisters—that it means not leaving the poor to the tender mercies of the state welfare bureaucracy.

> No one asked us to do this work. The mayor of the city did not come along and ask us to run a bread line or a hospice to supplement the municipal lodging house. Nor did the Bishop or Cardinal ask that we help out Catholic Charities in their endeavor to help the poor. No one asked us to start an agency or institution of any kind. On our responsibility, because we are our brother's keeper, we began to try to see Christ in each one that came to us. If a man came in hungry, there was always something in the ice box. If he needed a bed and we were crowded, there was always a quarter around to buy a bed on the Bowery. If he needed clothes, there were our friends to be appealed to, after we had taken the extra coat out of the closet first, of course. It might be someone else's coat but that was all right too (Day 1970, 60).

The Worker, then, would reject claims such as that of Ignatieff (1985) that it is acceptable to use the state as the mediator between oneself and the poor.

In asserting the need for assuming personal responsibility for the poor, Day frequently cited Dostoevsky's argument in *The Brothers*

Karamazov that love in practice is far more difficult than love in the abstract. To love the poor, one must meet the poor in daily face-to-face interaction. Anything else is love in the abstract. "It is not love in the abstract that counts. Men have loved a cause as they have loved a woman. Men have loved the brotherhood, the workers, the poor, the oppressed—but they have not loved man, they have not loved the least of these. They have not loved 'personally' " (Day 1970, 89).

The notion of personal responsibility also leads to the Catholic Worker's advocacy of the ancient custom of the Christ room, in which each family had a guest room to be used for the poor. Indeed, this, rather than the larger Catholic Worker House of Hospitality, was held to be the ideal.

> The city, the state—we have nicknamed them Holy Mother the City, Holy Mother the State—have taken on a large role in sheltering the homeless. But the ideal is for every family to have a Christ room, as the early fathers of the Church called it. It seems to me that in the future the family—the ideal family—will always try to care for one more. If every family that professed to follow Scriptural teaching, whether Jew, Protestant, or Catholic, were to do this, there would be no need for huge institutions, houses of dead storage where human beings waste away in loneliness and despair. Responsibility must return to the parish with a hospice and a center for mutual aid, to the group, to the family, to the individual (Day 1963, 192).

Implicit in this notion of personal responsibility is the belief that hospitality is not a specialized activity but something that anyone can do without training or certification. There is no esoteric body of knowledge needed to shelter the homeless and feed the hungry. Hospitality is not a profession; it is a universal human practice.

Personal responsibility, however, is more than just a moral imperative. For Dorothy Day and the Catholic Worker, personal action, whether taken individually or with a group, is the only real means to social change.

> What we would like to do is change the world—make it a little simpler for people to feed, clothe, and shelter themselves as God intended them to do. And to a certain extent, by fighting for better conditions, by crying out unceasingly for the rights of the workers, of the poor, of the destitute—the rights of the worthy and the unworthy poor, in other words—we can to a certain extent change the world; we can work for the oasis, the little cell of joy and peace in a harried world. We can throw our pebble in the pond and be confident that its ever-widening circle will reach around the world (Day 1983, 98).

In discussing the notion of personal responsibility as a means of social change Dorothy frequently cited the "Little Way" of St. Thérèse: "Today we are not contented with little achievements, with small beginnings. We should look to St. Teresa, the Little Flower, to walk her little way, her way of love. . . . Do what comes to hand" (1939, 74).

The notion of personal responsibility cuts two ways. Since social change is to be achieved by persons accepting personal responsibility to work for that change, persons must be free to accept or refuse that responsibility. "We are trying to work out the doctrine of gentle personalism, to live a life in which people do not do things by compulsion, but of their own free will" (Day 1939, 122–23). This approach leads to an anarchistic, noncoercive type of "organization" and its concomitant problems:

> The same difficulties take place in regard to the lack of rules save those set forth in the Gospel. . . . Because there is no compulsion, some will refuse co-operation. Those who co-operate scorn those who do not, as well as those responsible for not making rules to force the non-cooperators to co-operate (Day 1939, 123–24).

A crucial connection between Catholic Worker and European personalism lies in the notion that it is only through assuming personal responsibility that one becomes a person. This is articulated by Sandberg in his study of Worker thought:

> Just as there can be no person who does not respond to and take responsibility for others, the meaning of the terms person and personalism which are the foundation of the Catholic Worker's morality are always incomplete without the word responsibility. We become persons in relationship to others, and the deeper the relationship, the deeper the response and response-ability, the more fully we are persons and allow others to be persons (1979, 45).

Thus, it is in assuming personal responsibility that one becomes a person and it is in allowing others the freedom to assume or reject responsibility that one facilitates their becoming persons.

This philosophy interacts with hospitality in a number of ways. First, assuming personal responsibility for feeding and sheltering others is a means of becoming a person. Thus, hospitality has clear benefits for the giver. Second, in the conduct of hospitality, one must minimize any coercion of one's guests, so that they have the freedom to assume or reject responsibility.

> In its own practice of freedom the Catholic Worker in its various activities continually stresses that participation must be voluntary. The

food and clothes distributed in the houses of hospitality must be distributed with no strings attached. Those who wish to cooperate in the work are welcome to do so. There must be room for people to choose to do as little or as much as they are willing and able without fear of coercion. For it is only in this kind of freedom that people can choose to be persons and so accept personal responsibility (Sandberg 1979, 43).

Finally, personalism influences the style of hospitality. Personalist hospitality means that the host interacts with the guest in an I–Thou relation. Neither must be objectified into a social role (as is done with client and staff in bureaucratized social service). Rather, each must be free to respond to the other as a "thou."

The Works of Mercy

One cannot survey Worker thought on hospitality without reference to the Works of Mercy, a concept that encompasses not only hospitality but all aspects of Worker philosophy. One Worker defined the movement as "just doing the Works of Mercy."

The term "Works of Mercy" refers to a listing of meritorious acts that was codified during the Middle Ages. Thomas Aquinas refered to them as "traditional" in his *Summa Theologica*, although Augustine used a different listing. The Works of Mercy are divided into seven corporal works (feeding the hungry, giving drink to the thirsty, clothing the naked, sheltering the homeless, visiting the sick, ransoming the imprisoned, and burying the dead) and seven spiritual works (instructing the ignorant, counseling the doubtful, admonishing sinners, bearing wrongs patiently, forgiving offenses, comforting the afflicted, and praying for the living and the dead).[3]

The Catholic Worker understanding of the Works of Mercy differs from that of mainstream American Catholic thought in that the Worker takes the notion literally, particularly with respect to the corporal works of mercy. Feeding the hungry means feeding the hungry; sheltering the homeless means opening your home to the homeless; visiting the imprisoned means going to visit the imprisoned. This approach differs from the type of interpretation given the Works of Mercy by many popular Catholic writers. Statements such as "Those who provide comfortable and sanitary homes or apartments for the poor at a reasonable rent, deserve well of God and country" (Cassilly 1926, 59) hopelessly dilute the injunction to shelter the homeless. For the Catholic Worker, the Works of Mercy are commands to be taken literally and are as applicable to the technological society of today as they were to the society of two thousand years ago.

The whole Catholic Worker "program" can be incorporated into the notion of the Works of Mercy. Hospitality includes all of the Works of Mercy, spiritual as well as corporal. Peace witness and other protest for social justice are examples of "rebuking the sinner" (e.g., Day 1939, 138), while publishing newspapers is a means of "instructing the ignorant." It is the performance of the corporal works of mercy, however, that has always been the core of the Catholic Worker:

> Within *The Catholic Worker* there has always been such emphasis placed on the works of mercy, feeding the hungry, clothing the naked, sheltering the harborless, that it has seemed to many of our intellectuals a top-heavy performance. There was early criticism that we were taking on "rotten lumber that would sink the ship." As though Jesus did not come to live with the lost, to save the lost, to show them the way. His love was always shown most tenderly to the poor, the derelict, the prodigal son, so that he would leave the ninety-nine just ones to go after the one (Day 1970, 62).

Dorothy Day juxtaposes the Works of Mercy to "the Works of War," thus relating them to the Worker's pacifist stance: "The works of mercy are works of love. The works of war are works of the devil— 'You do not know of what spirit you are,' Jesus said to his disciples when they would call down fire from heaven on the inhospitable Samaritans" (1970, 61). A woodcut that is frequently reproduced in the *Catholic Worker* lists the (corporal) Works of Mercy followed by the Works of War: Destroy crops and land, seize food supplies, destroy homes, scatter families, contaminate water, imprison dissenters, inflict wounds and burns, kill the living (e.g., March–April 1984).

For Peter Maurin, the Works of Mercy have many functions. They are "the best practical way of making man human to man." They are the means for constructing social order and for achieving the Thomistic "Common Good." They are the most effective way to fight Communism, just as the first Christians used them to fight Roman paganism. The daily practice of the Works of Mercy by Christians is the only way to make the non-Christians say "See how they love each other." The Works are an expression of love. But most importantly, they are what God wants us to do; they are the right thing to do.

For Day too, the Works of Mercy are the ultimate answer to social problems, the bond that holds society together, the ultimate behavioral expression of one's Christianity. "The immediate solution will always be the works of mercy. We are commanded by Jesus Himself in the 25th chapter of St. Matthew to perform them. But there is more study to be done, a long-range view to take, to understand how far-reaching works of mercy can be" (1970, 63).

Since the Works of Mercy have traditionally been associated with the notion of charity, placing hospitality in this context raised a number of issues for the Worker, most notably the question of charity versus justice, the question of reciprocity, and the question of efficacy.

The Worker recognizes that there is a tension between charity and justice, a tension that occurs daily in the practice of hospitality. In her autobiography, Dorothy Day criticized Catholic charitable institutions because they ignored the issue of justice: "I felt that charity was a word to choke over. Who wanted charity? And it was not just human pride but a strong sense of man's dignity and worth, and what was due to him in justice, that made me resent, rather than feel proud of so mighty a sum total of Catholic institutions" (1952, 150). Although she reaffirmed this judgment in an interview with Robert Coles (Coles 1987, 57–58), she stated elsewhere:

> We must make it possible for people to fulfill the new commandment Jesus gave—that we love all men. Communists like to say that it is only charity (in its present ugly sense of a dole) that is enjoined, and they make charity seem ugly, and try to persuade men only to work for justice, when charity is highest of all and includes all (Day 1939, 138).

Thus, charity is higher than justice but must be practiced in the light of justice. The poor have a right to be sheltered and fed. Everyone has a right to survival. One must be sure that hospitality is practiced in such a way that it does not demean one's guests. Dorothy frequently quoted the saying of St. Vincent de Paul that "It is only by feeling your love that the poor will forgive you for the gifts of bread" (e.g., Day 1970, 62).

Perhaps because hospitality is a matter of justice rather than charity, one should not expect thanks for what one does, but should be prepared for anger and rejection.

> One must be humble from a divine motive, otherwise humility is a debasing and repulsive attitude. To be humble and meek for love of God—that is beautiful. But to be humble and meek because your bread and butter depends on it is awful. It is to lose one's sense of human dignity. So it is a cause for gratitude that [guests] . . . should feel free to assert themselves, not worrying about the trouble they cause (Day 1939, 97).

However, the performance of hospitality is not simply a matter of duty. "For a total Christian, the goad of duty is not needed—always prodding one to perform this or that good deed. It is not a duty to help Christ, it is a privilege" (Day 1983, 97).

By framing hospitality in terms of the Works of Mercy, the Worker also emphasizes the notion that the love of God is the true motive force underlying whatever good is accomplished. Hospitality is not designed to effect change in the guests. Personal change, development, and salvation depend on one's own will and on the power of God. The most another can do to facilitate this change is to provide the love through which the grace of God might begin to work. More direct efforts to change others, relying on one's own abilities rather than on God's grace for efficacy, are doomed to failure.

> Father Farina says that the only true influence we have on people is through supernatural love. This sanctity (not an obnoxious piety) so affects others that they can be saved by it. Even though we *seem* to increase the delinquency of others (and we have been many a time charged with it), we can do for others, through God's grace, what no law enforcement can do, what no common sense can achieve (Day 1963, 58).

The Worker, however, is not always successful in acting out this love and grace.

> It is too easy to forget that all we give is given to us to give. All we have to give is our time and patience, our love. How often we have failed in love, how often we have been brusque, cold, and indifferent: "Roger takes care of the clothes; you'll have to come back at ten o'clock." Or "Just sit in the library and wait." "Wait your turn; I'm busy." So it often goes (Day 1963, 171).

Other Aspects of Worker Philosophy

Hospitality is intimately related to other aspects of Worker philosophy, particularly its advocacy of anarchism, voluntary poverty, nonviolence, and agrarianism. The Worker's commitment to anarchism flows from its philosophy of personalism. In fact, many Workers dislike the term anarchism, preferring to use personalism. They are quick to point out that the two mean the same thing. Personalism means, first, a belief in taking personal responsibility to help one's fellow human beings and, second, a belief in the innate value of every person, a value far exceeding any abstraction. These two beliefs logically lead to anarchism—because a belief in personal responsibility implies that everyone should be free to assume or reject such responsibility (i.e., there should be no coercion) and because a belief in the value of the person implies that the person should never be subordinated to the abstraction of the state.

Perhaps the most systematic statement of Catholic Worker anarchism was presented by Robert Ludlow in a series of *Catholic Worker* articles in 1949 and 1950. Ludlow argued that the state sets itself up as God and is thus idolatrous. He also argued that the traditional Hobbesian justification for the state assumes that original sin necessarily triumphs over grace. This is an unacceptable position for a Christian: "It is because we despair of grace that we look to the State to restrain man" (February 1950). To believe in the necessity of the state is to deny the power of grace to conquer original sin. A Christian must work for a society that is based, not upon the assumption of a fallen, evil human nature, but upon the assumption of a redeemable human nature. Such a society is an anarchistic society.

> The Christian, if he is to take seriously the prayer, "Thy kingdom come on earth as it is in heaven," must have as a social goal an order that is inspired by the supernatural, and which consequently finds expression, not in Statism, but in the free society of Christian anarchism (February 1950).

> Therefore, there is an obligation on the Christian to hold as an ideal and to work towards a society, which indeed may not come about unless mankind is converted, but which nevertheless is the measuring rod to determine what direction we should go (April 1950).

However, one must make compromises. "This is the long-range view, and in our day to day existence we may have to make concessions in order to meet an immediate issue or solve a pressing problem. But we must not surrender our minds to the immediate" (February 1950).

The Workers themselves compromise their call for anarchy almost daily in the course of advocacy for the homeless with state welfare agencies.

> Even within ourselves we are trying to pull in two directions. The one leading to State Socialism, the other to Christian Anarchism. Consequently we both aid and oppose the State. The complexities of life sometimes make it inevitable, there are the pressing everyday problems of the poor and we cannot always be consistent in administering to a need that must be met at the moment. Nevertheless, if we forget the goal, or if we abandon the goal under pressure of the

moment we will, in the long run, have betrayed ourselves and those for whom we work. If we are not always aware that the redemptive powers of Christ can elevate human nature to the divine and that as we become more Christian just so much do we have need of less and less government—if we forget that it's possible to transcend original sin then indeed we will join forces with those who, however well intentioned, are leading the world into totalitarianisms where the State is all and all is contained within the State (September 1949).

Anarchism interacts with hospitality in several ways. First, it reinforces the notion of personal responsibility for the poor—one cannot leave one's brothers and sisters to the cold "mercy" of the state. Second, it reinforces the belief that bureaucratic forms of organization should be avoided at all costs in the Houses of Hospitality. Third, it enhances the adversarial nature of interaction with state welfare agencies in advocating for the homeless. However, as noted by Ludlow, the practice of hospitality—particularly the practice of interceding with welfare and health agencies on behalf of one's guests, necessitates a daily compromise with the principle of anarchism.

The Worker's advocacy of voluntary poverty has a profound effect on its style of hospitality. Perhaps the most unique feature of the Worker's advocacy of voluntary poverty is that, in contrast to traditional Catholic religious orders, the Worker's stand is that voluntary poverty should be both individual and organizational. Not only should individual Catholic Workers choose to be poor, but the house itself should be poor. Thus, Catholic Worker houses never apply for or accept permanent sources of funding from either the government or any private organization, including the Catholic Church. They follow the dictum of Gandhi that "it is not good to run public institutions on permanent funds. A permanent fund carries in itself the seed of the moral fall of the institution. . . . The ideal is for public institutions to live, like nature, from day to day" (Gandhi 1957, 198).

These notions have obvious implications for hospitality. Coupled with voluntary poverty, the ideal of Catholic Worker hospitality becomes not sharing one's largesse with the poor, but sharing one's poverty with them. Hospitality becomes living with the poor, in conditions of poverty. It becomes living with lice, roaches, and TB.

> Our poverty is not a stark and dreary poverty, because we have the security which living together brings. But it is that living together that is often hard. Beds crowded together, much coming and going, people sleeping on the floor, no bathing facilities, only cold water.

These are the hardships. Poverty means lack of paint, it means bed-bugs, cockroaches and rats and the constant war against these. Poverty means body lice. A man fainted on the coffee line some months ago and just holding his head to pour some coffee between his drawn lips meant picking up a few bugs. Poverty means lack of soap and Lysol and cleansing powders (Day 1970, 52).

I do feel strongly that we must put everything we have into the work in embracing voluntary poverty for ourselves. It is only when we do this that we can expect God to provide for us. If we do everything we can ourselves, He will supplement our efforts. This is one of the fundamental points of our work in stressing personal responsibility before state responsibility. It is only when we have used all our material resources that we feel it is permissible to call upon the state for aid, that in good conscience we can demand and expect help from the state (Day 1939, 60).

The Worker style of hospitality is also intimately related to the belief in nonviolence because the Worker advocates nonviolence not as a technique but as a life-style. The Catholic Worker is not only pacifist with respect to national policy; it advocates that all persons be nonviolent in their daily life. Thus, in practicing hospitality, Catholic Workers attempt to refrain from answering violence with violence.

Hospitality also provides Workers with a legitimation of their nonviolent stance on foreign policy. The experience of living nonviolently in a violent environment can strengthen individual Workers' commitment to pacifism. I, for instance, did not become comfortable with advocating a pacifist stance for this country until I found that I could survive the often violent life at Unity Kitchen and even contain incidents of violence without resorting to violence. Furthermore, the admittedly difficult work of providing hospitality to the homeless was used as legitimation for the Worker's pacifist stance. The classic instance of this was Dorothy Day's arguments on World War II:

Another Catholic newspaper says it sympathizes with our sentimentality. This is a charge always leveled against pacifists. We are supposed to be afraid of the suffering, of the hardships of war.

But let those who talk of softness, of sentimentality, come to live with us in cold, unheated houses in the slums. Let them come to live with the criminal, the unbalanced, the drunken, the degraded, the perverted. (It is not the decent poor, it is not the decent sinner who was the recipient of Christ's love.) Let them live with rats, with vermin, bedbugs, roaches, lice (I could describe the several kinds of body lice). . . .

> Let their noses be mortified by the smells of sewage, decay, and rotten flesh. Yes, and the smell of sweat, blood, and tears spoken of so blithely by Mr. Churchill, and so widely and bravely quoted by comfortable people (Day 1983, 263–64).

Perhaps most problematic is the relationship of hospitality to agrarianism, Peter Maurin's insistence that we must return to the land by creating farming cooperatives. The history of Worker efforts to create farms has revealed a profound conflict between serious efforts to farm and providing hospitality to those with no interest in farming. However, at least one Worker has articulated the notion that hospitality is a practice more congruent with agrarian communities than with modern cities (Naughton 1946).

Catholic Worker Hospitality in Cross-Cultural Perspective

In many respects the Catholic Worker stands in the mainstream of hospitality as it has been practiced across cultures and across time. There is a strong religious sanction. The guest is regarded as divine. Hospitality is closely tied to charity. There is little or no effort at conversion or rehabilitation. Hospitality is conducted in one's home. There are, however, two important respects in which it differs.

The first concerns the time dimension. Although many Catholic Worker houses place time limits on shelter, some do not. And, as far as I know, no house places time limits on sharing food: many guests eat daily at Worker houses for years or decades. This lack of a time limit leads to a tension between providing hospitality and building community, a tension I shall discuss in more detail in later chapters. Second, Worker hospitality is a full-time occupation, while in many cultures it is a peripheral activity.

A comparison with early Christian hospitality in particular is revealing, since the Worker claims early Christianity as its prime model and since both groups used the same scriptural references to justify and explain their customs. Both are examples of a subcultural hospitality that contrasts with the practices of the wider culture. In both, a large part of hospitality is directed toward the poor. In both, the Eucharist is linked to hospitality practice.

However, if the recent analyses of early Christian hospitality are accurate, there is a crucial difference in the function of hospitality in the two groups. For the early Christians, hospitality functioned largely to spread the Gospel. For the Catholic Worker, hospitality is largely a matter of redistributing resources. The two types of hospitality, then, are not synonymous.

Catholic Worker Hospitality and Rehabilitation

The essence of Worker hospitality may be revealed by contrasting it with the model of rehabilitation that holds nearly undisputed hegemony over the "helping professions" today. As many critics (Galper 1975; Bailey and Brake 1975) have noted, the rehabilitation model locates problems within the individual and sets about to change the individual, to make him or her more useful to society. Society itself remains largely unexamined.

Catholic Worker hospitality takes the opposite approach. The individual person is received hospitably, with no attempt at rehabilitation. The object of rehabilitation is society rather than the individual "client." This is true in two senses. First, through nonviolent protest, newspapers, "clarification of thought," and the example they provide, Workers attempt to rehabilitate society, to make it more human, to make it a society "in which it is easier to be good." Second, by their combined personal efforts, Workers do transform society to some extent. Thus, a handful of full-time volunteers, a hundred or so part-time volunteers, and a few thousand donors ensured that through Unity Kitchen the city of Syracuse in the 1970s was a community in which any man could find a free place to sleep and any person could get a free meal every day. From the vantage point of the poor, Syracuse was a different community than it would have been had Unity Kitchen not existed.

Thus, although the Worker effort at rehabilitation is largely by example, the example is not meant primarily for the destitute guest. Rather it is meant for those who have the social and financial resources to themselves become hosts to the poor. It is middle-class capitalist society that must be rehabilitated, not the poor.

One could say that the traditional rehabilitation model provides rehabilitation to the individual and hospitality to society in the hope of returning individuals to the service of society. In contrast, Catholic Worker hospitality provides hospitality to the individual and rehabilitation to society in the hopes of returning society to the service of persons. It is a profoundly sociological approach, in contrast to the psychological emphasis of the rehabilitation model.

Peter Maurin (1977, 94) expressed the contrast well:

The training of social workers
enables them to help people
to adjust themselves
to the existing environment.
The training of social workers does not enable them
to help people to change the environment. . . .
In Houses of Hospitality
social workers can acquire
that art of human contacts
and that social-mindedness
or understanding of social forces
which will make them critical
of the existing environment
and the free creative agents
of a new environment.

My Participant Observation at Three Houses

The next three chapters detail the practice of hospitality at three Catholic Worker houses that I observed between 1982 and 1984. Several methodological issues must be addressed before I begin the descriptions.

I will not discuss the arguments for utilizing qualitative rather than quantitative methods. These arguments have been amply covered in the literature (e.g., Taylor and Bogdan 1984; Blumer 1969). Instead, I shall discuss the ways in which my methodology differs from standard participant observation, and the strengths and weaknesses of my approach.[4]

I chose to observe each house for only two to three months for several reasons. The transient nature of residence in Worker houses allows one to become an insider within a month or two. It is common for people to volunteer at a house for a short time; thus, "temporary live-in worker" is an accepted role at most houses. The burden of the work ensures that responsibility and, consequently, insider status are quickly bestowed on a newcomer, particularly if she or he is "young and healthy," as one Worker put it. My two years of experience working at Unity Kitchen gave me a base of knowledge on which to draw in interpreting events at the houses and thus enabled me to make productive use of the relatively short periods spent at each house. Finally, my status as live-in researcher meant that I was doing participant observation twenty-four hours a day, thus drastically increasing the amount of contact with subjects per month over a traditional participant-observation schedule.

Although I went to the houses in order to study them, I adopted the role of Worker, rather than that of pure observer. There are many arguments against using this approach, but most focus on either the biasing effect of one's emotional reactions or on the reactive nature of participation. Emotional reactions can lead to bias. However, if recognized and reflected upon, your emotional reaction can be a valuable source of data. You don't fully understand the life situation of a Worker in the New York house until you come back from a night spent away from the house only to be told that your bed was given out to someone from the streets last night and "you'd better check it because he was really filthy and probably had lice."

Adopting a Worker role does make one's actions more likely to affect the setting. The other side of the coin is that others come to see you as a natural part of the setting and thus become less likely to alter their behavior in your presence. For example, on a return trip to the New York house, I mentioned to a Worker that I had met with another sociologist, who had begun studying the house using traditional participant observation shortly after I had left. The Worker responded, "That's interesting. I never thought of you as studying us." "Didn't you know I was doing my dissertation?" I asked. "Well, yes, but this puts it in a different light."

As a Worker I attempted to follow the implicit rules of the setting. By doing this, I gained access to a type of information not readily available through pure observation, namely, the reactions of others to my breaking of the rules. This is an excellent way of studying action and interaction, particularly if one accepts Peter Winch's (1958) argument that human action is essentially rule following.

When I met with the sociologist mentioned above, we talked for several hours and discovered that our observations generally meshed well, but with each of us occasionally revealing insights that the other had missed. One of the topics we discussed was the poor quality of the food. I told her that I had encountered resistance from within the house when I had tried a couple of times to give out better food to people who came to the door, food that was reserved for use by people in the house. "You mean there's food for people in the house and food for those who come to the door?" she asked. This was apparently a revelation to her, but had been a fact of life for me through much of my stay.

When I was at the Mustard Seed, I was told from the beginning that one person was in charge of the food. Because of my previous Worker experience, however, I misunderstood this statement. At other houses, when someone comes to the door and asks for food, the Worker who answers the door goes to the larder and gets them some unless there is some reason to believe they're "pulling a con." I assumed that, although Sally was in charge of food distribution, this general rule of operation held here as well. I was quickly informed of my misperception as soon as I acted on my interpretation of the rule. It was made quite clear to me that food did not go out of the house without Sally's permission. Since the rule was violated at times by veteran Workers, I may never have picked up on the force of the "All food goes through Sally" norm if I had not violated it myself.

Two types of rule breaking can be useful to a researcher. The first is breaking a rule because of misreading the rule. This serves as a valuable corrective to observations. The second is breaking a rule intentionally, as a sociological experiment to investigate the boundaries of the rule. Rule breaking serves not only as a check on one's misperceptions but also as a tool of sociological experimentation.

When a pure researcher asks a question, it is purely to record the answer as a piece of data. However, when the researcher is also a Worker, the question is often asked in order to perform the Worker role correctly. Responses to such questions may be more complete than responses to questions that are asked purely for research purposes. Adopting the role of a worker also leads to greater empathy with fellow workers. The élan at the Worker is something akin to that of the army. Workers face situations that are occasionally dangerous and usually demanding, and they resolve them by depending on each other. This greatly increases rapport.

Reflective analysis of the conflicts between one's role as Worker and one's role as researcher can provide valuable insights into the situation. My best example of this came from my Mustard Seed research. I discovered that some of the Workers were prepared to enforce social order with baseball bats. My socialization into the Worker had emphasized nonviolence, and my immediate reaction was one of shock and consternation. If I had been there purely in a Worker role I would have raised objections and probably been forced to leave the house. However, I rationalized that my role as researcher was to understand. Therefore, I muted my criticism after my initial broaching of the subject met with a none too cordial reception, and I remained in the house (although attempting to sidetrack violence in particular instances without overtly criticizing those who condoned it). Such situations enabled me to analyze my own conception of the role of a Catholic Worker.

Another difference between my approach and traditional participant observation was my decision to live in each house for the period
of observation. In part, this was a sine qua non of the research: I
couldn't have afforded to live elsewhere. Thus, the reciprocity involved in my research was considerably more intricate than that in
traditional participant observation—I contributed as a worker, but
I also received free room and board, something that I suspect few
researchers have received from their subjects. Catholic Workers are
so used to giving free room and board, however, that they scarcely
seemed to consider this a contribution they had made to me. It was
certainly never brought up, either explicitly or implicitly, in any of
the houses.

Living-in made it more difficult to keep complete, detailed field
notes, in part for lack of time. Furthermore, I had a very practical
difficulty with typing my notes in the house. When one tells one's
subjects that one is keeping a journal, they usually assume that one
is keeping a diary—an effort of a few minutes a day. In most studies,
nothing ever occurs to change this assumption. However, when I
began typing my field notes in Rochester, people began asking "What
are you doing?" after hearing me pound away several hours a day.
The situation became even more complex in Worcester, where there
was a strong worker-scholar split. I decided to handwrite my notes
because the sound of my typing would have labeled me as a "College
Joe," thus undermining my rapport with those who despised College
Joes. I continued the policy of handwriting notes in the New York
house, where it was nearly impossible to find a private place to spend
a few hours writing.

There are, however, some advantages to live-in research. It intensified the research experience, allowing me to limit my time at
each house to a couple of months. Furthermore, backstage behavior is much harder to conceal from a researcher when she or he is
actually living on the research site. An example of this is the extent
of drinking in the house. This is relatively easy to conceal from a researcher who appears only for limited periods, but almost impossible
to conceal from one who is living in the house.

In short, my field methods essentially followed the approach recommended by Mehan and Wood (1975, 227): "If the purpose of
the research is to know the reality work of a phenomenon, then
the researcher must begin by first becoming the phenomenon. The
researcher must become a full-time member of the reality to be
studied."

I followed the following procedure with respect to informed consent and confidentiality. I began by writing to each house, explaining that I wished to work there as part of a research project. After receiving permission (which was denied at a fourth house), I negotiated when I would work there. In the following chapters, I use the actual names of the houses and the cities in which they are located. I also use the actual names of persons who had been involved with the house but had died before my observations. (It seemed ridiculous to give a pseudonym to Dorothy Day.) I do use pseudonyms for persons who were alive at the time of my observations.

My observation reports focus on the practice of hospitality. Other activities of the house—newspaper publication, political protest, liturgies, spirituality—are largely ignored except insofar as they impact hospitality. For reasons of confidentiality, I have not treated topics of sexuality and intimate relationships at the houses. This omission does distort the portrait of hospitality at some of the houses a bit; however, it does not affect my basic argument.

These three houses are not in any way meant to be representative of all Worker houses. Instead, the houses are used to investigate variation in the implementation of the philosophy of hospitality. They merely establish that there is variation without providing any estimate of the extent of variation. I did not study Catholic Worker farms or houses outside the northeastern United States.

Any quotations not attributed to a particular author come from my interviews with house members. For the sake of readability of longer quotes, I have not indicated every omission by the use of ellipses. Quotations that include such punctuation are available in Murray (1987).

My periods of participant observation consist of but a brief slice of the history of each house. All of the houses have changed in important ways since I was there. One has burned down. Another has a different house director. A third has undergone a traumatic split over the issue of homosexuality. The snapshots I give of a house cannot be assumed to be generalizable even across the history of the house. Indeed, if I had changed the order in which I visited the houses, a quite different picture would have emerged. Two of the houses had undergone crises before my arrival. If I had arrived in the middle of those crises, the focus of my analysis may have shifted dramatically.

Since these three houses are not a representative sample, the basis for generalization must be the extent to which the social processes described are recognizable by those with experience with other Houses of Hospitality. The similarities I discovered give me hope that such recognition will occur.

4

The Flagship:
St. Joseph's in New York City

From the moment I knocked on the door at St. Joseph's House, I encountered the egalitarianism of Worker hospitality. Early in December I took the subway from Grand Central Station to Houston Street and stepped into the Lower East Side for the first time since my visit to the house in the mid-1970s. Although the neighborhood had become increasingly gentrified over the last few years, it still bore traces of its proximity to the Bowery, two blocks to the west. Shadowed by abandoned buildings, a small group of men huddled around a fire in a garbage bin. Two blocks to the east is an area well known as an illegal drug market. The Municipal Men's Shelter, Maryhouse, and the Hell's Angels' local headquarters were two blocks to the north, on Third Street.

The house was located on First Street, on a block that was generally quiet, although I once saw dozens of people literally running amok when drug dealers set up shop for the day in an abandoned building on the other side of the street. The block consists mostly of row houses, most residential, but some abandoned or commercial. St. Joseph's House itself was a narrow five-story row house.

The door was locked. An elfin woman with snowy white hair answered my knock. I told her I was the researcher they were expecting. She told me to wait and called Peter, a bearded, soft-spoken man in his thirties. I explained myself again. Peter said, "Oh yeah, you're coming the first. I had forgotten that was today." He invited me in and I followed him around as he answered questions from the dozen or so people sitting around the dining room.

He steered me to a table where Jack, a middle-aged black man, was sitting. Peter said to me, "He's coming in tonight too, so we may as well do this together." He turned his attention to Jack, "So you need to stay a week." "Right, I work at the Human Resources Administration, but I'm off for this week." "That's good because after a week I'll need the space again." Peter then spoke to both of us. "There's not much to explain here. Everybody does what they want in terms of helping." Jack said, "Good, I need something to do this week. I'll be willing to help out." I also expressed a willingness to help. Peter told Jack, "I'm not sure if I'm going to put you on the third floor or on the fifth. Harry will go on the fifth." Jack asked, "Is there a difference?" "No, just space. Why don't you come up and I'll check out the third."

On the way upstairs we ran into Harvey, a thin white man with unkempt gray hair, standing on a landing, talking engagedly to himself. Finally noticing us, he asked, "Which way do you want to go?" We said up, and he moved out of our way, talking to himself all the while. Jack, looking somewhat taken aback, observed to Peter, "You've got quite some people here."

Peter looked into the third-floor dormitory, decided it was already too full, and guided us to the fifth, where he gave Jack the bed of a Worker who was away for "awhile" and gave me a folding cot placed in front of the closet. He gave me clean sheets and a blanket and told Jack that the sheets on his bed, though a bit rumpled, were clean.

Here I was, a sociological researcher, arriving to study the Catholic Worker movement, and I was treated simply as one more person needing a bed. To the Workers, Jack and I had the same status and were treated essentially the same way. As happens disturbingly often at a Worker house, one could see the words of the New Testament enacted literally (in this case James 2:1–4):

> My brethren, show no partiality as you hold the faith of our Lord Jesus Christ, the Lord of glory. For if a man with gold rings and in fine clothing comes into your assembly, and a poor man in shabby clothing also comes in, and you pay attention to the one who wears the fine clothing and say, "Have a seat here, please," while you say to the poor man, "Stand there," or "Sit at my feet," have you not made distinctions among yourselves, and become judges with evil thoughts?

Although I hardly came in fine raiment, I did come with the social and educational credentials that often serve as its functional equivalent in our society. These made no difference in my reception at the Worker. Indeed, for the first week or so, my closest friends and companions were Jack and "Gimbel's Irv," a man who arrived seeking shelter around the same time. We were the newcomers, and that, rather than our reasons for coming, determined our status.

This is not to say that there were no permanent status distinctions in the house. Status was quite problematic, as I will explain later. Nevertheless, the house was a very serious effort to reduce status differentials between the rich and the poor—an effort that often succeeded in dramatic ways.

However, I was not too concerned with the issue of equality at that point. Despite the fact that I had lived at three other Worker houses by this time, I was a bit awe-struck at being here, at St. Joseph's, the "original" Catholic Worker house, the direct successor to the Teresa-Joseph Cooperative described in the previous chapter. Physically, of course, the house has had numerous incarnations—on Fifteenth Street, on Charles Street, on Mott Street, on Spring Street, on Chrystie Street, and, since 1968, on East First Street. Nonetheless, as a social entity, this house was "the original."

Strictly speaking, St. Joseph's House was only part of the original Catholic Worker community. In the mid-1970s, the New York Worker established Maryhouse two blocks away, on Third Street, as a shelter for homeless women. Dorothy Day moved from First Street into Maryhouse after it was opened and died in her room there. Also part of the original Worker community almost from the beginning was the Catholic Worker farm, which has also been at various locations—Easton, Tivoli, and, currently, Marlboro, New York. Finally, there was a beach cottage on Staten Island. These enterprises together constituted the original New York Catholic Worker community.

It has been this community that has produced the *Catholic Worker* paper for over half a century, that sent Workers to protest Naziism and assist in the Seamen's strike in the 1930s, to side with the grave-diggers against the Diocese of New York in the 1950s, to be arrested protesting the nuclear air-raid drills in the late 1950s and early 1960s, to join in the civil rights, anti-Vietnam War, and Farmworkers' campaigns in the 1960s and 1970s. (Such activities continue today. While I was there, the editor of the paper left for six months with Witness for Peace in Nicaragua.) It was the house where Dorothy Day, Peter Maurin, Stanley Vishnewski, Ammon Hennacy, Michael Harrington, and many others have lived and worked. It was the example that has inspired all other houses. I was anxious to see what it was like in the 1980s.

House Organization

As a sociologist, I was interested in how the house was organized. This question is particularly intriguing at St. Joseph's, given the anarchist philosophy of the Worker and the fact that the movement's charismatic leader had died just a few years previously. Indeed, one recent book (Aronica 1987) is devoted to the organizational effects of Dorothy's death. From my experience, it appeared that the house had two different levels of organization: one for major "policy-type" decisions, and the other for day-to-day decisions about hospitality.

Organization for Major Decisions

After living at the house for two months, I must confess that I had only the vaguest of notions as to how major decisions were made. My experience at the other houses had led me to believe that I would learn this aspect of the house without a great deal of effort. I found, however, that this was not the case in New York. In the first place, decisions could be made either at St. Joseph's or at Maryhouse, decreasing my chance of being present when decisions were made. Second, because there were so many Workers, I did not become as important a part of the community as I did at other houses and thus did not have as much access to decision making. Most importantly, the New York house has had a long history of dealing with visitors, students, and researchers. It long ago established techniques to preserve the backstage of decision-making (Goffman 1959). In any event, my primary interest was in the day-to-day practice of hospitality, and so I did not pursue the question too closely. Nonetheless, a few observations may clarify the situation somewhat.

The decision-making "system" combined elements of collective decision-making, authority by seniority, consensus among whoever happens to be around, and pure anarchy. The situation was complicated by the fact that some decisions were made jointly for and by both Maryhouse and St. Joseph's, others were made for and by the individual houses, and still others concerned the paper. When major issues arose concerning the house, there was an effort to call meetings of either all the Workers or all house members.

Two such meetings were held during my stay. The first, which I did not attend, was a meeting of Workers held in the apartment of one of the old-time Workers. A number of issues were discussed, including whether the soupline should be increased from three to four days a week. Several Workers later complained that, although the decision making was technically collective, "nothing happens unless [one of the senior Workers] wants it to happen."

A second meeting was held a few weeks later to continue discussion of adding a day to the soupline. This meeting was held in the house, and everyone was encouraged to attend—Workers, residents, and even temporary guests. After a half hour or so of discussion someone suggested that those who had not spoken be given a chance to voice their opinions, and all present did so. The general consensus seemed to be against adding a day—the argument was made that if the present glut of Workers disappeared this would leave the same old hands with more work. It was decided that people should ask the men on the line what they felt they needed, as well as going over to the Men's Shelter to see just what the city was now offering. It did seem to me that the word of the more senior Workers carried the most weight. The issue was finally resolved at a meeting after I had left—a meal was added on Thursdays.

There was, apparently, no one person formally in charge of the house, although the editor of the paper usually had a good deal of influence. Decision making was done collectively, although the group that formed the decision-making collectivity was not clearly defined. The house was an example par excellence of "negotiated order" (Strauss 1978). Given the strength of the commitment to anarchism, nearly everything was open to negotiation by almost anyone. Roles, rules, and statuses were negotiated in a way that does not happen in bureaucracy.

Organization for Day-to-Day Decisions: "Taking the House"

One cannot comprehend hospitality at St. Joseph's without some understanding of the notion of "taking the house," the rather curious way in which the New York Workers institutionalized anarchism. Essentially, they created a benevolent dictatorship that changed hands every five hours. There were three shifts a day (8–12, 12–5, and 5–10), each of which was covered by someone "on the house." The person on the house had near-absolute authority over what went on during her or his shift. She or he answered the phone, answered the door, decided who got in, who got clothes, who got food, and who was given overnight shelter, maintained order, and addressed any problems that arose.

Everyone was expected to defer to whoever was on house. This was a strong norm that held even when other people had vastly more experience. Thus, when I was "on the house," experienced Workers would turn problems over to me. During my first week or two of being "on the house," they would occasionally correct me; after that, however, I was pretty much autonomous. Enforcement of this norm was illustrated by a story I was told by a woman who had recently become a house Worker and who felt that one of the old-time Workers was infringing on her authority. She talked about this to another old-time Worker, who "taught me that when [she] starts [interfering], you just jangle your keys and say 'Do you want the house now?' Now I just jangle the keys. I don't even have to say anything."

Each shift included special tasks. The morning shift cleaned up breakfast (which was usually laid out by a man who came in from 7:00 A.M. and worked until 8:00 A.M.) and prepared lunch. On soupline days, the morning person was in charge of the soupline. The afternoon shift entailed responsibility for cleaning up after lunch and setting the tables for supper. The evening shift included cleaning up after supper and a brief cleanup just before ten. One's style of hospitality could be affected by how well one was doing in finishing these standard tasks. I tended to be less gracious to someone who came to the door if it was 4:45 and I didn't have the tables set for supper.

A wide variety of styles existed for taking the house, and the norm was that once someone was accepted as eligible to take the house, his or her judgment was respected. She or he was not constrained by any rules that had to be followed, but was expected to use "common sense" to react to any situation. Even when I pressed for a rule, I had a hard time getting one. One evening when I was on the house, a temporary guest went out, saying he'd be back later. I asked one of the experienced Workers what I should do if the guest came back drunk. He replied, "I don't know. Just use your common sense." After several more attempts to get something a bit more concrete from him, he said, "If he looks like he's going to just come in and crash out, fine, but if not . . ." His voice trailed off, implying that perhaps then I shouldn't let him in. And that was as close as I could get to a rule about a situation that arises several times a week. I noted in my journal: "Try as I will to get a rule articulated often it is 'use your common sense.' Several people have told me 'Everybody on the house does it in their own way' and this appears true. Everyone develops their own rules, sometimes discussing things with others, sometimes not."

Some people who took the house were relatively authoritarian, reluctant to let anyone in the door except for a "legitimate" reason. Others were very laid-back, allowing people to come in until the atmosphere of the house became a bit tense. In general, people from outside the house who worked one shift a week tended to be more lenient than Workers who lived in the house, and less experienced Workers tended to be more lenient than more experienced Workers. This was in part due to the effect of experience—since people created their own rules, those who had had more bad experiences tended to have more rules to prevent similar problems. It was also in part due to the emotional strain of taking the house. The experience was demanding, as one had to decide who did and who did not get such basics as shelter and clothes and had to put up with a certain amount of abuse. Someone who did it only once a week simply had more time to recover for the next shift. I felt emotionally exhausted after taking the house three days in a row.

The weekly schedule for taking the house was set up at the Sunday evening meeting of Workers. No one chaired the meeting, although someone would take responsibility for recording the schedule. The shifts that were covered regularly by volunteers were filled in first. Then Workers stated what shifts they would like to work. After everyone had volunteered, the group negotiated to see who would fill any gaps in the schedule. Generally, a Worker did between two and four shifts a week.

Theoretically, anyone could become a "house Worker"; however, while I was there, only ideologically committed persons took the house. In the past, however, persons who initially came to the house from the streets have taken the house. The process by which one becomes a house worker was fairly standard.

Generally, the candidate is a middle-class person who either moves into the house or begins coming regularly to help out. One does not move into a predefined role immediately; rather, one negotiates the role one will play by hanging out in the dining room and asking if anything needs to be done. On soupline mornings, the response usually is "butter bread," so one grabs a knife, sits down with other volunteers, and butters several dozen loaves. During the meal, newcomers are often steered in the direction of washing dishes; they may also ladle soup, wait on tables, or do a combination of these things. Roles are fluid and often change hands during the course of the two-hour soupline.

Given this situation, one's initial strategy is to observe what is being done, and step in and do something when needed. Gradually one becomes accepted as someone who knows what's going on and as a reliable Worker. All of this is a necessary prelude, a first step toward taking the house. Gradually, one can begin to advance the idea that you feel you are ready to take the house. This can't be done too soon. I offered within a day or two of coming and was told I should wait a week or two, "until you get to know the guys." Within the week, however, people became more open to my taking the house.

Your first "on the house" assignment comes at the Sunday evening meeting. Generally, you will have talked to a couple of Workers beforehand about your intentions. You volunteer to take a shift and if no one objects, you get one. For the first couple of shifts, a new Worker is apprenticed—assigned to a shift with an experienced Worker. This allows you to learn the role by example, sharing responsibilities and asking questions. This apprenticeship is the second stage of becoming a house Worker.

Training for the role is more aphoristic than systematic.[1] Even during apprenticeship, you are not given a list of rules but are told to use your discretion. In certain situations the person with whom you are working will give you hints, but no hard and fast rules. The norm is that accepting a person for the role means trusting them to use their own judgment. A wide variation in styles is accepted.

After apprenticeship is over, advice is usually accompanied by an affirmation that you are making the decisions: "It's up to you, but I would recommend not letting so many people in for coffee since you're new here," or "If I were you, given that you're new, I wouldn't do clothing today. Of course it's up to you."

The on-the-house structure resonates with the Catholic Worker notions of personal responsibility and anarchism in a number of ways. First, no one is assigned shifts, unless they have made it clear that they want to work but haven't yet indicated their preferences. People must choose to do shifts, and there is no pressure to do more than one has offered to do unless there is a real shortage of Workers. Second, there is a strong norm that once a person is accepted as an on-the-house Worker, his or her judgment should be respected. There is no system of rules for a Worker to follow—only a few aphoristic traditions of how things are handled. This gives maximum flexibility for a personal response to problems that arise.

Hospitality

St. Joseph's was open every day from 8:00 A.M. to 10:00 P.M. That did not, however, mean that the door was unlocked. What it meant was that during those hours someone was responsible for answering the door and deciding who to let in.

The door was the focus of hospitality. There was a group of people who had keys, a group that was always let in when they knocked, and the vast majority, who had to negotiate with the person who answers the door. Many who came to the door did not even ask to come in—they asked only for bread and butter "to go."

On entering, one would usually find several people, sometimes as many as a dozen, sitting around the tables, talking, and drinking coffee or tea. Some may be in the kitchen area cooking the next meal. Some may be waiting for the person who answered the door to get them some clothes. Others were waiting in line to use the bathroom. Most were ragged looking, often wearing overcoats even on warm days.

The dining room was small, containing five tables that seated only twenty-eight people. The neon lights on the ceiling were shaded by strips of faded flowered shelving paper, except during the Christmas season when the strips were replaced by Christmas wrapping paper from which paper snowflakes are hung. The room was painted yellow and a number of pictures adorned the wall—woodcuts by Fritz Eichenberg, a photo of Peter Maurin and one of Dorothy Day as well as several other religious pictures. On a slightly raised tile floor to the rear was the kitchen area, which contained a large black stove, a small round soup stove, a white refrigerator, and a three basin metal sink.

The daily practice of hospitality can be conceptualized in terms of the corporal Works of Mercy. The bulk of the work of the house consisted of feeding the hungry, sheltering the homeless, and clothing the naked or near-naked. ("Giving drink to the thirsty," perhaps because it was an unfortunate choice of words in this skid-row milieu, was unobtrusively incorporated into "feeding the hungry.") The other corporal Works of Mercy—visiting the sick, visiting the imprisoned, and burying the dead—were also considered to be part of Worker hospitality and were performed in a less routinized way as the need arose. Together with advocacy at social service agencies, they constituted the informal aspect of Worker hospitality.

Food

I felt a great sense of tradition at the soupline—in many ways, the operation had probably not changed much since the 1930s. Someone volunteered to get up early and make between forty and fifty gallons of soup, usually consisting of beans and vegetables, plus, perhaps, a bit of meat. The person taking the house organized everything else—buttering two huge trays of bread, setting the tables, getting the dishes and pots washed, and making coffee. If a new volunteer didn't know what to do, the house person would steer him or her toward one of these tasks—usually buttering bread. More experienced volunteers simply began work on whatever seemed to need doing.

By 10:00, everything was ready. A thirty-gallon pot of soup was placed on top of a metal milk basket in back of the serving table and someone volunteered to ladle. Just before the door was opened, the house person called everyone into a circle for a moment of prayer, usually asking for a peaceful meal. This prayer was an innovation adopted while I was there, decided upon in a meeting of house Workers. After the prayer, soup and bread were placed at each of the table settings and the person at the door let the first twenty-eight people inside.

It was a flurry of activity from then on. Two persons washed dishes, one watched the door, one ladled soup, the house person made coffee and made decisions about any unusual situations that arose. Everyone else waited on tables. If the house person allowed seconds, the waiters picked up empty soup bowls when a guest signaled them and they returned with a refill and perhaps two more slices of bread. As someone left, one waiter sponged off his place at the table and another brought a new place setting of soup, bread, and coffee cup. When they were finished, most guests took their dishes over to the dishwasher. The few who didn't were asked to do so; however, if they just walked out, the waiters cleared the space themselves. Guests often said a word of thanks to the dishwasher as they handed over their dishes.

Servers often duplicated tasks and got in each other's way. Waiters were not assigned to tables, so each tried to serve the whole room. Often two waiters brought bowls of soup to the same space simultaneously. If there were too many waiters, a competition developed among the less experienced to see who could get to a table first. Sometimes there were simply so many waiters that they tripped over each other. At these times, experienced Workers simply stopped waiting on tables and let the volunteers do it. At other times, of course, there were too few Workers to get the job done. One never knew how many servers would show up. Thus, the more experienced Workers showed up regularly, prepared to work if there weren't many volunteers or to sit around and chat if there were more than enough hands.

The soupline continued in this way for two hours. During this time, volunteers traded places, spelling each other at soup ladling or dishwashing. There was a constant stream of diners, mostly men, mostly black, in tattered clothes, often smelling of booze. Some stood out. Juan, a young Puerto Rican, would dash in, a bundle of frenetic energy. He wore a ski cap pulled completely over his head and often he carried around his neck a thick metal chain, which he might pull off and handle nervously. Everyone warned you to treat him carefully. Sometimes he left by dashing out the door like all the demons of Hell were after him, upsetting his chair as he went. While I was there, however, he never attacked anyone. Earl, an elderly man with wild white hair, would come in with the aid of a broken three-legged walker and rarely left without engaging in at least one screaming argument with Helen. Willie, a tall, rangy black man always came in carrying a bent, splintered, guitar that had once been bright red. He was a quiet man who stood out primarily because of his physical appearance. Tex, a tall, lean, one-eyed man with a Southern drawl, was someone I recognized from Unity Kitchen some years ago.

There had been one substantial change in the soupline since the death of Dorothy Day. In the summer of 1982 it was reduced from seven to three days a week. Those involved at the house at the time said that the complement of Workers was very low—down to three or four—that the soupline was getting increasingly violent, and that, with the sudden interest in the homeless, other souplines were opening. One Worker said of the decision:

> It was getting so people dreaded the soupline. And if you aren't enjoying it some, if you're just enduring, then there's something wrong. We thought we would do things better. We used to serve just black tea, dry bread, and soup, not coffee with cream and sugar, and bread and butter, like now. The meal used to be a lot more Spartan than now. So we aren't doing as much, but we are doing it better.
>
> It also has changed the rhythm of the house. Now the house revolves around the weekends—Friday, Saturday, and Sunday souplines. It used to be the same, day after day. No day was different. Now, there's a different rhythm, and that's good. It breaks the week up. There's change in the schedule.
>
> There were fewer people working then. You'd end up being on the house five days a week. It was just getting to be too much. We were doing it just for the sake of doing it. We weren't really looking at the guys' needs and whether we were serving them. It was just because it was tradition. I'm really pleased that we were able to make that decision.

Another stated:

> You should have been here a few years ago. We had the soupline seven days a week. I don't know how we took it. It was a hard decision to go down to three days. It was the first time the Worker didn't

serve every day. Everyone was running around feeling guilty and all. But the line had grown so much. And there were a lot of places springing up to feed people. People went around to find out about these places and decided that the weekends were the time when the fewest places were open.

After going down to three days, they experimented briefly with serving different types of meals—for example, hot dogs and beans instead of soup, but stopped this after a few weeks because there wasn't always enough to go around and "with soup you can always add more water."

Accounts of the change differed considerably. Workers tended to say that the problem of violence was so great that it justified the change and that the quality of the food had improved since. Residents tended to feel that the quality of the meal had declined. Some part-time volunteers were not convinced that the level of violence had justified the change.

There were several other ways in which food was distributed. Every day, from 8:00 A.M. until 10:00 P.M., people walked up to the door asking for food. A plastic container of buttered bread was kept by the door, and the person on the house gave a few slices to whoever asked. Occasionally, the house person invited someone in for tea and bread; usually, however, the bread was just handed out the door.

Not everyone was grateful for bread. One Worker told me that a recipient smeared the buttered bread on the door in disgust. Another Worker said that while she was walking toward the house one day she saw someone come away from the door with two slices of bread, throw them on sidewalk, and trample them. When he noticed her, he looked up sheepishly as if to say "nothing personal." I heard a few complaints about receiving only bread and butter myself. However, I was struck by the number who received this meager gift meekly, even thankfully. It made me wonder a bit about Edwin Meese's proclamation, made about this time, that there is no hunger in America.

Another means of food distribution was the house meal. Between those living in the two houses and the "friends of the house" who had standing invitations to the meals, sixty to ninety persons were at each meal. At St. Joseph's House alone, there were between twenty-five and forty.

Breakfast was a "pick-up" meal. The morning house person set out coffee, cold cereal, fruit, jelly, and bread for toast. Breakfast was available from 8:00 until 9:30, so it did not have the character of a group meal.

Lunch was more formal, usually consisting of soup, fruit, and, perhaps, cold cuts for sandwiches. The food was set out on the serving table and everyone helped themselves.

Supper was prepared in St. Joseph's House for both houses. Workers from both houses took turns preparing it. At 5:00, two Maryhouse Workers would appear with a shopping cart to take their share, after which the St. Joseph's House meal would begin. The cook and a couple of helpers dished out the food to two or three servers who would take it to the tables. The menu included meat two or three times a week and vegetarian meals the other nights. It was a full-course dinner, including vegetables, bread, coffee, and sometimes even desert. Persons off the street could be invited in to eat by the house person if there were leftovers.

One quantitative indicator I should have collected was my own weight. The only times in my life that I have lost weight have been at Catholic Worker houses. This was not because the food was of poor quality—on the contrary, it was often excellent. Rather, it was because at a Catholic Worker house you become painfully aware that every bite you take could be going to someone who is a lot hungrier than you. That second piece of chicken you want could be a meal for someone looking for leftovers. Sociologically, this points to the difference between face-to-face interaction and more abstract interaction. It is always true that the food I eat could feed someone who needs it more. However, it is only in the face-to-face situation that this fact affects my eating habits. The Catholic Worker places you in a situation of face-to-face contact with the poor where matters of distributive justice are as concrete as the food you eat.

Shelter

Shelter at St. Joseph's was a rather unstructured affair. There was no space reserved for "shelter guests." Rather, guests were given whatever bed was available, whether that be a bed in which guests usually slept or the bed of a Worker who was gone for the night.

The upper three floors were sleeping quarters. Each floor contained a dormitory with about half a dozen beds, two private or semiprivate rooms, a bathroom, and a kitchen. The fourth floor was for women, the third and fifth for men. Private and semiprivate rooms appeared to be assigned largely by seniority, regardless of one's status as Worker or resident. The most recently arrived Workers lived in the dormitories.

There was also one long-time resident who lived in the basement. He came to the house over a decade ago and lived in an upstairs dorm.

After his habit of collecting, repairing, and playing TV's made him persona non grata in the dorm, he was moved to the dining room, where he lived for a few years on top of a desk surrounded by his TV equipment. When this proved unsatisfactory, his desk was thrown into the basement, which then became his kingdom.

The person on the house decided who would be admitted into shelter. There were no rules as such about accepting or rejecting persons, although there were some unwritten and largely unspoken norms. The most important of these was that shelter should be given only to someone who could convince you that they had only a temporary need for shelter. Generally, guests were limited to one or two nights, although they could stay for a week or even a month if they could convince Workers that they had a plan that they could implement in that time.

Two types of negotiations for shelter occurred: negotiation for the initial offer of shelter and negotiation for extension of the stay. Both types of negotiation occurred between those wanting to stay and whoever was on the house at the time. Generally, the initial offer of shelter included a time limit, but many guests treated this as negotiable once they had achieved entry, and Workers often did negotiate extensions.

Negotiations could occur over the phone, at the door, or inside the dining room. A person was most likely to be rejected over the phone, particularly if an agency was calling for the person. This was because it was easier to reject a person over the phone and because it was felt that the house does not exist to help agencies "pass the buck" for someone with whom they didn't want to deal.

Whether or not a person was accepted for shelter depended on a number of factors: if any beds were available, the "psychic space" in the house (i.e., whether Workers felt overburdened by the guests already there), the weather, and the self-presentation of the potential guest. If no beds were available, the person was usually turned away. There were two exceptions. First, mattresses could be laid out in the front half of the second floor in an emergency. This had to be cleared, however, with Robert, who was in charge of mailing out the paper, because he had to wake them up early so that he could begin work there. On two bitterly cold nights when two men asked to stay after all the beds had been filled, I asked Robert about using the second floor, and he replied quickly, "On a night like tonight, I say let as many come in as can fit. It's too cold for people to be sleeping out. Just tell him that I'll wake him up at seven, so I can get to work."

This space is not used often, however—less than seven nights in the two months I was there. It was treated as an emergency alternative because it disrupted the work of putting out the paper.

A Worker who had a private room could also allow someone to sleep on the floor there. The night after I arrived, a well-dressed white man appeared, claiming that he had just arrived from Texas for a job interview at Gimbel's but had been mugged, losing all his money. All the beds were full, so George, who was on the house, told him he could stay on a mattress in his room until a bed opened up. "Gimbel's Irv" stayed there for several days, then moved into a bed in the dorm, remaining with us until just after Christmas, when he left under less than auspicious circumstances.

On the other hand, a person could be told that "the house is full" even though beds were empty. When tensions in the house were running high and Workers felt they couldn't deal with the additional psychic burdens usually brought by a "wounded person" from the streets, the house was deemed full. This was usually done informally by discussions among several Workers rather than at the initiative of the person on the house.

Finally, and perhaps most importantly, the negotiation was affected by the way in which the guest presented himself or herself. The operative rule was "we already have enough permanent residents." The person most likely to gain shelter was someone who presented himself or herself as in need of shelter for only a limited time because he or she had a realistic plan for getting shelter elsewhere. Persons who were regulars at the soupline were not likely to be offered shelter, except perhaps for one night in an emergency. Those selected as guests tended to exhibit more middle-class attributes than "men on the line." Andy's story illustrates the negotiation process.

It had been raining off and on all day, and I was on the house for the evening. A short, bedraggled white man in his early thirties came to the door wearing two ragged, filthy sweaters in place of a coat. Andy said, "I talked to a priest. He told me to come here—that this was a community that practiced nonviolence and peace. I'd like to join. I'm a fallen away Catholic, but maybe I could join the order or something." I invited him inside and asked him if he stayed at the shelters. "I don't go there. I don't have anything against them, you know. They're nice places, but it gets violent there, so I mostly live on the streets."

I offered him tea and a sandwich. He seemed like a meek, harmless guy, albeit a bit befuddled. I told him we had no space; however, since this was one of my first evenings on the house, I decided to check with one of the other Workers. George came down and talked to Andy awhile, then said to me, "It's clearly no. He's been coming around for awhile. Some guys just want to join to get the benefits. He's expecting more than a night or two." He gave Andy a list of emergency shelters and went back upstairs. Andy finished his meal, wrote down a few numbers from the list, and asked if he could use the phone to call his brother. I told him I would give him change to use a pay phone. (Persons off the street are not allowed to use the phone.) He left, but returned occasionally for meals.

The other type of negotiation was for extension of one's stay. In most cases, a length of stay was agreed upon when the person first arrived, and this agreement was adhered to. However, some experienced street persons could exploit the on-the-house system to extend their stay far beyond the original agreement. Trapper Bill was an expert at this. He was a muscular white man in his thirties, balding but with longish brown hair and a scar above one eye. He was given shelter one night by Don, who left shortly thereafter for a brief vacation.

After two days, I asked Bill if Don had told him that he had to leave. He replied, "Oh, yeah, they told me I had to check every night to see if there was an empty bed. Is there one tonight?" I said I would check with Peter, who was on the house. Peter said he didn't know anything about Bill's situation, but that there was an extra bed so he may as well spend the night.

After Bill left the room, Gimbel's Irv came over and told me that he was sure Don had told Bill that he couldn't stay beyond last night. On hearing this, George said he was upset with Bill because he was exploiting the house. "This is his last night. He's trying to stay indefinitely. He's already stayed longer than we let most people."

Over the next week, Bill was repeatedly told by the person on the house that "tonight is your last night." However, he was able to utilize the gaping holes in the on-the-house authority structure to extend his stay far beyond the initial agreement. He would simply wait until the next evening and ask the person then on the house whether he could stay just one more night. This person would usually know that Bill was reaching the end of his stay, but would not have been informed that the person on the house the night before had given him "one last night." Thus, Bill was able to prolong his stay for a considerable length of time.

Bill was not the first, nor, I'm sure, was he the last, to negotiate the on-the-house system this way. All Workers knew its flaw—that the lack of communication let people get things from one Worker that another had already denied. However, they didn't see this weakness as grounds for instituting the type of ordered system necessary to prevent such situations. The cost in terms of personalist style to achieve such efficiency was simply too high. Moreover, the current system gave the guests the maximum number of avenues to get what they need. Unlike most bureaucratic social services, if the guest didn't receive satisfaction from one Worker, she or he could simply try the next Worker, who probably wouldn't even know about the first attempt. This maximized the guest's chances of getting what she or he wanted, and may have been part of the unconscious logic behind the "system."

The real burden of giving shelter was not the filling of an extra bed, but the extra social effort required to accommodate a new guest, particularly one with psychological or alcohol problems. Even without emergency-shelter guests, the house was committed to providing hospitality for the residents, many of whom needed little care from the Workers and indeed contributed greatly to the work of the house. A few, however, required a substantial amount of assistance from the Workers. One man who lived at the house for years had to be bathed and shaved by the Workers. One woman regularly came in drunk, screaming racist slurs at any blacks who happened to be present. She also had to be taken to the hospital whenever she fell down and hurt herself. These were persons to whom the house had made a commitment over the years, and who were not likely to be asked to leave in the forseeable future. Their care had to be balanced with the needs of emergency guests.

Clothing

There were actually two clothing distribution systems at St. Joseph's—one run by the Workers and one run by Mother. Mother was a powerful-looking woman with two black beauty marks on her cheeks, a gruff, commanding voice, and a heart of gold—a combination that could be both exasperating and an oasis of cheer and goodwill in a desert of despair. Mother would scour the streets and trash bins for cast-off articles of clothing for "my boys," bring them to the house, and place them in a heap on the front windowsill for "her boys" to pick through. People would come in and look through the pile, occasionally taking an article, although the more discriminating guests wouldn't go near it. If there was a particularly loathsome stench emanating from the pile, an intrepid Worker might risk Mother's wrath by surreptitiously disposing of the offending article or perhaps the whole pile. If Mother caught him or her, she would most likely roar out, "What are ya doin? That's for my boys. That's good stuff!" But the Worker usually prevailed and some of the clothes would be removed. This alternative clothing distribution system was apparently a tradition at the Worker, and no one made a serious attempt to interfere with it.

"Officially," clothing was distributed at 2:00 P.M., Monday through Thursday—the days the soupline was closed. Unofficially, clothing could be distributed at any time by the person on the house at his or her discretion, although the norm was that this should be done only in "emergencies" (a term deliberately left ambiguous).

What happened during the official clothing distribution time depended largely on the discretion of the person on the house, but the procedure was usually as follows. Whoever was on the house would bring piles of clothing upstairs from the clothing room in the basement and lay them out on the tables. At 2:00, people would be let in to pick through whatever was on the tables and take whatever they wished. Items that were in short supply and great demand—underwear, socks, shoes, and winter coats—were not brought up. Instead, guests had to ask the Worker to go down and get them. Coats and shoes were especially hoarded in the winter, and sometimes the person requesting such items would be asked to trade in what he was wearing.

An incident that illustrates the Worker approach happened while I was being apprenticed with Ken, a young Worker who had been there a few months. A half dozen men were inside looking through the clothes. A sharp looking man asked me to go down and get him a red coat that he had seen someone trying on. It sounded suspicious to me because I had seen this man talking to Ken just a bit earlier and it had sounded like he had been asking for a coat. I asked Ken, "Where did you put that red coat? This guy wants it." Ken said to me, "Don't get him a coat. That guy sells clothes. He has a good coat. He took it off." I told the man I couldn't get him the coat and he began to complain, "Why not? You get coats for other guys." "You already have a coat." "So do other guys," he grumbled as he left.

Afterward, Ken told me, "He comes in here and cleans us out all the time. I saw him selling clothes on the street once. It's good that he cleans us out sometimes—we've got to get rid of the stuff. But things like coats are in short supply." Thus, there were two categories of clothes. Those in abundant supply were freely given to whoever wanted them, short of clearing out the whole supply. Those in limited supply were rationed to preserve them for people in real need. Even this rationing, however, was not very systematic.

Workers did not follow the official schedule for clothing distribution too strictly. If the day was too hectic and it didn't look like there would be time between lunch and supper to do the clothing, guests simply were told to come back the next day. On the other hand, one volunteer who regularly was on the house Sunday afternoon always gave out clothes on his shift, despite the fact that it wasn't an "official" clothing day.

At times, giving out clothes could be extremely frustrating. You gave a pair of dry socks to someone, simply to send them back into the rain with leaky shoes. Other times, however, it appeared that a set of clothes could make a difference. One evening when I was on the house, a young black man came to the door asking for clothes. He said he had just been told by his sister that his boss wanted him to come back to work. He had been laid off from a job in the garment district seven months earlier and was living on the street. He wanted the change of clothes to wear to work tomorrow. His elation at this turn of fate seemed too genuine for me to doubt the story: "Another week and no more living in the streets for me. I'll get my paycheck and get a room. This is fantastic." He thanked me profusely for the change of clothes. As much as the Worker ideal is not to expect thanks, occasional incidents like this made the work much easier.

Informal Hospitality

Food, clothing, and shelter were distributed in a somewhat organized fashion. Other aspects of hospitality, however, were not organized at all. Individuals could choose to visit guests who were in hospitals or prisons. Ideologically committed Workers were not the only ones to do so. Some "residents" had people who they visited regularly. Visiting guests in hospital or prison had a different character than visiting a stranger. For the hospitalized guest, such a visit was a sign that the Workers really cared about him or her as a person. They were not coming to visit him as "someone who is sick," but as Bob, their old friend. And this was a rather accurate perception of how such visiting occurred. There was no listing of persons in jail or hospital and no organized system to make sure they are visited. Rather, the onus was on the individual Worker to go and visit someone. Guests treasured these visits. In perhaps the most lucid conversation I ever had with Harvey, he said to me:

> When I was in a New York City hospital, two people came to visit me, and one of them was that woman [pointing to one of the Workers with a look that revealed the great esteem in which he held her]. The other was Father Gregory. Father Gregory got mugged one day. I have no use for those muggers.

Harvey seemed to have trouble at times remembering where he was. He was quite clear, however, about who came to visit him when he had been in the hospital some time ago. For the homeless person, cut off from past social ties, receiving a hospital or prison visit from a Worker he or she knows can be a crucially important affirmation of his or her worth as a person. These visits may be the most hospitable acts performed by the Worker.

Hospitality also entailed advocating for guests with welfare and health bureaucracies. While I was there, several Workers were doing a great deal of advocacy with the Department of Social Services for two former guests, a woman and her teenage son. Unable to find an apartment for the amount welfare would pay, they lived in a welfare hotel for months at a cost to the city of $63 per night for a dingy room that, for the first few days, had no lock on the door. A Worker accompanied the woman on each trip to the welfare office, mainly to keep her from giving up. I went with her once and found out why she was near despair. We arrived before 8:00 A.M. on the day she was told to pick up her check. We sat in a waiting room with about thirty other people, many of whom knew each other quite well from whole days spent together previously in this same waiting room. Although we had come in as soon as the office opened and she had been one of the first to sign the list, she was not even called until 11:30, when a social worker told her that her regular worker was out but that she would try to see her before lunch. She didn't. If I had not been there to go out and buy her a cup of soup, she would have had no lunch; if she had left the waiting room and they called her name, she would have been moved to the end of the list and probably would not have received a check at all. The people were trapped in the waiting room just as surely as if a barred door had been locked behind them. We did not receive the check until after 4:00; a total of eight hours waiting for a check she had been scheduled to pick up that day. (It appeared that no checks were issued until after the banks had closed, so that everyone had to go to a check cashing place and pay a few dollars from their check just to get it cashed.)

Workers often took guests to hospitals to help them get service from emergency-room personnel who were sometimes reluctant to serve drunken alcoholics. Our Christmas party was delayed while the two coeditors of the paper took one of the female residents to the hospital after she had come home dead drunk with a gash on her knee and refused to let the ambulance drivers do anything for her. Upon their return they were jubilant that they had had to wait only two hours.

This type of unscheduled response to situations that might occur at any time of the day or night were the soul of hospitality at St. Joseph's. Food and clothing were regarded as a matter of right, not to be denied to anyone if they were available. Shelter, too, was a matter of right, although it was rationed. The other acts of hospitality were more spontaneous and responded to the situation and the person involved. As such, they seemed to be the most often remembered and cherished by the recipient.

Typifications of People

Although a personalist approach to hospitality emphasizes treating the guest as a whole person, as a thou, it is impossible to conduct social relations without some sort of mental scheme of "types of persons" (Schutz 1967). It is inevitable, therefore, that even with the avowed purpose of treating others as pure thous, the Workers would develop schemes for typifying persons. As I will show, however, both the type of schemes used and the way they are used differ from those of bureaucratic social-service agencies in a way that facilitates the grasping of the other as a thou.

An important distinction to make at the outset is that the typifications of people at the house take the form of ideal types rather than categories. By this I mean that idealized pictures of various types of persons are created, but real persons are not expected to correspond to any one type. In an ideal-typical scheme, an individual person may have elements of several types and be considered under different types. In a categorization scheme, classes are created for the purpose of placing people into one group or another. There may be occasional ambiguities, but for the most part the placement into groups is clear-cut. In an ideal-typical scheme, on the other hand, ambiguity is the order of the day.

The distinction between ideal types and categories may be made clearer by comparing the Worker to a conventional social-service agency. The Worker's ideal-typical scheme of "Worker and guest" corresponds to an agency's categorization of "social worker and client." However, there is an enormous difference in how these schemes operate in everyday life. At the social agency, the social workers are paid employees. The records of the agency verify who is a paid employee. The agency maintains listings of clients. There is, then, a written source by which one can determine whether a given person is social worker or client. Moreover, the social workers are distinguished from the clients by numerous social cues. Social workers have offices, or at least desks. They are better dressed than clients. They have an air of authority. Even an inexperienced outside observer can distinguish the social workers from the clients after a few minutes at a welfare office. At a halfway house, it might take a bit longer, but the distinctions would still be clear.

At St. Joseph's none of this applied. Workers were paid $10 per week "ice cream money"—but so were a number of guests. Workers wore clothes from the same clothing room that supplies the guests, usually had a very unassuming air about them, and, except for the "business manager," had no desk. An observer can be at a house for days and still not be absolutely sure who is Worker and who is guest. There were a number of persons who had attributes of both ideal types and who most persons in the house were reluctant to classify as one or the other.

Workers at St. Joseph's employed three schemes by which they typified persons with whom they came into contact. The first scheme concerned persons' relationship to the house; the second typified persons in moral terms; and the third distinguished types of deviants. The first scheme created types of persons according to whether or not they were living in the house and the history of their relationship to the house. Under this scheme, there were several ideal types of persons.[2] I will begin with types who lived in the house.

The first type of person living in the house was the ideologically committed Worker, someone who had come to live at the house out of a belief in the Catholic Worker approach. There were nine such Workers, seven men and two women. All were from the middle class, white, and between twenty and thirty-five years old. Except for the editor of the paper, no one had lived at the house for more than two years, most for less than a year.

The next type was the resident—about a dozen persons who lived in the house, considered it their home, who had come to the house in search of shelter. They were from a variety of ethnic groups (including Asians, Latin Americans, and Africans) and ranged in age from late twenties to late sixties. Many had lived in the house for years, or even decades. It is difficult to think of them as a category because of their range of personalities, abilities, and relationships to the house.

Some residents took no part in the activities of the house. One, in fact, was so seldom even present that it took me over a week to realize that he lived in the house. Others played a major role in putting out the paper. One was in charge of distribution, a position of some authority. Another "took the door" during every soupline, a key position since he had to maintain order in the line and keep out people who seemed to be in a violent mood. Others worked the soupline regularly. Thus, the residents varied greatly in their relationship to the house, so much so that it is only with great reluctance that I group them together. Each contributed to the house in some way, yet some were clearly analogous to "clients" in a halfway house, others contributed as much to the house as they received, and still others were somewhere in between. They were often both receivers and givers of hospitality. A few individual portraits may help the reader to understand them a bit.

Harvey, the man we met on the stairs when I arrived, lived at the house for several years. Before he became a resident he had lived in a flophouse and come in daily to sweep and mop the second floor. At that point he was "less far gone than now." On a freezing night in February he disappeared. The Workers called hospitals and even the morgue, but did not hear from him for weeks. In March they got a call from a hospital saying, "We have a Harvey Lewis here, and he claims he knows you." They went to visit him and were told that his body temperature had been 80 degrees when the ambulance had brought him into the hospital. Gene, an old-time Worker, said:

> I don't know how he survived. He stayed in the hospital a while longer, but he was never right after that—he was like he is now. He used to be weird, but now it was all the time. When he left the hospital he moved into the house. He had no place else to go. That was when we started giving him a shave and shower every week. I've got to do it tomorrow. It used to be Don and I split the duty on that, but since I went away [for a vacation], Earl has been doing it with Don. Now that I'm back, Harvey wants me to shave him, but I've been too busy. Well, I'll do it tomorrow. A haircut too.

Harvey wandered through the house at will, apparently oblivious to everyone around him. He talked to himself constantly. Once I heard him say to himself, "I'm putting my hand on the doorknob. I'm turning the doorknob. I'm opening the door." It was as though he was trying to convince himself of the reality of his actions. Another time, he announced to the air, "I'm expecting! I'm expecting!"

Although Harvey seemed oblivious to what was going on, he perceived much more than one would expect. He was sensitive to rebukes, often leaving the floor if he was told not to do something. He maintained relations with a few of the old-time residents and Workers, particularly Jones, who always threatened to stuff him in one of the huge canvas bags used for mailing the paper, much to Harvey's delight.

Helen, the woman who answered the door on my arrival, was under five feet tall, slightly stooped as a result of a childhood illness. She had been living at the house for about two years, but had been associated with it off and on for many years before that. She liked to tell about the time the YWCA had her arrested for vagrancy while she was in Pittsburgh during World War II looking for construction work.

She was at her finest during the soupline, waiting on tables, cleaning up messes, screaming to the dishwasher that we need silverware, admonishing a new volunteer on proper technique, and, especially, breaking up arguments among the guests. All of the guests knew her, usually as "Ma." The volunteers all knew her too. She was the first person to welcome a new volunteer.

But it was in troublesome situations that she really showed her mettle. If two guys in line started arguing and were about to come to blows, the experienced Workers called in Helen. She would come over to the troublesome person and say "Come over here. I want to talk to you." She would ask how he was doing, have him sit down with her, and, after a bit, guide him out the door. Once, I was told, she came up to a huge drunk who was trying to attack someone and challenged him, "You wanna take it outside with me?" He broke out laughing. Even a roaring drunk couldn't take on a little old lady. She could get someone out the door painlessly in cases where the Workers would have to drag the person out.

Harvey and Helen were by no means representative of the residents. If anything stood out about the residents, it was their individuality. There really was no resident "role"—each resident negotiated his or her own role. Harvey's role was akin to that of a resident of a nursing home, although with a bit less systematized care, a lot more freedom, and far more genuine love. Helen created a role in which, for all that she may have been disgruntled with status differentials or the way the house was run, she knew that she was contributing something valuable to the house. Hers was not an artificial dignity created for her by the staff of a nursing home. She had an important role in the overall functioning of the house and she knew it.

Treating the residents as a group does reveal the role of reciprocity in Worker hospitality. Reciprocity is gratefully accepted but not required in return for hospitality. One need not reciprocate to remain a resident.

The next type of person living at the house was the emergency-shelter guest. This was a person who had been accepted for shelter for a limited amount of time—perhaps for a night or perhaps for a couple of weeks. Like the residents, they may or may not reciprocate by helping out around the house, but whether or not they did so had no effect on their length of stay.

Another type of person was the short-term Worker, someone who came to the house to live and work for several weeks or months, generally because of a desire to try out the Worker style of life. This was the type into which I fit. Although there was only one other person of this type at the house during my stay, it was evident that this was a regular type, with which the house had had a lot of experience.

A final type of person living in the house was the visitor. Visitors differed from emergency guests in that they came not in desperate need of shelter, but rather to see the house for a variety of reasons. Generally, they stayed a few days. Visitors included middle-class persons wanting to "see" the Worker for a few days, former New York City Workers, Workers from other houses, and friends or family of Workers. Again, reciprocity was dependent on the visitor. Some helped out for their whole stay; others did little. One visitor was a priest who stayed for a weekend. Although he attended a Friday night "clarification of thought" meeting, he expressed little interest in the work of the house, not coming to a soupline until his third day. It seemed to me that he was using the house simply as a place to stay until some friends of his returned to town and he could stay with them. No one seemed to mind, though.

A number of important types of persons lived outside of the house. First, there were the Workers and residents of Maryhouse. As at St. Joseph's House, most of the Workers were in their early twenties or thirties and had been there less than two years. There were also several older Workers who had been there much longer. The house had about thirty residents, all women, many older, almost all with mental problems. Maryhouse did not do emergency shelter, so there were rarely any emergency guests; there were, however, a number of visitors, who often helped out at St. Joseph's as well.

Another important type was the Worker living in a nearby apartment. Around a half dozen Workers who had lived at the house for a number of years moved into their own or shared apartments, many of which were owned or paid for by the Worker. Some worked at the house regularly, others stopped by less frequently, but all were still actively involved in the house and would be brought into any important decision making. Most of these Workers were in their thirties and had been involved in the house for a decade or more.

Still another type of person was the "friend of the house." This type of person lived outside the house but, due to a historical relationship to people in the house, had relatively free access to the house much of the time, had a standing invitation to house meals, and frequently helped with the work—particularly the ubiquitous task of folding *Catholic Worker* newspapers. Friends of the house tended to be older, lower-class white men and women. (Nearly half were women, although there were very few women "on the line"). Many of them had a room or apartment of their own. They had been around the house for years; sometimes, their relationship to the house predated, and was only vaguely understood by, most of the Workers in the house.

Finally, there were the men "on the line," the thousands of homeless New Yorkers who came in for soup, to use the bathroom, to get clothes, or to get bread and butter to go. Many were regular characters, known to all and familiar with the ways of the house. Others were known only by the longer-term Workers. Still others were nameless, coming to the house a few times and then disappearing, or even coming for months without standing out from the crowd in any way.

A special subgroup within the men on the line were the window washers, a group of relatively young black men who lived on the corner of Houston and Bowery, huddling around a fire in their garbage can, who dashed out to wash the windshields of cars stopped at the red light in search of some spare change. Most were alcoholics and drug addicts, but they were a unique group of street men. They were among the few homeless persons who talked in terms of a future and were still able to project themselves as returning to "normal society."

They conceived of themselves as entrepreneurs, operating a business whose services were no more imposed upon customers than are the more extensively advertised goods of "legitimate" corporations. They had a special relationship to the house. It was their bathroom, their place to get in out of the cold. Workers came to know them better than most meal guests. As one Worker noted, they respected the house—they knew when they could stay and chat and when they should just use the bathroom and leave. When the police began harassing them that winter, breaking up their fire, destroying their windshield-washing equipment, and telling them to disperse in the middle of the night, the *Worker* ran an article on their plight.

The second scheme for typifying persons was a moral scheme. Persons, particularly guests, were typed according to certain moral standards. Unlike professional social workers, Catholic Workers felt free to think of people in moral terms, to describe them as violent or greedy or gentle or generous. The two major negative moral typifications (violent and greedy) were related to daily problems at the house—maintaining order and rationing the goods to be distributed.

There were a few guests who, on the basis of repeated incidents, were typed as violent. As one old-time Worker put it:

> Some guys are violent. They tend to react to their inner tensions
> by hitting someone or worse, rather than verbally. We've had some
> violent guys. One big black guy from Alabama sliced open June [a
> Worker] above the eye and punched out this guy [another Worker]
> who was with us. The tension had just been building up for weeks
> and it exploded. . . . Ninety-five percent of the guys are great. It just
> takes two or three to start trouble.

One person in particular was regarded as violent. According to one Worker, "Jim is a very sad person who's been with us a long time. We usually don't let him in because he tends to flip out and can start throwing punches." Another described him as "an old friend," who he generally didn't let inside the house.

Those who were typed as violent were more likely to be kept out of the house and given food "to go." At the other end of the moral scale from violent are those who were construed as "vulnerable." This designation seemed to be applied most often to younger white men and to the elderly.

The second major moral type was greedy or exploitative. One young man was so typed after he had taken a taxi to the house without money, expecting the Workers to pay the $10 fare. The fare was paid by the Worker, but all agreed that the lad was "exploiting the house" and resolved not to do it for him again. A related type was the fraud. Gimbel's Irv stands out in my mind here. Irv stayed at the house for a month to save enough to get his own place. He was well liked and accepted by all in the house, buying presents for a few of the residents, and even buying some Christmas decorations for the house.

Just before I left for the Christmas holiday, he offered to use his employee discount on a present for my wife. I went with him to the store, picked out something, and gave him the money to get it the day before I left. We arranged to pick it up together on my way to the train station (so it wouldn't get stolen at the house). He never showed up, so I returned to Syracuse *sans* present. Upon my return after Christmas, I was told that he had disappeared, taking with him $100 in house money from George's room. George was quite upset at the betrayal of trust, particularly since he had befriended Irv and let him sleep in his own room. Others in the house were mystified that Irv would spend four weeks setting up a situation that netted him less than $140. One old-time Worker said simply, "Maybe someday he'll come back and be sorry for what he did."

Those typed as greedy were not excluded from the house, but were watched more carefully than others. The young taxi-user was allowed into the house regularly after that incident just as if it hadn't happened. Irv never came back, but I suspect he would have been welcome for the soupline, at least.

Workers also applied positive moral terms to persons rather frequently. Guests were "all right" or "good guys" if one could trust them. Some were generous; some made one feel welcome.

The final typification scheme utilized conventional deviant labels. Persons coming to the house might be classified roughly as alcoholic, crazy, or drug addicts. The terms were not used in any professional or scientific way, but rather, in a commonsense manner. There was no attempt to grasp the medical dimensions of alcoholism or to understand the precise differences between schizophrenics and manic depressives. Rather, such general terms as alcoholic and crazy were sufficient to the Worker's needs. These terms were applied as typologies of everyday problems in running the house. Alcoholics were those who snuck bottles into the house or came in drunk and rowdy. Crazy persons were those who "acted out," talked to walls, and so forth. Addicts were persons who presented the Workers with a problem because they shot up in the bathroom.

Although Workers were generally sensitive to the effects of labeling, they did not rigorously abstain from using standard labels. They
sometimes used "very scattered" or "strange" instead of crazy or
mentally ill; however, most were not rigorous about language. One
Worker told me of a time when he was arguing with a helper who had
a history of mental problems. The helper screamed at him, "You're
crazy!" to which the Worker replied "I'm crazy? *You're* the one who's
crazy!" In general, Workers would argue that the way one interacts
with a person, and the fact that one is willing to live with that person,
is more important than the terms one uses.

The overall approach to typification is related to the personalist
philosophy of the Worker. The ideal is to grasp the other in his or her
fullness. As Schutz has shown, however, one cannot operate without
making typifications of others, typifications that hinder one's ability
to grasp the other fully. The Worker approach, implicitly recogniz-
ing this, attempts to maximize interpersonal relations in three ways.
First, none of the schemes use jargon. Terms used come from the
common English vocabulary and are applied for the most part without specialized meaning for the setting. Moreover, the terms are not
based on any special theory. Second, the typifications are ideal types
rather than categories. There is no need to classify everyone into one
type or another. Ambiguity is tolerated, even welcomed. Third, the
emphasis among Workers is on personal history rather than type.
Workers are expected to "know the guys." One need not know any
theories of drug addiction. One should know that when Abe asks to
use the bathroom, he is probably going to try to shoot up there. One
need not know the difference between paranoia and schizophrenia.
One should know that it is no problem if Harvey chooses to talk to
the doorknob.

The Worker approach to typification, then, is designed to maximize appreciation of the guest as a whole person. As such it contrasts
with both the bureaucratic and professional models, which use jar-
gonistic categorization schemes to describe persons, an approach that
Workers would argue restricts one's ability to grasp the other as a
person.

Problems of Status

St. Joseph's is an amazing experiment in egalitarianism, attempting to bridge one of the widest social gaps in America—that between
the middle class and the homeless. To observe that there are still status
distinctions within the house is by no means to judge the experiment

a failure. The traditional class divisions of American society are diminished to a remarkable extent by sheer willful effort, although they are still discernible in subtle, often disturbing ways. One of the ways the house seems to have attenuated class distinctions is by creating a second status distinction that conflicts with, and thus undermines, the first. The distinction that reflects social class is between those who come to the House out of ideological conviction and those who come out of need. The distinction that undermines social class is between those who are "in the House" and those who are "on the line."

The Worker–Guest Distinction

Worker houses vary greatly in the extent to which they try to eliminate distinctions between the largely middle-class Workers and their homeless guests; however, each house makes some effort in this direction. The very act of living together eliminates many distinctions. Residence is an important element of social class even though it is often ignored in sociometric scales. Classes do not generally share neighborhoods (unless "declining" or "gentrifying"), let alone living quarters. Living in the same household as another, even sharing a room, makes it difficult to maintain many of the differences in lifestyle that are essential elements of class distinctions. Furthermore, the middle-class Worker and the resident from the streets perform many of the same tasks every day—washing dishes, mopping floors, folding newspapers, cleaning tables. Thus, two major elements of class distinction—residence and occupation—are largely eliminated by the Catholic Worker approach.

Other class differences do remain, however—most notably education and the fact that a middle-class volunteer has social margin, that is, social acceptance that will facilitate reentry into "normal society" (Wiseman 1979). Workers are aware that this distinction is never eliminated. A Worker at another house put it well:

> There is one tension at this place that is probably more important than any other. It's between the plight of the staff and the plight of our guests. It's irreconcilable.
>
> We've chosen to be here, and that's a luxury of the class, culture, economic system (or whatever it is) into which we were born. At any moment, we know, we could leave West Fifth Street for a clean, air conditioned place where we would be welcomed and loved. They can't (Garvey 1978, 96).

Many in the Worker movement, both middle and lower class, state that the ideology versus need distinction is inaccurate—that everyone at a Worker house comes out of need, whether that need be physical, psychological, social, or spiritual. A common theme among Workers runs, "If we fit into regular society, we wouldn't be here." There is, then, a continual debate within the movement as to whether there should be a distinction along the lines of ideology versus need. Nonetheless, in each house I have visited, this distinction is made to some degree.

Ken stated the problem this way:

> There is a sort of second-class citizenship here. It's subtle, but it's there. I mean there's volunteers like me and then there's the residents. Maybe it's somewhat the residents' choice. I mean Norb [one of the residents] isn't interested in helping out in the soupline. But it's not very egalitarian. And after awhile you start to make assumptions that, of course, residents don't do this or that.

A Maryhouse Worker defended the notion of a distinction with respect to practical matters such as alcohol:

> Some people feel there should be no distinction between guests and Workers, but I don't see it that way. Like alcohol [which is forbidden in the house]. One time [a Worker] had a friend visiting and they were in my room and wanted to have a beer. So I said sure and they went out and got a can of beer each. [Another Worker] heard about it and got all upset. She wouldn't come to me. Finally she told me that she was upset and I said yea, I heard. She told me why and I said "You have every right to think that. I understand your position. But this is my room, so you should let me do what I want to here." So we made our peace. She didn't complain when we had alcohol here at her going-away party.

Thus, a distinction exists between Workers and guests—with respect to participation in decision making and with respect to privileges. But it exists in tension with an ideal of egalitarianism and is thus often muted. Major decisions about the house are often made by the ideologically committed Workers or even by a subgroup of the most experienced Workers. However, there is an effort made to include residents in such decisions, as in the house meeting described previously.

The distinction is further blurred by the fact that there are a number of status indicators that partially blur the distinction. One such status category is "on-the-house Worker." While I was there, only Workers took the house. However, this apparently had not always been the case. Once, while a couple of us were discussing a particularly troublesome and withdrawn guest, one of the Workers commented, "How far he's fallen. Do you know that at one time he took the house?" A second category is the group receiving "ice cream money"—the $10 per week stipend. All Workers receive ice cream money, but so do a number of residents. A third category is the group that has keys to the front door. Again, all Workers are given keys (eventually—it took two weeks in my case), but so are a number of the residents. Thus, all Workers enjoy the status privileges of ice cream money and a key—and so do a number of residents. This fact has two implications. First, it partially mutes the Worker–guest distinction. Second, it suggests that Workers and guests are ideal types rather than categories. Some of the ambiguities involved are reflected in the career of Gene.

Gene was an aging gentleman who came in during lunch on Super Bowl Sunday. He was neatly groomed, wore a suit, tie, and overcoat, and spoke in an educated manner. He returned later that afternoon while we were on the second floor watching the game. He asked me, "Is it safe to leave my clothes out here while I take a shower?" I said, "I guess so. Did [the person on the house] tell you you could take a shower?" "Yes." He took a shower, something that simply isn't done by persons not living in the house. A few people, myself included, looked quizzical, but no one said anything since it was the responsibility of the person on the house. In any event, breaching the shower gap was his first major step into the house. He said he would leave a shirt here to dry and be back for it in the morning. "It isn't all that difficult walking the streets. And I can go to Penn Station and sleep there. Nobody bothers me."

This, apparently, was Gene's way of surviving on the streets— look and act middle class in order to create enough role confusion so that people didn't perceive him as a street person. Thus, he could stay at Penn Station because he didn't look homeless. Similarly, his demeanor threw us off a bit at St. Joseph's—we didn't know quite how to respond.

A few months later, one of the Workers updated me on Gene's story. He kept coming around the house and eventually was allowed to stay. He soon began acting like he was in charge of the place. Because of his appearance, the guys on the line accepted him as an authority. The Worker recounted, "If someone came in for clothes and I was on the house, he would tell me, 'Why don't you run down and get him some clothes. I'll keep an eye on things up here.' Or he would tell Ken, 'Son, why don't you do this for this poor guy.' "

He began answering the door, which is the most jealously guarded prerogative of the person taking the house, and was told not to. However, "He still would act like he was in charge when the guys came in. We finally asked him to leave. He came back three days later with a broken foot. We didn't want to take him back, but what could we do? And within a few days, even with all that, he was acting like he ran the house again. We had to ask him to leave."

Gene's story illuminates the nature of the distinction between Worker and guest—the line between them is often vague, but it does exist. I find it hard to imagine him being able to act as he did for even an hour at any social-service agency, where the staff-client distinction is firmly fixed, a gap rivaling that between Dives and Lazarus.

The In-the-House/On-the-Line Distinction

The most important status distinction at St. Joseph's was one not derived from the class structure of the larger society, but rather one that was particular to the house itself: the distinction between those "in the house" and those "on the line." The distinction did not refer so much to whether one was actually living in the house as to whether one was automatically allowed in the door. If one had to explain why one wanted to come inside, then one was not "in the house." This is illustrated by the time when I answered the door and found a middle-aged man I'd never seen before. When I asked him what he wanted, he replied, "I'm a friend of the house," with just the right tone of indignation to let me know I had no right to question his right to enter. I immediately let him in.

Perhaps the most obvious consequence of the in-the-house/on-the-line distinction had to do with food. The better food was usually reserved for those "in the house." Those off the line were given bean soup, bread and butter, and coffee during the soupline. At other times they were given bread and butter. Occasionally they were allowed tea or coffee depending on the discretion of the person taking the house. A few were allowed in to eat the supper leftovers if there were any. If cold cuts, meat, desserts, fruit, or vegetables were donated, it was expected that these would be saved "for the house" and not be given out to those who come to the door during the day or used for the soupline meal. One volunteer told me that she had gone to some butchers and begged two hams, which she planned to use for the soup on her shift. She left them in the cooler with a note saying they were for the soup. As she finished the story, "When I got in the next day they were gone. The people in the house had eaten them.

Now, whenever I want meat for the soup, I bring it in under my arm the day I'm going to put it in."

Those on the line were expected to understand the distinction. And most did. People came in to use the bathroom even during supper and left immediately after receiving some bread and butter, while those "in the house" continued with their meal almost oblivious to the outsiders. During the times between meals, people in the house sat and drank coffee although none was offered to those who came in to use the bathroom. Those who challenged the distinction could be labeled troublemakers. One afternoon a man came in, somewhat drunk, to use the bathroom. When he was done he asked the person on the house, "Can I have a cup of coffee?" She replied, "No. That's for the house." He began cursing her and left. Shaken by his anger, she characterized him as a troublemaker.

There was a similar distinction in terms of space. Those on the line were almost always confined to the first floor. Anyone found on another floor would almost always be challenged.

Other privileges and rights also accompanied the distinction. Packs of Tops tobacco were meant for distribution to residents and friends of the house. It was a rare occasion when a pack went to someone on the line, and woe be to the Worker who was caught in the act of giving it to a homeless person by one of the residents.

The force of the distinction could be influenced by the person taking the house. In general, those who tried most to mute the distinction were the newer Workers and the part-time volunteers. These tended to offer people coffee when they had time, and often tried to give out something better than bread and butter, such as adding some peanut butter to the sandwiches. One Worker responded when I brought up the issue, "Well, I guess one thing you can do about having two classes of people is to try to alleviate the difference. You can invite people in while you're making them a sandwich, and not make them wait outside."

Those who did try to mute the distinction, however, came under heavy fire. The strongest defenders of the distinction were the residents. My field notes are full of situations where I was criticized, or saw another Worker criticized, by a resident for giving someone off the streets a privilege reserved for those in the house. Once, a bag of pastries was donated during my shift and I gave some of them to some street men who had come in to use the bathroom. One of the residents said to me the next morning, "Why did you let those bastards off the line have those sweet rolls last night? We could have had them for breakfast. They were for us, not for those bastards." Another time, when a young black man was sitting drinking coffee at my invitation, a resident came down and said to me, "That guy shouldn't be roaming around here. He's off the line." Still another time, I came down to help cook the supper and found the cook (a resident) in a frenzy because the person on the house had let several people in for coffee. "You've got to get these people out of here! I can't cook with them all in my way."

Perhaps the most amazing example was the day I destroyed my relationship with Brother Francis. Brother Francis was an older man who lived in one of the flophouses nearby and had been coming to the Worker for over fifteen years to take care of the garbage and feed the cats. He conceived of himself as another St. Francis, friend to all animals. When he gathered enough slop from the meals, he would try to convince someone to drive him to a nearby park where he would strew it on the ground as food for the birds. He loved his cats, crooning to them and telling them (just loud enough so everyone could hear) that they were infinitely superior to the humans in the house. Every Worker felt the lash of Brother Francis's tongue. I, however, began on his good side, largely because, on my first time on the house, I did not object to his taking a slice of liver to feed his beloved felines.

My falling out with him came one afternoon when I was on the house. He came in to find the dining room empty except for one little old bag lady I had allowed in for some coffee. Although she was a "friend of the house," she was no friend of Brother Francis. He began screaming at me in his high voice. "She shouldn't be in here. She stays at the women's shelter. She comes in and sits around all afternoon. You shouldn't have let her in!" His vision of perfect hospitality, it seemed, was a house containing only himself and the cats.

Residents were not, however, the only protectors of the distinction. Workers constantly balanced the interests of "the house" with those of the people off the line and usually resolved matters in favor of the house. During one soupline when it was cold and raining outside, Ken and I decided to try a different approach to handling the line. Rather than make people wait outside until spaces opened up, we told them to come in and wait on the stairs. The situation was crowded, damp, and a bit unruly; however, it was all we could think of at the time. A more experienced Worker commented: "You shouldn't put people on the stairs because they get slippery and someone like Mabel might fall coming down. We usually just make people wait outside on days like this. But we should have had one or two people outside to watch the line to prevent people from crowding and shoving at the door."

At a meeting in which we discussed adding a fourth day to the soupline, one newer Worker suggested having coffee and bread one or two mornings a week as an alternative. A more experienced Worker replied, "That time—seven-thirty to nine—is breakfast time for the house and there really isn't any other space for that. We have to consider the people in the house."

Despite the strength of the distinction, the barrier between those on the line and those in the house was not impenetrable, as illustrated by the story of Donald. Donald was a small, balding man in his forties or fifties who started coming to the house during my stay. He stuttered on occasion, or perhaps it was only that he was constantly shivering. When I asked him where he was staying, he would respond, "I've got a cold-water flat." From the way he shivered it was more than the water that was cold there. When I was on the house I'd always let him stay in longer than normal to get warm. A few times he asked about staying in the house, but was told that he could not, for fear he would become a permanent resident. Eventually, he began coming to house meals regularly.

A few months after I left the house I asked one of the Workers about Donald. She told me that he was still coming around, not only for lunch and supper but also for the soupline. She said that his situation was brought up once at a Sunday night meeting. People were wondering how he had come to be a regular at the meal. Ken said he thought he had let him in first. Another person said she thought he was one of Sue's friends. No one was quite sure how he had achieved the de facto status of friend of the house, but no one wanted to take the responsibility to tell him he couldn't come anymore, so he kept coming. I suspect that many friends of the house achieved their status in a similar way—at least to the extent that no one was quite sure how they became "friends."

By far the harshest critique of the in–out distinction came from one of the guests, an electrical engineer in the defense industry who had quit his job and taken to the streets after a religious conversion experience. I will piece together here a few of the comments he made:

> I thought if one were to follow Christ one must empty himself, forget matters of status. But here, you still make judgments—judgments about status, about propriety, in answering the door. Here the companionship, the service, is for the people inside. The Crispy Rice is

for the people inside, for the guys who work at Gimbels. I have a
great sin on my soul just being inside this door, but I'm too weary to
care. This place is too near the Ritz, too near the downtown businessman who doesn't want his life interrupted by those on the outside
so he puts a doorman at the door to keep them out. It's lukewarm.
This morning I waited until everyone had come in [for the soupline]
before I came in. I didn't feel that I could say "I'm special" and cut
ahead of the line and just walk in. I don't feel comfortable with the
door here—the difference between those in and those out. That's
why I loathe being in this place. [It's] a country club inside with a
few crumbs going out the door. I see very little of what I'd perceived
to be the spirit of Dorothy Day here.

In the course of his critique, he made it clear that I was as guilty as
anyone else: "How many times have I heard you tell someone, 'You
have to leave because I have to clean up now,' when in your heart
you were thinking, 'You have to leave so that you won't be in here
when we eat.' You say you understand about the door, but then you
do the same thing as before. What good is it if you understand but
don't change what you do."

How did such a sharp status distinction come into being? What
functions did it perform? A few partial answers present themselves.
In the first place, the very act of giving shelter to some homeless
people creates an important status distinction between those who
are given shelter and those who are not. Once this distinction is
made, those who have been granted the higher status have an incentive to maintain and reinforce it. The residents of the house see a
sharp distinction between "in" and "out" because that is the major
status distinction between them and "those bastards on the street."
Middle-class Workers need not be as committed to the distinction
because there are other status differences between themselves and
those on the street—their education, their middle-class upbringing,
their social margin. In short, those on the line are not a reference
group for the Workers, but they are for the residents.

The situation is intensified in New York City by the sheer number
of homeless. St. Joseph's is faced with the immense problem that its
meager resources can't possibly deal with the thousands of homeless
people in the city but Catholic Worker ideology forbids making re-
strictions on who is given food. The solution, as will be discussed
below, is to reduce service quality in order to reduce demand. There
is, however, no need to reduce quality of food and other services to
those actually living in the house. Thus, the economics of supply and

demand work in this case to sharpen the distinction between those in the house and those off the line.

Methods of Restricting Demand

There were over twenty thousand homeless persons in New York City. The dining room at St. Joseph's House seated twenty-eight. This posed a problem. Catholic Worker ideology demanded that no one be turned away when they come asking for food. This exacerbated the problem.

The realization that there were countless hordes of homeless persons "out there" permeated life at St. Joseph's. It was illustrated every time the soupline got overcrowded, which was fairly often. When the weather was good, the person at the door simply allowed between thirty and thirty-five people inside at a time. The others waited in line outside the door. When it was raining or bitterly cold outside, however, the person at the door often let another ten or fifteen people crowd into the dining room, where they would stand two or three deep by the walls waiting for a chair to open up. Everyone became more tense, more irritable. When so many crowded inside, there was no system to assign chairs on a first-come, first-served basis, so there were innumerable arguments over seats. Guests who were already emotionally high-strung became even more so. This tension level could not be maintained throughout a two-hour soupline without the possibility of serious violence.

The person taking the house was responsible to deal with the situation. The accepted solution was to eliminate the serving of seconds. If anyone wanted seconds on soup or bread, they got back in line. This reduced the time a person spent eating and increased turnover—within fifteen minutes, the crowd usually thinned out.

Thus, the strategy for coping with the immediate problem of excess demand on the soupline was to restrict supply—to restrict the amount each person could eat, rather than the number of persons allowed to eat. However, the house's approach to the larger problem of infinite demand was different. The Workers tried to decrease the demand itself by either decreasing the quality of the service or food or making its distribution so erratic that people couldn't depend on it.

One example of this was the quality of the soup itself. It was almost always a bean, split pea, or lentil soup. Meat, if any, was generally leftover from previous house dinners. The oral history of the soup was interesting—old-time Workers claimed it was far better than it used to be when Dorothy was there; however, old-time residents claimed that the quality of the soup had gone down considerably in the last few years. I have no way of determining which account is correct. It does seem, though, that the quality of the soup was kept low primarily out of fear that if it was better the house would be overwhelmed by hungry homeless persons.

A second example was the food that was handed out at the door. Almost invariably this consisted of bread (often stale) and butter. I once suggested to Ken giving out peanut butter and jelly sandwiches instead of bread and butter. He replied:

> That would cost a lot. But maybe cost isn't a problem. I don't know. The argument that would be used against it is that too many people would start coming. There'd be a crowd of people all the time if we gave out peanut butter and jelly. In the summer we gave out tomato and mayonnaise sandwiches, which I guess have more nutrition than bread and butter.

A few days later, I was downstairs and found him giving out tuna fish and cheese sandwiches made from leftovers from the house dinner. He invited several people in while he made up the sandwiches. Six or seven newcomers arrived within a couple minutes after the first left. One of the window washers came in with a big smile, saying "I just got it on the wire that you have tuna fish." The tuna fish was gone within fifteen minutes. Ken turned to me and said, "That's one of the arguments against giving out peanut butter and jelly: this sort of thing would happen. People hear there's something good and they all come." A third example is the distribution of house money to those who come to the door. Every evening the person taking the house is given an envelope with about $10 in it to distribute as she or he sees fit. (The first evening I was given the money, I was told, "The house money is to be given out on the basis of need and, in a few cases, on the basis of tradition, which bears little relation to need.")[3] Usually it is given out to people coming to the door asking for "car fare," a dollar or less at a time; however, sometimes one gives away three to five dollars if someone's story sounds somewhat realistic. Many, if not most, of the people asking for money, however, are turned down. One Worker told me, "The only way we avoid being swamped is by being erratic in who we give money to."

5

In for the Long Haul:
St. Joseph's in Rochester

I was amazed at how easy it was to convince the Workers at the Rochester St. Joseph's House to let me study them. There were only three Workers at the time. The director was Barb Tompkins, a nun who had worked at the house for about four years and had been director for two. Louie, the cook, was a wizened little man, a sixty-year-old alcoholic who had been at the house for eight years. John Baker, a tall man in his late twenties, was a carpenter's apprentice who had come to the house a year and a half previously, largely through his involvement in the peace movement. The reason they were so quick to accept me was that Barb needed to take a month off to do some work for her religious congregation, and they were desperately seeking someone to help John with the house during that time. If I was willing to do that, they said, I could study them all I wanted.

Although I did not begin with the same feeling of awe as I did in New York City, I soon discovered that this St. Joe's, too, had quite a long and interesting history. Dorothy Day was invited to speak in Rochester by the Catholic Women's Club in 1933, the same year that the movement began. Inspired by the talk, a group of local seminarians created a Catholic Worker study group. By 1937 there were three Catholic Worker study groups in the city, two associated with colleges and one meeting at a downtown library. In late 1937 they were allowed to use a house owned by the St. Peter Claver Society, located in a poor black neighborhood. Here they held weekly meetings, conducted Sunday-school classes for black children, and distributed clothing and food baskets to people in the neighborhood.

In 1939 the group acquired a house of its own and began a meal program. An early report said they were feeding five. By the fall, however, a flyer reported that they had served over 11,000 meals. The same flyer gave their purpose as follows:

> Many ask why we run this House when the Salvation Army, the Rescue Mission, etc. will take care of them. Most of these ambassadors are Catholics; they are our own. No institution can adequately take care of Catholics unless it is run by Catholics. If we care for our fortunate Catholics, why not care for the unfortunate ones? They, too, have souls to be saved; and if they are sunk in vice or their "sins are as scarlet," it is only the more reason why we should try to aid them spiritually. And as for an impersonal, machine-like, mass-production, public Social Agency caring for them—May the good Lord deliver them!

At this point there were still no full-time Workers at the house. Rather, students and members of the original group came in whenever they could to keep the meal going. In contrast to New York City, none of the founders lived in the house. The next year they moved again, renting an abandoned Episcopal church hall, where one of the founders remembered them feeding about 250 men per day.

In 1941 they bought their own house, an ancient three-story brick building, and named it St. Joseph's House. They also took a step at this point that branded them a deviant Worker house, a house that was "looked at askance" by the New York house. On the advice of a lawyer, they incorporated and formed a board of directors. On March 18, 1941, St. Joseph's House of Hospitality was incorporated with a five person board of directors—two women and three men. Two of the male directors moved into the house, although one moved out shortly thereafter.

Incorporation was viewed as a dangerous compromise with the capitalist system by other Worker houses, which had not incorporated.[1] The Worker norm was well expressed by the story of a huffy social worker who visited Martin de Porres Hospice in Washington, D.C. Exasperated by the lack of efficiency and organization, she asked Llewellyn Scott, the house director, for the names of his board of directors. Llewellyn pointed to the statues of the Blessed Lady, St. Joseph, and Blessed Martin de Porres arrayed on the mantelpiece and said, "There they are."

One Worker wrote to Dorothy defending the incorporation: "You know we incorporated when we bought this House, but only because we had to in order to be granted an exemption from taxation, and could see no objection from the CW program to our buying the

House. . . . I did, however, and do still regret the necessity of incorporation" (Catholic Worker Archives, Marquette University, Series W-4, Box 7).

The new house brought with it a rash of plans—for a farm, for providing shelter as well as food to the men, for a chapel, and for various other improvements. The chapel was built, and a farm was begun, but the house never opened a shelter. Other than the one Worker who lived in the house, it was rare for more than four or five street men to sleep there. St. Benedict's farm was opened in 1942, but after a few years only one of the original farmers remained and it became his private farm rather than a Catholic Worker venture.

World War II and Dorothy Day's pacifist stance brought dissension to the house. The Workers, who still met weekly at the house, split into a pacifist and a "just-war" camp. Several became conscientious objectors, one going to prison, another to a C.O. camp.

In 1944, Tim (the Worker who had been living in the house) left to get married, and several desperate letters were sent to Dorothy Day asking that she send someone to run the house. No one was sent and, although one of the conscientious objectors returned to live in the house for awhile, the house basically struggled along with no ideologically committed live-in Workers. During this time they ran two meals—breakfast and supper—feeding about eighty men at each. In 1948, Tim returned, now with a family, as resident director of the house until 1952.

When Tim left for the final time, the house entered a period in which, for over fifteen years, the day-to-day operation was handled by men off the soupline, supervised by one of the original board members, who came in almost daily after his regular job. Occasionally young people would come to live at the house, but none for long. The situation was helped by a Legion of Mary group that met in the house once a week and helped to serve the meal, inviting the men to pray the rosary with them afterward.

In 1968, the son of the chairman of the board, returning from a Peace Corps stint, moved in to become resident director. He revitalized the house and moved it, for the first time in its history, into an uncompromisingly antiwar stand. He went on trial for draft resistance in 1969 and was sentenced to do public service at least fifty miles away from Rochester. He remembers fondly that many of the men from the soupline showed up at his trial.

> A good many people from the house came down to the trial, and came to the celebration party we had afterwards, and so I felt living at

the House all during that period of time and having extended myself somewhat towards helping some of these individuals, [that] then, when my future was somewhat on the line, being able to sit there on the witness stand and look out in the courtroom and see a lot of the gentlemen sitting out there and saying, "Oh, oh, good for you," you know, and "Sock it to 'em," was really supportive to me and I felt like it was a kind of an unsolicited paying back of me for ladling out the soup and handing out the overcoats over a period of months before that.

About a year later, the son and daughter of another of the original founders moved into the house and ran it for about a year in what was known as "the hippie era." Several of the guests still had fond memories of that era when I talked to them over a decade later. Nonetheless, some members of the board of directors had less affection for this new crew and by at least one report (Bishop 1982) were not unhappy to see them leave.

The house again went into a period of decline in which it was basically run by some men off the line and directed from afar by the same chairman of the board who had shepherded it through the 1950s and early 1960s. A professor from a nearby university worked at the house for a semester-long sabatical during this time (Bishop 1982).

This period of decline ended in late 1976 when Patrick Grady, a young seminarian, who had spent some time living at the New York house in the early 1970s, moved in and became director. He arrived just as the board was about to let the house close down. He reorganized the soupline. When he arrived, they had a system by which the men were given numbers while they were in the waiting room, and then came in to get their soup when their number was called. "One thing I did want to do as soon as possible, and it was a symbolic thing for me, was to get rid of those numbers. So, at the first opportunity, within a month or so, those numbers disappeared. I began to do symbolic things that would evoke my understanding of hospitality and the Works of Mercy."

As he recalls it, he just worked on the meal and was receptive to anyone who wanted to help, whether homeless or middle class. Soon, several of the guests moved in with him—one doing repair work, another (Louie) cooking, a third making signs. He also involved the house in political activism, particularly the migrant-worker and nuclear issues. People active in those movements began to come around and help out at the house as well. In 1977 he began a summer program in which several volunteers spent the summer living at the house. Out of this project a second Catholic Worker house, Bethany House for women, was begun.

Pat was ordained in October 1978. Barb Tompkins, who had been one of the summer volunteers, became a regular worker in 1980, coming in daily, although living in a community of nuns rather than at the house. Soon thereafter, Pat was assigned to a parish, leaving the running of the house to Barb. John soon arrived, and, with Louie, they formed the staff I met in 1982.

By the time I arrived at the house, however, there were several other persons involved. Barb had recruited Pete, a big, affable man who had lived at the house previously, to live at the house while she was away. Barb's order sent Marie as a temporary replacement for her. Like Barb, she did not live at the house but came to work from 9:00 to 5:00, Monday through Friday. Kathy was a college student from Notre Dame who worked at the house every day as part of a summer volunteer program. Mike, a tall, skinny alcoholic, about forty, had begun staying at the house and helping out about a month before I got there.

The day I moved in, two young women moved into the third floor. They had been running Melita House, a Catholic Worker house for pregnant women. The day before I arrived, the house had been taken over by the Sisters of Mercy, and the Workers who had been running it moved into St. Joe's while they decided what to do next. Their relationship to the house was left vague, although they both helped out at times.

Physical Description

The house was a three-story, red-brick, century-old building that had changed little since the 1940s. There was a new facade to the first floor, paid for by a construction company after their crane had backed through the front wall a few years previously. The inside had been remodeled a few times over the decades, and the equipment was certainly not the original. However, the picture of the Holy Spirit painted on the dining room wall in the early forties was still there.

St. Joseph's was not located in a skid-row area. Rather, it lay on the edge of a poor residential area that was rapidly being gentrified, the so-called South Wedge. The house was bordered on the left by a small shoe factory and on the right by a paved parking lot owned by the Worker.

The house was divided into two sides, each with a separate entrance. The right-hand door led into two sitting rooms containing numerous well-worn chairs and couches, a 1950s-style red barber chair and a barbershop wall cabinet, and an old TV. On the left was the entrance to the main dining room. This room contained eight new round tables, each with six chairs of molded colored plastic. At the far end of the dining room, set off a bit by a large counter, was the kitchen area, containing a huge black stove, a three-door refrigerator, and a new three-compartment sink.

The second floor contained living quarters for the staff, a five-bed dormitory for overnight guests, an office, and a chapel. Only half of the third floor was habitable, used by the women from Melita House. The other side of the third floor was in disrepair, with gaping holes in the walls—it looked as though it hadn't been used in decades.

House Organization

The house was organized quite differently from St. Joseph's in New York City. The board of directors, which had been formed in 1941, was still in operation, and the house had a director, who was formally in charge of day-to-day decisions.

The board of directors was responsible for major financial and policy decisions. "Major" was not defined, but there seemed to be general agreement between the Workers and the board as to what should be brought before the board. Indeed, the full-time Workers were all on the board, which also included former Workers (including two of the founders) and volunteers who had shown interest in the house. Barb, the house director, was chair of the board; however, at a meeting I attended after I left the house, she resigned and one of the original board members was elected as chair.

Over the years the board has exercised power in the house in a manner reasonably similar to boards of directors in traditional human-service organizations. The use of house funds was restricted by the original 1941 statement of purpose. For instance, the house had a surplus of funds in 1982, a situation that is considered a major problem in the Worker since it contradicts the ideal of organizational poverty. Board members argued that the house could not avail itself of the traditional Worker approach to getting rid of a surplus—sending a donation to another Worker house or to someplace like Mother Theresa's organization—because such a use of funds was not encompassed under the statement of purpose.

There were many ways, however, in which the board did not

operate like a conventional board of directors. The majority of the board consisted of persons who worked, or had worked, in the house. Historically, it does not seem that the board sustained the house. By all accounts, when the house was weak, the board too had been weak, often not meeting for years. An incident at a board meeting I attended indicates that the Catholic Worker spirit still affects the board. At the beginning of the meeting, the chair asked, "Do we have any bylaws?" Everyone looked confusedly at each other. Finally, one of the original board members said, "No, we never made any up. All we have is our statement of purpose." The director said, "Maybe we should make some up."

In terms of daily decisions, there was no parallel to New York's "taking-the-house" system. The director was responsible for daily decisions; however, she encouraged collective decision-making for day-to-day matters. Meetings of Workers were called whenever a situation arose, usually attended by whoever was there at the moment. Thus, authority rested in the director rather than in a series of persons taking the house. If the director was not present (which was true for much of my stay), decision making was more collective.

The house also differed from New York in that Workers did not volunteer for the shifts they wanted to work. Rather, Workers were expected to work five days a week, at least from 11:00 A.M. to 3:00 P.M. Thus there were usually at least two Workers present when the house was open, rather than one person "taking the house."

There was one role at the house that approximated a role in a bureaucracy—that of house director. The only real distinction between the director and other Workers was greater responsibility for decision making. Otherwise, the director had the same responsibilities—meal preparation, keeping order, being present, sweeping floors—as all other staff. Nevertheless, the consensus on the board was that the house must always have a director, and it was this commitment to find a replacement when a director left that made this role unusual in a Worker house. This can best be seen by contrasting the directorship with the "role" of cook. For many years, cook was also a specialized position in that Louie did all the cooking except on his day off. While I was there, however, he divided cooking days with Pete. The difference between the roles of cook and director was revealed by what happened when Barb and Louie left the house. When Barb left, a search was instituted for a new director and one was finally chosen, even at the cost of paying him a subsistence salary to support his family. When Louie left, the cooking was divided up among the other staff and among some of the volunteers. No new cook was chosen. Thus, house director was a role in the bureaucratic sense that it outlasted any particular incumbent, while cook was a role that Louie negotiated for himself, which disappeared when he left.

A final aspect of St. Joseph's organization was the remarkable fluidity of the services provided by the house. Over the years, services would expand and contract with the number of Workers. This was especially noticeable with respect to shelter. When there were several Workers, shelter was offered to more people; when there were very few Workers, shelter was curtailed. This flexibility has probably contributed to the survival of the house since it prevented Workers from overextending themselves for long periods, as happened at Unity Kitchen.

Hospitality

In the Rochester house, simply taking a shower was an act of hospitality. You had to trudge down to the cellar, past the rows of canned goods, into a dingy little room that contained the shower, a sink, and a washer and dryer. It was the same shower stall that was used by guests to wash off the accumulated dirt of days or even weeks on the streets. Sometimes they used it to delouse themselves. And you had to drag your middle-class body into that tiny, sometimes grimy stall if you wanted to get clean. The experience teaches you more about equality than all the books ever written.

For me, the shower was a symbol of Catholic Worker hospitality. Worker hospitality extends to the most private aspects of one's life. Its essence is daily face-to-face interaction with the poor, with little possibility of retreat to the safety of one's office (for one doesn't have one) or even one's room (for one may be sharing even that with one of the guests).

As at the New York house, formal hospitality centered around food, shelter, and clothing. Also like New York, however, hospitality involved far more: visiting hospitals, advocacy with social agencies, burying the dead, and even picnics with the guests.

Food

Daily life at the house revolved around the 1:00 P.M. meal, which was served Monday through Saturday. Louie, the cook, was up every day before 8:00, putting down the chairs that had been stacked after yesterday's meal and beginning to prepare the meal for the day. Although soup was served two or three times a week, the majority of the meals were "family-style" dinners—goulash, chicken, casseroles, and even pork chops about once a month.

Workers began drifting down soon after 8:00 to fix themselves breakfast. Overnight guests, if there were any, usually left by around 9:00—they were supposed to be out during the day. Workers often started helping Louie cook, if he needed help, or started doing dishes or cleaning. Often visitors dropped in to chat and share a cup of coffee.

The house opened officially at 11:00 A.M. Usually there were a few men waiting by then. They came into the sitting rooms, turned on the TV, and settled down in the old-fashioned overstuffed chairs and couches to watch. A few snuck bottles in and sat in a corner nipping at them when the Workers weren't looking. Often a Worker set out snacks, usually day-old donuts.

All types of people came in—young and old, black and white, male and female, alcoholic, insane, crippled, or simply out of work. The overwhelming majority were black males, however. Some had been regulars for years. One of the founders told me once that as he came in he had greeted three men he had known for over thirty years. Many were native Rochesterians; others were transients or migrant workers from the fields around Rochester, or had moved from other cities. While I was there I met half a dozen guests who I had known in Syracuse, including one we knew as Tom but who was called Ed by the Rochester Workers.

Around 12:45, people crowded around the door leading from the sitting rooms to the dining room. At about 12:50 the steaming food containers were carried to the serving table. From there, Workers and volunteers took the plates of food to the empty tables. When all the places had food, a Worker would tell the waiting crowd, "OK, you can come in now." Occasionally there was some pushing and shoving, but usually people entered in a fairly orderly fashion. Forty-eight were seated at a time. Those who couldn't be accommodated in the first sitting went back to the sitting rooms to wait for the next. Toward the end of the month, there were sometimes three sittings.

Usually, several of the volunteers who helped set the tables were guests who then ate during the first sitting. The other volunteers and Workers served as waiters, refilling tea, water, and salt shakers, wiping up spills, and serving seconds. A guest signaled for seconds by holding up his or her empty plate. The cook usually decided whether seconds were allowed—generally they were only if there was enough food to give firsts to everyone.

If there was food left over, guests were allowed to take some home in jars. A huge amount of bread was donated every week by a nearby monastery; thus, the house usually had bread left over for guests to take with them. In giving out food to go, the emphasis seemed to be on getting rid of the supply rather than on equitable distribution. Those who asked first were often given as much as they wanted, with the result that "them that eats the fastest gets the most."

There was not much concern with saving food for latecomers. In fact, latecomers were discouraged, even harangued at times—"You know we serve at one. Where were you?" Nevertheless, they were given a meal if there was food left. If the regular meal had run out, they were given peanut butter and jelly sandwiches.

As the final sitting began to clear out, tables were cleaned off and chairs stacked to one side. After eating, most guests left the house, although some returned to the sitting rooms. The floor was swept and mopped, often by one of the meal guests.

When the dishes had been washed, the Workers and volunteers sat around the serving table for a cup of instant coffee or tea. This after-dinner tea time was important for many of the volunteers, since it was one of the few times they could sit and talk with the Workers in a relaxed atmosphere. It was also a mark of status among guests to be welcomed to join in for some coffee, although the same privilege was often granted to a drunk who simply barged in. Conversation ranged from the events of the day to issues of war and peace to gossip about the diocese.

The sitting rooms remained open until 3:00 P.M., at which time a Worker would go into the rooms, wake up those who were sleeping, and ask whoever was still there to leave. Mike then swept and mopped the sitting rooms. At this point the main work of the house was done for the day. Often Workers would then take someone to welfare or a hospital or to look for a room, or would visit someone in the hospital. If there were enough people in the house, someone would cook a communal supper; if not, everyone was on their own. If new guests were staying, at least one of the staff would make it a point to remain in the house.

Although the vast majority of the food was distributed at lunch, food did get distributed in other ways, usually when someone came to the door asking for some. Men from the street might come by after hours asking for a sandwich or a carton of milk. If someone was around to hear the doorbell, they would usually invite them in, fix them a peanut butter and jelly sandwich, and let them eat it inside. A few families from the neighborhood occasionally asked for food and were given a grocery bag full from the stores in the basement.

Shelter

While the meal was considered to be the primary mission of the house, shelter was a secondary task, one that could be cut back or eliminated if it became too much of a strain. The day I arrived, John asked Pete and myself to sit down with him to decide what we were going to do about shelter. He began by saying, "With this new situation, we'll have to talk about housing men at night. I figure at most we could do it Monday through Friday—with Pete being gone Saturday and Harry Sunday. But we'll have to talk about it and see how everyone feels." We talked for half an hour or so and decided that we would do some shelter, but that it would be a limited amount until we got a feel for how much we could handle.

We did not give shelter to anyone during the first week. One person asked and was told he could stay, but did not show up that night. During my second week, however, we had a few guests. Giving shelter was a much different affair than at the New York house. Because there were both fewer Workers and fewer guests, interaction with each guest was more personal and often more draining. The events of the first evening give some idea of the type of negotiations, uncertainties, and interactions that accompanied taking in new guests.

About 5:00 P.M. Mike answered the doorbell. A young white man announced, "RPC [Rochester Psychiatric Center] sent me here. They said you'd give me a place to stay for the night." Mike replied, with some hostility, "No, we don't do that." The guy continued to press his case. Mike finally said, reluctantly, "You can come in just for a minute." I came over and the man said, "The police sent me here. They said you'd give me a place to stay." I replied, "Well, we don't usually do that anymore." "Then why did the police tell me that?" "Well, we used to let people stay but we've been low on staff so we haven't been doing that much lately. What's your situation?" He said, "I'm supposed to got to Norris [an alcohol clinic] tomorrow. I just need a place for the night." I said, "Let me go get the other staff and we'll see what we can do."

I found Pete and John, who came down with me. John introduced himself and asked the guest his name. "Tom Rotthan." John asked what his situation was. "I was over at RPC and a cop there told me I could go to Norris tomorrow morning and I could stay the night here." He pulled out a plastic ID card and presented it to John, who just laughed and waved it away. Tom looked perplexed and John explained that we didn't require documentation: "I'm just laughing because you're obviously here—you don't need to show us that. We can see you. Are you going to go to Norris then?" "Yeah." John looked at Pete, who said, "I don't see why not." John said, "OK, you can spend the night." Pete added, "But we don't want you going out again tonight. You're here and I think you should stay here." "That's fine with me." John helped Tom get a shower and some clean clothes.

Pete said to me, "I saw that guy once when I was tending bar. He came in so messed up, all beat up and really wasted, that we couldn't even serve him. Maybe he's trying to get himself straightened out."

John left on his bike to visit Bethany House. Eventually the rest of us sat down to supper. Tom was introduced to everyone, and he took a lead in the conversation, talking mostly about rock and new-wave music and about how he was a black belt in Tae Kwon Do karate— "the sun source of the martial arts." After dinner, Tom talked to me for quite awhile, mostly about his experience in Vietnam and his college career. Although I responded to him seriously, I became increasingly skeptical about the veracity of his tale. There were simply too many stories, too eagerly told, for me to take them at face value.

A monsignor from a local church telephoned to ask if we had received a call from a young black man named Jim looking for a place to stay. I said no. He said, "I just had a call from him and told him to call you. He asked me to call first. He's a student at [a local business school] and his landlady threw him out." I said, "We're pretty limited in how much hospitality we can do, and we already have a couple of guests, so I'm not sure what we can do." "I understand. We're all limited in what we can do. We'll have to do more for you. Our church already sends donations but we need to do more for you. This guy really needs someone to talk to him. He seems like a very agitated young man. Do you have a black staff member?" "No." "Well, that might have helped. I had a hard time understanding him over the phone." I said, "Well, I'll see what I can do. I'm not sure if we'll be able to get him a place to stay, but I'll certainly talk to him if he calls."

I told Pete about the call and he was agreeable to taking in another guest. The phone rang again. It was Jim. He explained that his landlady had thrown him out. "Can you get here by ten?" I asked. "Yeah."

Meanwhile, Tom asked to go out for a walk. Since we had told him he couldn't go out alone, I decided to accompany him. On the walk he asked me about the people in the house, apparently trying to find out who held the real authority. When we returned, Pete pulled me aside and said, "I don't think this guy's on the level. Mike said he's a real bullshitter and that he's been shooting up recently." I said, "Yeah, I saw some marks on his arm but they didn't seem all that recent." (He had told me he had done heroin in Nam but had kicked the habit.) Pete continued, "Mike also said that he really wasn't set up to go to Norris. He was never at RPC—he just talked to some guard on the grounds."

Shortly after our return, Jim arrived, carrying a satchel with his school books. He was a thin man in his thirties—older than I had expected. Pete asked him about the situation with his landlady. His explanation was hard to follow, but it seemed that he had been doing work around the house for her and that she had been lenient about the rent, but trouble arose when he refused to do any more work: "She was always telling me to do this, do that. I couldn't take it." Pete asked him if he needed clothes, but he replied, "I got loads of clothes. I just ain't got no place to put them." He asked if he could be awakened at 6:00 A.M. because he had to be at school at 8:00.

Tom went up to bed. A few minutes later, Louie came down and said he had told Tom to stay on his side of the floor, that the other side of the floor was for staff members, and that if he wanted to use the bathroom he should use the one downstairs. Louie then said something to Pete and went back upstairs. Pete told me that Louie had caught Tom going into Pete's room and had told him to get out. Pete shrugged and added, "Oh, well. It's just for one night."

Jim went into the sitting room to watch TV with Mike. Pete and I went upstairs. I asked him, "When we have guests do we stay up late or all night to make sure things are all right?" He said, "No, we just go to sleep when we want to, and if anything happens we take care of it when we find out."

After John returned and everything had apparently settled down for the night, Pete and I went out for a few beers. When I got back, John was still up. He said, "I hear our guest shoots up." I said that seemed to be the case. John said, "I'm not too good at asking those kinds of questions. Barb is much better at it. I figure more you take someone or leave them in [their] totality. If you accept them then you find out what the problems are." I went to bed. Both Tom and Jim were gone before I got up.

Although it would be difficult to call this or any other night "representative," this one does illustrate some key points about shelter at St. Joseph's. There was no formal intake procedure—no set of questions to be asked, no forms to be filled out, no identification required. However, not everyone who asked was accepted. The guest had to negotiate his way in with whoever answered the door. When other staff were in the house, they were often called into the negotiation process since all had to live with the guest. Indeed, the entire process of offering shelter was one of negotiation. Besides negotiating entry, guests and staff negotiated status, role, and even territory. Often decisions about whether the guest would be allowed to stay beyond the amount of time initially stated (usually from one to three nights) were negotiated among staff based on the first evening's interactions with the guest. Offering shelter could mean making an intensive commitment to face-to-face interaction with the guest as practical problems must be solved and personal relationships established. This reality informed the staff's decision. If no one responsible was there that evening or if everyone was too exhausted to deal with the problems that may come with the guest, shelter would probably be refused.

After Pete left, John and I were the only ones willing and able to take responsibility for guests. Thus, to accept someone for the night meant that either John or I had to commit ourselves to being there for the night. If we wanted to go somewhere together, we couldn't accept guests for the night.

As in New York City, shelter was not usually given to meal guests. One might even say that the overnight guests and the meal guests were drawn from two largely separate populations. Very few meal guests asked to stay, even though they were sleeping in the weeds, vacant buildings, and the old, abandoned subway tunnels. When they did ask, they were often turned down. There were only a very limited number of spaces for shelter—the five beds in the second-floor dormitory. If one accepted the regular meal guests for shelter, the dorm would be quickly and permanently filled—a condition that the staff did not want. Even if one allowed "needing a few days' break from the streets" as a legitimate reason for shelter, the dorm would be constantly full. The staff tended to prefer men who either were just passing through town or who had a definite plan to achieve some type of long-term arrangement. Thus, the men accepted for shelter tended to be strangers. The preference for travelers was illustrated by the ease with which I convinced the staff to allow persons to stay who

I had known from the Oxford Inn and who I was confident would soon return to Syracuse.

The preference for those with plans was illustrated when Dan was accepted into shelter. After John had talked with him and told him he could stay, Jane asked, "Does he have any plans?" John said, "He's going to look for a job." A collective moan arose—everyone understood that that meant he was going to try to stay for an indefinite amount of time, because the chances of him getting a job other than day labor were slim at best. The same preference was reflected when Barb visited a couple of days after we had taken in Johnny, an alcoholic friend of the house. "You old softies," she reprimanded us gently. Then she went in to talk to Johnny. "But what is your plan? How do we know that this isn't just going to be a few days off the streets?" "You know, at the unit, you can't go there unless you're in withdrawal. I've graduated from that program two times already anyway. And you can't get into detox unless you're drunk." "But you're not telling me what I asked. What's your plan?" The conversation went on for half an hour without a plan emerging.

The overnight hospitality I have described reflects how the house operated during the spring and summer. During the cold months, more formal shelter was offered. The winter after my stay, the house sheltered up to fifteen men per night, with one live-in staff person and one or two volunteers responsible for keeping order. In addition the workers helped to coordinate a city-wide network of about half a dozen churches, each of which provided shelter for about a dozen homeless people.

Perhaps the main difference, other than numbers, between summer and winter shelter was that during the winter the house was committed to having a worker or volunteer up all night. Since no one was responsible for staying up all night in the summer, there was an incentive to accept primarily guests who would not create situations in which someone had to stay up.

Clothing

Normally, during the summer, there were only two or three people waiting outside the door when the house opened. But on Tuesday mornings there were often twenty or thirty, milling around and pushing to be the first inside. Usually, they would be greeted by John, wearing a tie over his T-shirt, calling out, "Now don't shove." Phil, an enormous, friendly young man who often managed to be at the head of the "line," would respond, "Don't worry, as long as there's shovin', I'm not gonna move, and if I don't move, nobody's gonna move." As soon as there was a bit of order, or maybe even if there wasn't any, John would turn around and begin marching in an exaggerated, toy soldier fashion through the two sitting rooms toward the door of the clothing room. The crowd followed in a ragged line.

Once the line got to the door, a worker asked each person in turn what articles of clothing they would like and wrote this on a scrap of paper and handed it to the guest. Inside the clothing room were five workers. Each worker met one of the first five guests at the door, took his or her slip, and helped them to find the clothes they had requested. When a worker's guest left, the worker would get a new "customer," until all had been through.

There were well-defined rules for clothing distribution: a maximum of one set of underwear, socks, pants and two shirts per man. Women were free to take whatever clothes they wanted from the women's table—there the supply exceeded demand. Workers had different styles with their guests. Some Workers played a watchdog role, making sure a guest got no more than his due. Others enacted the role of salesperson in a clothing store, showing off their wares to customers. Still others played a laid-back role, letting the guest fend for himself.

For the purposes of the clothing room, workers generally typed people into two categories and interacted with each type quite differently. The majority were characterized as cooperative and grateful. With these, the roles adopted by the workers were either laid-back or salesperson. The entire clothing room interaction was sometimes carried out in mutual parody of a clothing store, with the worker trying to convince the customer that an article was "right" for him, and the guest responding light-heartedly as a customer out to get the most for his money. After selecting his clothes, one man said jovially to John, "I like how you treat your customers," to which John replied, "The customer is always right." Other guests were simply meek and thankful, like the middle-aged Spanish man who had requested a shirt, shoes, and a pair of pants but was able to find only a shirt. He left thanking me profusely.

On the other hand, perhaps a half dozen guests were typed as greedy and demanding. These guests, I was told as soon as I was paired up with one, must be watched closely lest they walk out with everything. My very first "customer" was a tall, middle-aged, rather well-dressed black man. He handed me his slip when he walked in the door and then asked me to find him a shirt while he found a jacket. Out of the corner of my eye, I noticed him stuffing suit coats into a large plastic trash bag he had brought in with him. I didn't interfere at that point. Florence whispered to me, "Watch that one. He'll take you for all he can get." After a minute or two I said to him, "Well, are you about through?" He said he was and started to leave. Then he saw a man with a suit he liked and said, "Where'd you get that suit, man? I didn't see that." He began looking in the section the other man was in and soon found another suit he liked, which he started to stuff in his bag. Florence whispered, "He can't have that." I told him "If you want that one you'll have to give back the other coat." He did so and left.

Although I had played a relatively laid-back role with the gentleman, others assumed a more aggressive watchdog role whenever he came in. A few weeks later he came in and was paired with Louise. Earl, a feisty older man who came in to work in the clothing room almost every week, kept after him from the moment he came in the room, allowing him no chance to take anything not on his list. He did this even though he wasn't assigned to him. He said to Louise, "Watch him." The man said to Earl, "You telling her to watch me?" Earl replied, "Yeah, you. You'd take the whole store and then ask for more on the way out." The man did seem to take less than usual this trip.

The presence of people who demand a great deal of clothing presented a problem of distributive justice—a tension between the Worker anarchist philosophy and the pragmatic desire to ration clothes so that the first did not get everything while the latecomers were left with nothing. For instance, after John had told one customer that he could have only two shirts, rather than the four he wanted, the man complained, "What do you have all this stuff for? You should give it out to people instead of just keeping it." John said, under his breath, "Yes, but fairly." The guest was using a common argument—that the goods the Worker distributes do not belong to the Workers, but are given to them to be passed on to the poor, so why shouldn't the poor themselves determine how the goods should be distributed. Although this argument appeals to Catholic Worker philosophy, Workers often reject it because such an approach inevitably results in some guests getting far more than they need, while others must go without socks or underwear or winter coats.

The clothing room was one of the least favorite activities for the Workers at St. Joseph's. Several frankly stated that they hated it. I found it a draining task. The current procedure was but one in a series of attempts at arriving at a just system of distributing clothes. This approach was more organized than is normal for a Catholic Worker house, but was justified because the one-to-one contact was more personal. John stated:

> We've had a variety of systems over the last few years and all of them had their drawbacks. We tried letting five persons in for five minutes each, then we tried letting someone in as someone else left, but found that some people stayed in forever. The men didn't like this system at first, but now they appreciate its order. Also, it's more personal— each staff member gives one person individual attention.

In addition to the "official" Tuesday clothing room, guests could ask for clothes at any time. As at the New York City house, the norm was to give the person clothes if they were in real need, but there was no articulation of what this meant. It was up to the Worker in such cases whether to take the person into the clothing room or have him wait in the sitting room while the Worker got clothes.

Other Aspects of Hospitality

As in New York City, there were a number of ways in which hospitality was extended in addition to the meal, shelter, and clothing distribution. Perhaps the most unusual institutionalized type of hospitality was barbering. Every Thursday at 2:00 P.M. a local college professor came in and cut hair for free, using the old barber chair in the sitting room. About half a dozen to a dozen men took advantage of the service each week. The barber observed:

> I've been cutting hair here since October 1975. I like it here. You get a great variety—young and old, black, white, Puerto Rican, Indian. It took them years to learn to trust me. You know, they thought just anyone was coming in cutting off hair. I do it any way they tell me. At first they would be skeptical [and] just say to do it any way, but I made them tell me how they wanted it—it's part of their self-respect. I would do it any way they tell me. Some of the requests have been pretty weird but I've done them. I'm used to doing baldies now— shaving it all off. A few years ago I thought it was weird but now I'm used to it. One man—he was a young man—asked for a crewcut. That wasn't so weird, but he asked me to shave off a strip halfway up the middle. I kept asking him if that was how he wanted it and it was, so I did it.

Picnics were a second institutionalized activity. The house held an annual picnic at a nearby park on the Genesee River. They rented buses, and around a hundred guests were driven to an afternoon of hot dogs, baked beans, salads, and drinks (all nonalcoholic, except for the bottles slipped in by the guests). The picnic was the big event of the season for both Workers and guests. It was talked about and planned for weeks in advance. A number of guests teased Kathy, a young college student who worked there, about how they were going to "get her" with water balloons at the picnic. Kathy took pictures, which she arranged on a big sheet of paper and hung in the dining room.

In addition to the big picnic, the Workers tried to have small picnics about once a week in which a couple Workers took four or five of the meal guests out to a park. Usually we would try to sign up people in advance, although sometimes we would just ask around the day of the picnic and take the first five who wanted to go, as long as they weren't too drunk or belligerent. The general idea of these picnics was to let the Workers and guests get to interact in a smaller, more personalist social setting than the regular meals. The ones I went on were generally pleasant and relaxed. They did help me to come to know some of the guests a bit better.

Many guests used the house to clean up. They were allowed to use the shower in the basement and could get new clothes if they were taking a shower. They were discouraged from using the washer and dryer, especially if they were drunk (since there had been some disastrous results from such usage in the past). They would also come in to use the shaving equipment, sometimes requesting help. I once shaved a week's stubble off one of the guys, a difficult task since he was stone drunk and his head kept weaving.

Advocacy could include helping someone find an apartment, pleading a case before welfare authorities, or taking someone to a hospital. Sister Marie's first experience was memorable. Johnny had been on a drunk for days, and he was wandering around with stitches in his head, which he should have had out some time ago. He came in late one afternoon. He was drunk, but Marie volunteered to take him to the hospital to get the stitches out. The next morning I asked her how it went.

> Awful. He created a scene, called a guard an "asshole." I was so angry at him and then angry at myself. I had to spend so much time trying to calm down the hospital personnel. And he was so loud in the waiting room. They told him that the doctor was suturing another patient and would see him as soon as he was done. Then I found out that he hadn't even had his stitches put in at that hospital. They didn't have

anything about it on his record and finally he said, "I can't lie to a sister. I had the stitches put in at another hospital." I got him to go outside and told him to wait right there. The doctor came out and was ready to see him, but when I went out to get him he was gone. We were so close. I was so angry.

Several days later, Pete took Johnny to get his stitches removed.

Some almsgiving was also practiced at St. Joe's; however, the house had the most stringent policy about giving or lending money to guests of any house I've seen. Almost without exception, the guest had to have a demonstrable reason for wanting money. Spare change was rarely given out since it could be used for drink. Instead, almsgiving often took the form of in-kind gifts. The house maintained an account with a local hotel and could issue vouchers for people to stay there if they had a need for a place for a night and the house couldn't accommodate them. Occasionally, the house would bail someone out of jail, expecting to be reimbursed.

Burying the dead was another type of hospitality. I went to a memorial service for one of the men who had lived in the house. Father Pat gave the eulogy, remembering Vince as a "giver of gifts." It seemed ironic that this man, although near destitution, received something that most of the middle class never gets—a memorial service officiated by a priest who had known him personally. This was one of the most dignifying things the Worker could give its guests— the hope that one won't die alone and forgotten.

Finally, the house often held people's money, checks, or valuables. A few men had their checks mailed to the house. These arrangements often caused problems for the Workers. Once Mex, an older alcoholic, came in drunk to get his check. Reluctantly, John gave it to him. He was back in a few hours, demanding his check. It apparently had been lost or stolen, but he thought it was still at the house. Fortunately a neighboring businessman came by a bit later with some papers Mex had dropped by his establishment. The check wasn't there, but when I searched the area more thoroughly, I found it lying in some bushes. When Mex returned still later, again demanding his check, we decided not to give it to him until he sobered up. But when he returned with the police, we gave it to him. Another time, a younger alcoholic came in roaring drunk, demanding a pair of boots he had left at the house a year ago. When we could find only one boot, he went into a rage. Fortunately, we eventually found the other one stashed in an obscure locker.

The style of hospitality at the house also deserves some treatment.

There was certainly more attention to cleanliness and to serving balanced meals than I was used to at Unity Kitchen. However, it was the type of interaction the Workers had with guests that really impressed me.

For one thing, Workers did not content themselves with simply breaking up an argument or fight. After intervening in an argument and cooling things out, John or Barb would pull up a chair and talk with one of the offending parties—not to criticize, but just to establish more contact and provide some time for tempers to cool off. If someone was asked to leave, they might go out and talk with the person for awhile. One time a young black man came in really drunk and started several fights. We finally dragged him off someone and hustled him out the door. Rather than retreating inside, John stayed out with him, stroking his back and saying, "You're a good man, Dwayne. Don't forget that—you're a good man." This supportive, affirming approach to even the most troublesome of guests seemed to affect the whole atmosphere of the house, which seemed far less violent than Unity Kitchen had been.[2]

A related aspect of style was the continual emphasis on finding and affirming the positive characteristics of individual guests. I think that I heard Workers at this house refer to specific guests as "gentle" more often than at the other houses. A guest who was not violent was often characterized as a "gentle person."

There was also a great deal of care to introduce oneself to a guest one did not know and then ask the guest's name. This was done without being intrusive. Giving one's own name first was important in that it established an equality of exchange of information. One was not being asked to give one's name to an anonymous authority figure.

Finally, there was careful attention to the quality of the meals. St. Joe's proved to me that one could serve family-style meals of good quality in a relatively peaceful setting without restricting who was allowed to come to the meal. One important part of the solution was to have repeated servings, so that everyone could eat, but only a certain number would be allowed in the dining room at any given time.

Typifications of People

Rochester Workers used basically the same three schemes for typifying persons as did the New York Workers: relationship to the house,

moral qualities, and deviant labels. The schemes were also ideal typical rather than categorical. There were, however, some important
differences.

As in New York City, persons were generally considered either
alcoholic, crazy, or neither, and the terms were not used with any
technical precision. There was little talk of addicts as a separate type—
addiction was not seen to be the common problem that it was in New
York City.

Also as in New York City, Workers talked about guests in moral
terms—some were greedy, others violent, still others gentle. One
unusual aspect of this house was that guests were rather frequently
characterized as gentle. The term seemed to be the unconscious result
of a desire to have a positive moral term to contrast with "violent."
Another interesting moral consideration concerned whether guests
were trustworthy. When Workers called someone trustworthy, they
did not usually mean that the person was considered totally trustworthy, but rather that they felt they knew in what ways she or he
could or could not be trusted.

As in New York City, the most important typification scheme was
relationship to the house. Rochester Workers even employed many
of the same terms as those in New York City, including "friends of
the house." An interesting divergence from New York City was that
the term "staff" was often used as a synonym for "Worker." The most
significant difference, however, was that there was no type known
as "resident"—long-term guests who participated in the life of the
house. As a consequence, the distinction between Workers and guests
became quite problematic, largely due to the presence of a couple of
persons who in New York City would have been termed residents.
Since no one conceived of the house as having residents, these persons existed in a very uneasy type of limbo. They had no established
social role—no expectations for how they should act.

The distinction between "working" and "helping out" helped to
draw the line between Worker and guest at St. Joseph's. Working signified that someone was entrusted with responsibility for the house
and for keeping order—that that person could be left alone by other
Workers to "run" the meal. It was a position of full trustworthiness.
"Helping out" signified that a person assisted in preparing and serving
the meal, but was not entrusted with keeping order and would not
be left alone in the house. The distinction was never formalized, but
it did exist in the minds of the Workers. Thus, when someone commented, "I hear so-and-so is working at the house now," a Worker
immediately replied, "No, he's just helping out."

The stories of three men—Louie, Angelo, and Mike—reveal even more sharply the ambiguities involved in the Worker versus guest distinction.

Louie was introduced to me as staff. He was one of the three persons who met with me to discuss my coming to St. Joe's, although he didn't say a word in the meeting. He had come to the house eight years previously, a man off the line who had volunteered to do the cooking. He was the lone person from Pat Grady's time still living and working in the house. However, some time after I left, he accepted a job cooking at a local rectory. One of the Workers reflected at the time: "I wonder what the house's responsibility to Louie is if he comes back." Eventually, he did leave the job, but the last time I saw him he was "helping out." I asked one of the Workers where he was living and was told, "In the weeds. You ask him and he says 'Oh, here and there.' " The house made no move to take him back as a Worker. Even his apparently clear status as Worker was always somewhat ambiguous, for in the final analysis he was a guest. His story is a warning for those social scientists who place too much emphasis on the language used to talk about a person—Louie was always called a staff member, but in a real sense he wasn't one.

Angelo's story illustrates the ambiguities in the process of deciding whether an applicant was a legitimate candidate for staff. He was an African college student, staying at the YMCA, who came to the door one afternoon. From the beginning he had a difficult time communicating with everyone in the house—perhaps because of cultural differences, perhaps because of his own psychological differences. I offered him food, which he accepted, but then he said he wanted to work here. I told him we needed help serving the meal in the afternoon, but he said he wanted to do more. John and I showed him around the house, and it soon became evident that he didn't want to leave. Eventually he did, but he returned the next day. By this time we realized that he wanted to become a staff member. We hedged on responding to that, not wanting to turn him down outright, but not sure that he would "fit in." We invited him to "help out," but somehow he didn't fit in at that role. The regular helpers complained that he was constantly in their way. Angelo complained to me about how the place operated. He said he would institute more order. Nonetheless, he kept coming back to help out, always gently reminding us that he wanted to be staff when his time at the YMCA ran out in a week or so.

Angelo presented a problem in that Worker ideology requires that one accept offers of help freely, but no one in the house thought

Angelo would "work out." We held repeated discussions about what to do. Marie suggested that we take him into hospitality and let him help out. John replied, "That won't work here. He wants all or nothing. He wants to be a staff member." Later, John said, "I don't like to judge anyone. Sometimes you have a feeling, but I don't like to preclude things." We decided to tell him that we couldn't make a decision until Barb returned, hoping that the problem would resolve itself in the meanwhile. He eventually realized that we did not want to include him as staff and began to come around less frequently. He did raise troublesome questions about the staff–guest dichotomy, causing one person to reflect: "What is a staff member here anyway? I'm not so sure."

The story of Mike is even more complex. Mike carved out a role for himself, somewhere between Worker and guest, a role that was often problematic for everyone in the house. Mike was about forty, an alcoholic, and had been living in the second-floor dormitory for about a month. He did a lot of work at the house, washing dishes and cleaning the sitting rooms.

My first intense encounter with Mike came the second evening I was at the house. I found him on the first floor with several friends. He was obviously intoxicated. After his friends left, I said that I had thought drinking was against the rules, and he replied that no one else had ever criticized him for it. We argued awhile; then I went upstairs leaving the issue unresolved. As Pete and then John came back, Mike screamed at them to "keep that asshole off my back! I do my work!" Both decided to let the issue ride. When I talked with John the next morning, he said, "Well, I'm not sure what to do about it. He made some good points: 'I'm an alcoholic and I'm going to drink and I pull my weight around here.' " He said that this was the second or third time Mike had done this, but that the other times were "just for a day" and "hopefully this will be too."

Mike's drinking continued sporadically for the next several weeks, however. We had repeated confrontations with him, especially about his harassment of the women from the third floor when he was drunk. It soon became clear that his drinking was, in part, a negotiation tactic—a sign that he was unhappy with recent changes in the house, specifically the arrival of myself and the women, all of whom he saw as threats to his status.

Indeed, two separate negotiations were going on. We were negotiating with Mike about the drinking rule, and he was negotiating with us about status. Mike had created his own role in the house, a role that lay somewhere between Worker and guest. He did too much work to be considered simply a guest; however, because of his drinking, no one wanted to consider him a Worker. Thus, he considered himself a Worker while the Workers essentially considered him a guest. No attempt was made by the Workers to clarify his position until a crisis arose.

My arrival exacerbated Mike's situation. My threat to him was the most direct, and not only as a result of our early confrontation over drinking. From Mike's perspective, I had come long after he had, did essentially the same work, and yet was clearly treated as staff. I was given a staff room, while he slept in the guest dormitory. I was included in decision making, while he usually wasn't. As Pete observed, Mike was in a precarious position at the house—his role was neither clearly defined nor comparable to anyone else's. The dilemma was brought to a head by the arrival of "mental health days."

"Mental health days" was a recent tradition at St. Joe's. At the beginning of every second month the house closed down for about three days. The Workers felt that everyone needed a break every once in awhile and that the first part of the month was the best time since many people received income maintenance checks then. Some of the guests saw it differently. One helper stated:

> Mental health break. That's bullshit. You want to know how that started? Things had been kind of crazy for a few months around the first of the month. People were coming in with bottles and all. So they decided to close for a few days around then sometimes. To justify it they called it a mental health break. Other people accepted it and then they accepted it and they came to believe they needed it. They get three weeks vacation, are open six days a week and take another day off, and they need a mental health break every couple months? Hell, back in the late sixties when Larry and I were running this place we were open six days a week every week. Just the two of us.

Mike's crisis occurred because John and I both planned to leave for the break and had to decide what to do about Johnny and Mike. Johnny was an old friend of the house who had been living in the dorm, staying sober, and helping out for several weeks. Mike, of course, had not been staying sober. To allow them to stay would have left them alone with the women and Louie. We had several discussions about this issue, which culminated in an informal meeting of John, myself, one of the women, and eventually Louie.

The first idea we discussed was to ask some other man to stay at the house, but we couldn't think of any likely candidates. Jane then said, "What did you do before when the house was closed? Didn't you ask everyone to leave?" John said, "Yeah, but Mike's been helping out a lot." Jane replied, "He's got places to go, doesn't he? They'll survive a few days on the streets." We continued the discussion until Jane said, "Louie, what do you think?" Louie came over and replied, "Mike gets drunk and invites his friends in. Sunday night he invited in that guy who had been so drunk the day before. I had to raise my voice and say 'The house is closed 'til Monday morning.' You weren't there, John. He left but I came down later and he was back. Mike wanted him to spend the night. I had to really raise my voice and say the house was closed."

John asked, "That was last Sunday?" Louie said "Yes. And the way he gives out food and clothes—bags of canned goods just walking out the door. I don't think house guests should be free to give out food and clothes. I think only staff should do that. When you and Harry aren't here, I have to be here to protect the girls. I won't go out of the house if I know the girls are alone up there." Jane said, "It wouldn't be much of a vacation for Louie if they stayed." Swayed by Louie, we decided that Johnny and Mike should be asked to leave for the break. John said that he would tell them.

Both took the news quietly at first, but their resentment came out in various ways. Mike's came out that night. He came storming into the house, literally roaring drunk: "This is my last meal coming up! My last meal!" He yelled that he would fix himself a "special meal" and went downstairs and got a can of minced clams and some noodles. He tore angrily around the kitchen speaking to none of us in particular until John came home, at which point he verbally assaulted John.

First, he objected to the way he had been informed: "You could've shown me some respect. Did you have to ask me in front of those people? Couldn't you have taken me aside? I'm not complaining about your asking me to leave but about how you did it. All I want is to be shown a little respect." After John acknowledged that he should have taken him aside, Mike continued, "Why can't you ask me before you bring people into the dorm? That's where I live. You could at least show me that much respect." John asked if he had had problems with some of the guests. Mike replied, "That's not the point. You keep changing the rules. First you say no more than three people. Then there's four, five. Why don't you bring them into your room, John?"

Mike then moved on to the subject of me and the women. "How long will he be here?" he asked, pointing to me. John replied, " 'Til the end of August." "How long will the girls be here?" "The summer." "How long am I here for?" John replied, "I don't know, Mike. Originally, you were going to stay until you were ready to go into the Emergency Treatment Facility." "That doesn't matter. Barb told me I could stay as long as I wanted. They're temporary. I'm permanent."

John said, "Well, there's a problem in that you drink. We have a rule against drinking." "There's no rule about that. So I drink, so what?" "There's two rules here—no drinking and no fighting. Those rules don't change." "Have I ever been violent?" "That's not what I was talking about. I'm talking about your drinking." "Well, I don't like your just eating vegetables. I don't like not having meat. I need a piece of meat once in awhile." John replied, "We fix meat some of the time at dinner. My not eating meat doesn't affect you." "It affects me like my drinking affects you. There's going to be a third rule here— you have to eat meat." "You don't make the rules here."

The above represents only snatches of the conversation, but covers the main points. Mike was, of course, quite drunk; nevertheless, the course of the argument is instructive. John emphasized issues of rules and rule breaking. Mike, for the most part, emphasized status and role.

The next day, Barb came back and discussed matters with Mike. She strongly agreed with the decision to ask him and Johnny to leave during the break. After talking with Mike in private, she came down and reported to us, "Now, I hate to make chasms, but Mike was considering himself a staff member. . . . He wanted to decide who would be allowed in the dorm. I told him that I considered him a guest. That was how he originally came. I said 'If things have changed since then, then we have to talk about that, but if you want to be a staff member you'll have to become more involved in the community. And, of course, stop drinking.'"

Mike came back to the house after the break was over, but problems continued and Barb eventually asked him to leave. He came back, however, and helped at the house for quite some time after I had left. In a later discussion, one of the Workers created a whole new term for Mike's role—"disenfranchised staff." When I went back for John's wedding, Mike was there, dressed in a suit and very pleased to be invited. Later, however, he broke ties with the house rather decisively by throwing a rock through the front window; he is now clearly a guest.

Tensions in Hospitality

Two important tensions characterized the hospitality of the Rochester St. Joseph's House. First, there was the tension between the vision of the house as community and the vision of the house as service; second, the tension between hospitality and political activism. Although these tensions were not as divisive as those one finds in many houses, they still convey important insights into the Catholic Worker notion of hospitality.

Community versus Service

Over the past decade a rather subtle debate has been waged in Rochester over the vision of Worker hospitality—between the house as community and the house as service. Each vision was associated with a particular director.

The vision of house as community was exemplified by Patrick Grady. His vision was of a community in which both persons off the street and persons from middle-class backgrounds lived and worked together to provide hospitality. He states:

> I do believe that in sharing a household together certain dynamics occur, be it dynamics of fellowship, sharing of beliefs—similar or dissimilar—sharing of interests, sharing just of one's self because one's so close. Fellowship does emerge when men and women are together in a household. My experience with the guys from the street is that there's a very clear articulation, when given the opportunity, of somebody's most basic needs before God. I'm hungry or I'm frustrated and God why did you abandon me? . . . So I think there can be a connectedness based on our common humanity. In effect you can be pretty surprised [at] how this starkly poor transient street woman can inform and can evangelize and can bring truth to the apparent[ly] together intellectual giver. . . .
>
> I come out of the New York experience. I think there is a sense of history that is important to let inform you out of that household there. And I was very impressed and touched by, well, certainly the chaos of struggling for the very diverse personalities to come together in a very fragile community where it's not rare that at a Friday night meeting someone who is crazy will get up and go off about something that makes no sense. That's all right. That's all right. I guess I'm saying that that doesn't happen in many places. And I don't think it's something you can calculate or organize or systematize. It's attitudinal, a perception, an experience. I guess you can create systems around the attitude so that it's much more possible to give others

responsibility. But it begins with an attitude though, a perception of hospitality.

I think there always will be [a distinction between homeless persons and Workers]. But I think there can be a movement toward more inclusion.

Catholic Worker hospitality as community, then, envisions accepting certain of the men as equals, or as nearly equal as possible, and forming a household in which both ideologically committed persons and persons from the street join together in providing hospitality to other homeless persons. In practical terms, this meant accepting Karl and Louie and a number of others into the house as roughly coequal workers. Pat gives his view of the other vision of Worker hospitality, that of service:

> Then there is the perception that goes something like this. We are a community called to serve. We are Catholic Worker [and are] going to make a commitment to do this for X number of years. And three or four people, they come together to do this work and all of what it entails and [say] "we are gonna make commitments to one another and this is our community, and others of like minds and like spirits can join this." But I think that's too narrow an understanding of what this Catholic Worker openness in terms of extended family as a community is about. It's practically an antithesis to mine.
>
> Two clearly different schools of thought have emerged. And one of our running debates, either verbally or nonverbally, is the one centered around community. The past few years seems to be a community forming around the committed volunteers, where the men are not included in that. They don't have a place in that. And I would say they have a very important place.

Barb, John, and others committed to the vision of service would describe it a bit differently. To them, the ideal is to provide the best possible hospitality to all guests. This means the best food possible plus personable, gentle interactions with the guests. Including too many homeless persons as members of the serving community almost invariably results in rougher treatment of guests, receptions that are not always too hospitable, and less appetizing food. The portrait of Pat's approach painted by almost everyone I talked to was that he gathered a group of men off the streets to run the house while he was often engaged in political activity.

The community that Pat created had its rougher edges. One Worker described the old community as follows:

It was a matter of turf, the territorial imperative. Everyone had their own little bit of turf. Louie used to steal things from people just for revenge. He's done a complete turn around now. That's because he was insecure about his position. There was Jack, the old guy who came to dinner the other day. He was the painter, but he used to bitch and talk behind people's backs and cause a lot of dissension. It really was a House of Hostility then. And there was Karl. He used to get drunk and get violent and throw people out. He was finally asked to leave. Howard was there too. We buried him a year or so ago. He had cancer of the throat. He used to wear his collar to cover it up. I used to take him to bars. We even let him drink in the house those last months. The doctor said it was medicinal—just to ease the pain.

Although it appears that the vision of community is egalitarian while that of service is elitist, the reality is a bit more complex. Each vision involves a profound status distinction. The vision of service makes a fairly clear distinction between staff, who have generally come for ideological reasons, and guests, who come out of physical need. The vision of community reduces the distinction of ideology and need, maintaining that all come to the Worker out of need, be that need physical, emotional, or spiritual. However, as was evident in the New York City house, this vision produces a status distinction between those inside and those outside the house. Only some of the guests are chosen to be part of the community, and they then work diligently to maintain the distinction between themselves and "those guys off the street." This status distinction can become as sharp as that entailed in service, as explained in the previous chapter. In effect, then, the vision of community moves to eliminate the original status distinction between rich and poor, but at the cost of creating a new status distinction in terms of attachment to the house itself.

Hospitality versus Peace Witness

Most Catholic Workers would list three major missions of the movement: hospitality, newspaper publishing, and peace witness. However, few would deny that there are profound conflicts between these missions, particularly between hospitality and peace witness.

Hospitality and peace witness are somewhat analogous to the micro–macro problem in sociology. Both dimensions are deemed essential, yet it is extremely difficult to do justice to both at the same time. Hospitality is the microresponse of the Catholic Worker to social problems—it deals with problems by face-to-face interaction with persons experiencing problems. Peace witness, or, more broadly, political witness, is the macroresponse, attempting to reach the societal problems that the Workers believe lie at the root of the very personal misery that appears daily at their door. To the Worker, the two are inseparable; however, they are extremely difficult to reconcile in practice.

The very rhythm of hospitality differs from that of peace witness. Hospitality is a day-to-day, cyclical activity—requiring a constant, continual commitment simply to be present in the house and deal with whatever situations arise. The heroics it requires are simple, everyday heroics. Its primary virtues are patience and fortitude. Peace witness, on the other hand, is an occasional activity. It too requires some continual effort—in terms of attending meetings, planning, "spreading the word." However, a major aspect of peace work consists of the demonstrations that occur on an irregular basis. These are the major events of the movement, the periodic gatherings that, as Durkheim (1915) observed, renew the spirit and solidarity of a group. The rhythm of peace witness revolves around such events. Peace witness, then, involves an alternation between ordinary time and special events; hospitality, however, occurs entirely in ordinary time.

The conflict between the two occurs on many other levels as well. In the very busy life of a Catholic Worker house, they constitute conflicting demands on one's time, pulling workers in one direction or the other. Even on the day of the biggest, most important demonstration, someone has to run the soupline. If someone does civil disobedience (CD), they run the risk of being absent from hospitality duties for weeks, months, or even years. Decisions to do CD, then, affect the whole house since they place additional burdens on everyone else involved in hospitality.

Historically, the Rochester house has largely eschewed peace witness in favor of hospitality. With the exception of a very limited and divided peace activism during World War II, the house nearly abstained from political involvement for its first twenty-five years. One informant even reported that a young man who carried a "Rochester Catholic Worker" sign at a civil-rights demonstration in the early 1960s was reprimanded by some board members. This situation changed temporarily in 1968 when Ted Parker became director and involved the house in his trial for conscientious objection to the Vietnam War. The house continued to have some involvement in antiwar issues for several years. However, after the countercultural Workers left, the house reverted once again to its apolitical stance.

This situation changed again when Pat Grady arrived in 1976 and involved the house in the farmworker and antinuclear campaigns. When Barb Tompkins became director, she showed comparatively little interest in politics and placed the primary emphasis on hospitality. This reversion was not complete, however, because of the arrival six months later of John Baker, who had been involved with the antinuclear movement for several years.

John came from a small town near the Seneca Army Depot, which is the primary storage facility for nuclear weapons on the East Coast. For over three decades, the depot managed to maintain a very low profile—few knew that nuclear weapons were stored on its ten square miles. Many people credit John's investigations with uncovering and publicizing the fact that nuclear weapons are stored there. He published an article on the topic in the house newsletter, which was shown to a Rochester reporter who then wrote a prizewinning article on the depot for a local paper.

John's struggle with the depot was based on his vision that the depot constitutes "Auschwitz in our own diocese." The presence of nuclear weapons within the Diocese of Rochester places grave responsibility on all Catholics in the diocese because the weapons lie within their spiritual community. The responsibility is the same as was that of the diocese in which Auschwitz was located because the weapons are a global Auschwitz waiting to happen.

John carried on a very personal witness at the depot. In the days before the Women's Encampment began in the summer of 1983, many areas of the depot that are now off-limits to outsiders were open. One of these areas housed the chapel, where John would stop to attend Mass whenever he traveled from St. Joe's to his family home. After Mass, he would often engage the chaplain and the base commander in discussion of his religious objections to nuclear weapons. This personal witness had at least some effect on the depot personnel. Someone reported seeing a photograph of him on the wall of the security office. The last time I was arrested with him, the new base commander drove over to meet the man he called "the infamous John Baker."

John worked with a local Rochester group called CANA (Catholics Against Nuclear Arms), trying to inspire them to a campaign of civil disobedience at the depot. This campaign got off the ground during the summer I was there. Although John had not succeeded in convincing anyone to do CD with him, he decided to "take a walk" on the depot grounds by himself to observe Hiroshima Day. About two dozen of us accompanied him to Saturday evening Mass at the chapel, after which we proceeded with him as far as the guardhouse. As he approached, the guards closed and locked the gate, so he sat down in front of it to see how long they would keep it closed. By sunset he was still there, but his supporters, not prepared for a long seige, began to leave. I sat with him after everyone else had left. We were joined about 3:00 A.M. by friends from Rochester and from Syracuse (an event that got the guards a bit nervous). I left with the Syracuse car about 7:00 A.M.. When the two friends from Rochester left in the afternoon, the guards carried John off the depot. He decided that seventeen hours had been enough and hitchhiked home.

The CANA group consisted of a number of individuals and couples who were associated with the house. Most of them attended the Saturday evening Mass at the house regularly. This, however, did create some tension because few of the peace activists took any role in the hospitality. The Saturday Mass became known as their Mass, and many who were involved primarily in hospitality were reluctant to take part in it. A discussion between two helpers revealed sentiments that I heard echoed a number of times. Mike said, "Those people who come to Saturday Mass, they're a little strange." Abe replied, "Yea, they're nice enough, and they say 'Come join us,' but they're a tight little clique."

Even those who were in sympathy with the peace group were disappointed that they did not get more involved in hospitality. One stated, "Those people don't really know what goes on day-to-day at St. Joe's. I wish some of them would get more involved in the day-to-day activities. They're into different things. And that's good in a way for me to be exposed to that, but . . ."

This gulf between those involved in peace work and those involved in hospitality apparently narrowed after I left. When the house began sheltering people the next winter, a number of the members of the peace group volunteered. (Most could not volunteer at the meal since it was in the afternoon and they worked nine-to-five jobs). Further, a number of new full-time workers became more involved in peace witness. CANA began to stage several demonstrations a year at Seneca Army Depot, and both Workers and members of the peace group joined John in civil disobedience. This resolution of the tension was due in large part to John, the one person while I was there who seriously attempted to carry out both missions of the Catholic Worker.

Tension between those involved in peace work and those involved in hospitality is by no means unique to Rochester. It was evident at both the Mustard Seed and St. Joseph's in New York City. Cleavages in Worker communities often seem to occur along a peace work–hospitality line. Joe Torma, a professor involved with the Rochester house, gave me insight into this tension: "A true Catholic Worker should embody that tension within himself. It should not be an external tension between a hospitality group and a peace group. It should be an internal tension." This, I think, is the ideal of the Catholic Worker. It is not that there should be no tension between its twin missions of hospitality and peace witness. Instead, the tension should be personal, a conflict within each member as to allocation of time and energy to the two missions, rather than social (i.e., reflected in the existence of separate groups for each activity).

6

A House of Penitents:
The Mustard Seed in Worcester

When I write about the Mustard Seed I am very conscious that I am writing about the past. The house I lived in for a summer burned down less than a year later. Although a new building was built, the setting I describe is gone forever.

The day I arrived at the Seed, the house manager said to me: "You'll find we're different from the other Worker houses—we're loose here—real loose." In the months to come I was to find that those words were far truer than I could have imagined. Perhaps the primary way in which the Seed was different from most Worker houses is that it was run by people who had been homeless. The last of the ideologically committed founders had left about a year before I arrived, and the work of the house was carried on by persons who had once been considered guests but had become part of the Catholic Worker movement.

The fact that the Workers had been homeless themselves seemed to contribute to a sense of social equality that was unparalleled even in other Worker houses. For the most part, Workers did not sneak off to see movies or discuss scholarly books that held no interest for their guests. Their leisure time was spent in the same type of activities their guests enjoyed—which could include drinking, vociferous arguments, and occasional fights. One former Worker perhaps put it best: "People read about the Catholic Worker and think it's a community of saints. At least the way the Seed is now, people can't think it's a community of saints. They have to look beneath the obvious to see what's really going on."

Another former Worker was less sympathetic, telling me, "You should go and study a *real* Worker house." Although she was not the only one to express such criticism, there were others who felt the house was in the spirit of the Worker. The truth of such claims depends on one's vision of Worker hospitality.

In this case differences in vision led to bitter strife. A few months before I arrived, several peace activists had tried unsuccessfully to unseat the house director, resulting in a schism of the Worker community. Wounds from this event were still raw, to the point that some would not talk to me about it even after I had been at the house for three months. Perhaps because of the depth of the conflict, the Mustard Seed reveals more starkly than the other houses some of the tensions implicit in the Worker model of hospitality. In order to understand these tensions, we must begin with the history of the Catholic Worker in Worcester, Mass., a history that predates the Mustard Seed.

The first Worker house in Worcester was Matt Talbot House, which opened in 1938 but lasted less than two years. St. Benedict's Farm began in Upton in the same year and is still lived on by a couple who had been part of the Worker movement. After the closing of Matt Talbot House, however, there was no Worker house in the area until the opening of the House of Ammon in 1971. In many ways, the history of the Seed begins there.

The House of Ammon

By all accounts, the House of Ammon was a bold experiment in anarchy. The only rule was that there were no rules. One Worker remembered that "there were no locks on the doors until the motorcycle gang moved in, and then they put locks on *their* doors." Another Worker described the house as "the streets with an umbrella over it." Exguests told of week-long drinking parties held in the house. I can't verify these accounts personally—the house burned down six years before I arrived. However, everyone to whom I talked agreed that no rules were enforced—at least not by those who "ran" the house.

The house was started in early 1971 by Father Barry Peters in the town of Hubbardston, about twenty miles outside of Worcester. Peters was the "radical priest" of the diocese—a close friend of Abbie Hoffman and a veteran of the civil-rights movement who was transferred out of one parish because of his activism. In the year prior to starting the House of Ammon, he lived in a Catholic Worker-type commune in Athol, Mass., True View Farm. There he came to know two people who would be the mainstays of the House of Ammon throughout its eight-year existence—Mark Jaworski and Ann Lally.

The house was founded on the Worker ideal of anarchism. In a letter to Dorothy Day, Father Peters stated:

> As you know several of us have been talking, more dreaming, about a Catholic Worker House here that would accept ABSOLUTELY the whole platform without any hedging. . . . Naturally, the house of hospitality will be just that. The sky and the cops will be the limit. But we do not want the community to grow too rapidly. Many young people want in right away, but in fairness to them I think we should take only a couple at a time. We want to give them careful attention—really try to teach them what we have been so slow to learn (Catholic Worker Archives, Marquette University, Series W-4, Box 2).

They found a fifteen-room farmhouse, which predated the War of 1812, and purchased it for $12,500. It had neither plumbing nor central heating, but it did have an old barn, outhouse, and three acres of land. Father Peters and five others moved in that winter, with high hopes for starting an agronomic university of the type Peter Maurin had advocated. From the start, there was a firm commitment to equality:

> We know that this poverty is the only indispensable precondition for our survival under God; and it is also our best guarantee that never in this house will some people be more equal than other people. Not that we even imagine a day coming when some would be treated as second class citizens. No. But we are keenly aware that one or another might become a big shot of sorts. And that would be the end of all being equally equal. . . .
>
> Again, though it seemed obvious that a photo of the *"founders"* (big shots?) should be taken in front of the run-down property . . . no picture was ever snapped. Day after day we said "We'll have to get together for a picture." We even brought the silly camera to the house. But God kept us busy enough that we are not blushing now. No picture. No Founders.
>
> The same spirit of poverty that prevented the group from becoming "big shots" seemed to have ruled out the possibility of anyone becoming "boss." There have been very few big decisions to be made apart from the selection of the property and the constitution of the community—but always the decision comes from consensus. And this almost informally, surely without voting. After a bit of discussion for the clarification of thought, it becomes clear that one person is more competent in this area and the others ask "Well, why don't

you take care of it and whatever you decide is fine with us" (quoted from an Easter Week 1971 mimeographed sheet, Marquette Archives, Series W-4, Box 2).

There was great energy in the first year. The Sunday Mass was marked by marvelous song. Father Peters remembers that Dorothy Day was "very, very, very taken" with the music on her only visit to the house. Prayer was held every night, with Bible reading and song. Fields were planted. Mark installed indoor plumbing (they never did get central heating). Four issues of a newspaper, *Carry it On*, were published. In October, they opened a free store in nearby Clinton. A chapel was built on a neighboring farm. Three community members were arrested in Washington in an antiwar protest. Father Peters made a public offer to take over a financially troubled local college for no pay and staff it with two dozen university professors who would work for room and board. And clarification-of-thought meetings were held, one of which was particularly memorable.

Margaret and John Magee, veterans of the original Worcester Worker, spoke about the conflict between raising a family and running a House of Hospitality. Father Peters recalls:

> The point that Dr. Margaret and Dr. John made is all the while they were at the Boston house falling in love and at the Worcester house and at the Upton house getting married, there didn't seem to be any problem. But once the children started, they knew that they could not raise a family in a CW community. . . . She remembers very well what her judgement turned on. It was milk for the children. She had to be sure she could put milk in the refrigerator, that it was her milk and nobody would take it. She saw that she'd never be able to do that at a Catholic Worker.

A letter from Father Peters to Dorothy the next day gave the reaction of the community: "John pushed it further saying that Peter taught that married people (families) HAD to own, etc. Nobody at our house bought that. We were polite but forceful and unanimous in our disagreement."

Meanwhile, hospitality had become serious business. A letter from Father Peters to Dorothy dated November 12, 1971, states:

> During the summer some nights we had as many as sixty sleeping in the house, around the house in tents and cars, and in the spacious barns. More than our share of romantic hippie types looking not only for free food, free booze, free drugs, free sex etc. but also, to some extent, looking to see as Allen Ginsberg says, if anybody has a vision. A

few saw that we had one and stayed on. A few others, like the young man in the Gospel, saw we had one and, weak of heart, moved on. At night prayer we remember one and all.

Last night two dozen slept in the house and barn. That's about the number we've had since schools started up and the cold weather set in. Roughly half take some measure of responsibility for the house. A few of these are students at Worcester colleges. One, Kathy, works at a nearby computer factory and gives over what she makes to help run the house (Marquette Archives, Series W-4, Box 2).

The same letter indicated some of the issues involved in giving open-ended hospitality:

Right now we have 4 homeless boys ages 14, 15, 16, 17 living with us. Two are from Tennessee of all places!! They pose a great problem. If we ask too many questions they either lie or clam up. On the other hand Massachusetts law is very strict on the harboring of minors and we could get into trouble. What to do? Surely we cannot force them out into the cold. The fact is they have no homes. Really. Their parents or guardians are interested in them only to the extent that Welfare sends money for their care. Already I have been summoned to the local court (I refused and got away with it) for a case involving a minor and the local police are always at the door. Thank God the police, like most of our Hubbardston neighbors, think well of us and though we never turn anyone in, we always tell the truth. They respect us for this. One officer who had been very hard on us (traffic laws, etc.) came one night to take a kid away and he apologized saying "This is a shame, the kid is better off here with you than where I have to take him" (Marquette Archives, Series W-4, Box 2).

Father Peters recalled that the Catholic Worker farm at Tivoli used to send them guests: "They used to send up the people they couldn't handle at Tivoli. They'd say go to Hubbardston. One time Dorothy herself sent up this couple—what terrors they were! And everytime I saw her, she would ask 'And how are so and so?'—as if she had sent up her aunt or something!"

By late 1972 the situation in the house had changed considerably, as reflected in a letter from Father Peters:

The house has changed a great deal since spring. Many of the "community" have left in one way or another for one reason or another. (Let's face it. It ain't easy.) This is, of course, a great sadness for me, but I see so clearly the hand of God in my suffering. With fewer of the family taking up space, we have more room for the poor. The booze-ridden, drug-ridden, sex-ridden poor. The old, the sick, and the hopeless poor. Both the deserving and the undeserving poor . . . are received as Christ. Thank God we don't have the problems of the Social Workers trying to decide which are which. All are welcome here. Naturally, though, with fewer Catholic Workers on the job, the burden falls heavy on a few (Marquette Archives, Series W-4, Box 2).

By March 1973 the situation sounded even worse:

> I guess you could say we have been blessed with failure. The guests have been unbelievably destructive, many of the original community left in confusion and the farm was neglected. But there are a few of us still here and we refuse to quit.
>
> Why? It's largely because we have no place to go and still remain honest. But there's more to it. We have read the Gospel carefully enough to know that it is a call to poverty, humility and the folly of the Cross. After all, we are on pilgrimage. . . .
>
> Clearly we are not making Peter's dream of the agronomic university come true in Hubbardston—but maybe, as God sees things, we are helping a little. At least we are trying (Marquette Archives, Series W-4, Box 2).

By late 1973 the motorcycle gang had moved in.

There are very few written sources available after 1973. One newspaper article in November 1976 noted that Ann was running the house herself because Father Peters was in the hospital. Fortunately, however, a frequent activity around the Seed was reminiscing about the House of Ammon, so there is a fair amount of oral history about the later years.

Perhaps the major theme among ex-Workers was the anarchy of the house. One discussion went as follows:

Father Peters: At the Mustard Seed, it's always been someone being asked to leave, meetings, someone forced out. It was never like that at Hubbardston. No one was ever turned away. The doors were open 24 hours a day. They just arrived and if they liked it they stayed.

Mark: Yeah, if they didn't get the shit kicked out of them.

Father Peters: Yes, that did happen.

Young Jim (who had lived at the house as a runaway teenager): I remember a lot of people getting their asses whooped.

Mark remembered that Father Peters was the one who always insisted that there be no rules. "He was like a rock on that point." I asked if the Workers did break up fights. He said, "It depended on where it happened. It was a big house. Sometimes a lot of things went on. There was a lot of evil in that house, as well as a lot of good."

Chris, who had worked at the house for a few years, noted: "It wasn't Barry's house. It was God's house. There were a lot of things that went on that Barry wouldn't have put up with if it was his house, but he felt it was God's house and that was how He willed it." Mark replied: "It was an experiment in anarchism; no, an experience." Chris added: "No, it was an experiment and it worked."

Ann recalled one incident as particularly galling:

> What got to me was when I came back and found Arnie chopping up my bed for firewood. "You weren't using it, and I was cold," he said. A five-hundred-dollar bedroom set and he's chopping it for firewood. They cut up the hardwood floor in the living room for firewood. They had all summer to chop wood, but they used the floor. They could have used one of the floors in the barn, but they had to use the living room.

Another theme was relations with the neighbors. Some neighbors, particularly those in a house across the street, were friendly and helpful. The town as a whole, however, was hostile.

Raids by the police were common, searching for criminals and stolen goods. Mark remembered: "It wasn't that the house didn't deserve being raided. It did deserve being raided. The stuff that went on there. About two-thirds of the people staying there were wanted for something." Barry noted:

> The public health department was friendly at first, but then became embittered. We were a shame to them, and I can understand that. But as I reflected on it, we were a shame to them because we were sick and we were poor. The sickness of alcoholism, and the poverty that was too great to hide. We were like everyone else, but didn't hide it, and so we didn't come up to their standards.
>
> The people in Hubbardston thought the people who stayed at the house were from California or Borneo or someplace exotic coming into their town. But they weren't. They were Bud and Tim, the local boys, the boys from the town. Oftentimes the families of those who were staying here were leading the opposition.

Workers talked about the house in terms of a coming to grips with the reality of evil. Barry said that the house taught him the reality of evil and spoke of it at times as "that dark night of the soul." Ann noted:

> Barry thought if you treated people right, they'd treat you right. How naive that was. What we didn't realize at first was that someone was

making the rules—it just wasn't us. People would get thrown out of the house by the strongest people there. We just moved the streets inside. It took me ten years to realize that.

A major topic of conversation was the fire that destroyed the house. The official version was that a drunken guest knocked over a candle one night. A couple of guests who were there that night believed that townsfolk burned it down. All agreed that the fire department took their time putting out the blaze—at least until one of the guests came out the door in flames. One guest recalled bitterly: "Remember Bob coming out? I'll never forget it. You ever see someone's skin melting? And they threw a wool blanket over him. They call themselves firemen."

The house was gutted and soon torn down. When I visited the spot, it was a field of goldenrod, shoulder high. All that remained of the house was a low stone wall, the stone steps to the side door, and a capped-off gas line. There was a small wooden cross lying, broken, in the grass. Young Jim said someone had put it up in memory of Bob, who had died in the fire.

But to the Workers, the fire was not entirely a tragedy. After the fire, Ann went to the New York Worker, where she has remained to this day. She recalls: "When I came to New York, people were telling me how sorry they were about the fire. I would tell them it was the best thing that could have happened. Their jaws would drop open. You can't run a house like that—without rules." Barry recalls: "I knew it was the end before the fire. I knew that I could not go on in Hubbardston, that the experiment was over in some way, that Ann could not go on in Hubbardston. And she knew it. But we were really waiting for a court case to put us out of business. The court case never came about."

The court case concerned a rape that had occurred at the house. For Barry, this had been the incident that convinced him that the experiment had to end: "A woman was gang raped. . . . It was in all the papers, 'Gang Rape at the House of Ammon.' The bishop called me in and told me I would have to close, as he had done before. I told him I wasn't the only one involved in that decision. I would have to talk to Ann and others. I offered no defense. I had none." Barry sums up the experience of the house as follows:

> Oh, Hubbardston, oh, it was a great trial. And as I said, Dorothy so often says "Our faith and love has been tried by fire." Ours was tried by fire in more ways than you can imagine. Certainly more ways than

the obvious. We were burnt out. And something had to give. And there was this dramatic sign from God that our work there was over. And that we would be able to go on with the same work but more relaxed. . . . Not so radical. Not so radical in the no rules. But radical, more radical in all the important ways. More radical in the no judging. And more radical in the contemplative life.

And the main Workers at the House of Ammon did go on with the work. Ann went to the Worker in New York City, where she became Dorothy's constant companion in the years before Dorothy's death. Barry and Mark became mainstays at the Mustard Seed, where Barry was chaplain and Mark treasurer.

History of the Mustard Seed

The Mustard Seed was opened as a storefront in November 1972 by Gary and Don, two former Holy Cross students active in the antiwar movement. Concluding that their movement work left them "out of touch" with people, they decided to try something that would involve more direct contact. A later Worker interpreted the founding as follows: "As a response to the Vietnam issue, they wanted to do the works of mercy as opposed to the works of war."

Seeking a spiritual base, they went on a retreat (the same retreat at which I met them and was introduced to the Catholic Worker). Coming away from the retreat "real excited and determined to do it," they soon found a storefront, which they rented with money from Gary's job. Gary remembered:

> And what we had decided during the retreat was that we would not even do food and clothing or anything like that. We would just open up the storefront. There wouldn't be anything in it; it'd just be a big open, empty space. And we would let people start to determine what we should do with it. We would just be there. So, we rented the place and we fixed it up a little bit . . . and we just sat around. And, slowly, people would open the door and say, "What are you doing here?" and we'd say "I don't know, what do you think we should do?" We figured that people wanted us to do food, shelter, clothing, or some variation, but we weren't convinced, you know, and so we were just going to wait to find out.
>
> Mostly it was older folks who were stopping in. We picked that corner because there was a lot of drugs and there was a lot of harassment of people on that corner, older folks. There was an elderly highrise actually not far away, and it was kind of a midpoint between downtown and the high-rise. And they just would sit down, take a

breather from trying to walk over the hill to the high-rise, have a cup of coffee, talk.

Don and I must have hung around there a couple of months anyway not doing much, and we slowly got into just playing chess. People'd see us playing chess [and] they'd start coming in. It's not exactly clear to me exactly how it happened. The next thing that happened was it was just a mob scene. There were all kinds of people; there were piles of clothes; people were bringing in food.

It became a place where people kind of hung out for some of the day or some people for all of the day—a place where people could go and just sit, play cards. They knew other people were going to be hanging around. . . . And everyone seemed, anyway, to really enjoy it, you know. It was just a nice place to be.

They started a campaign against a local slumlord. Students from the local colleges began to help out. In the meantime, some problems were developing. Gary noted:

We were really naive, you know. People would want keys and we'd make keys and they'd have keys and you'd find out later on that people were sleeping in there. I don't even know who slept there, who was around. I still to this day don't know because I didn't want to know. That was the only stipulation the landlord gave—that no one sleep there, so I didn't really want to know anything about it.

There was also a lot of drinking going on behind the backs of the two Workers. Finally, dissension arose about decision making, as several guests urged that Don and Gary turn the place over to them.

How leadership gets determined is always somewhat vague. People, since I was there and Don was there from the beginning, obviously felt that we ran it. As long as we were there, even if we weren't paying any of the bills or whatever, I think people would have felt that we were running it, you know, whatever that meant.

It's funny because so many poor folks have such reactionary politics. I mean they're just *so* reactionary that a clear power structure seems really important and [when] you're coming out of a radical or leftist head and you're not trying to set up a pyramid-type power structure or anything like that—you're trying to develop circular models and do things like that—and yet you keep getting pushed in, or people keep trying to take that place [of authority]. It seems to be people feel there's a vacuum there. I'm sure it's not just with people who come to the Worker houses, or poorer folks, or whatever.

In any event, one man began "harassing people" to let him run the place. Shortly thereafter, there was a fire in a trash can that burned part of a wall, as a result of which the landlord asked them to vacate. Gary is still unsure whether the fire was an accident or a result of the incipient power struggle. In any event, the storefront Mustard Seed closed in November 1973.

Although Don left the area shortly thereafter, Gary began meeting with two persons who had expressed interest in the Seed—Henry, a student at a local college, and Peg, a school teacher who had spent some time with Catherine de Hueck Doherty's community in Canada—to plan the reopening of the Seed as a house. In January 1974 they purchased a house on Piedmont Street. Peg recalls that they didn't know who was going to sign for the house until they were in the lawyer's office about to close the deal.

> We were in the lawyer's office before I ever knew that Gary wasn't gonna sign. Well, it turned out he couldn't sign, because he's a tax resister and had been all along. It was like who's gonna sign for this? . . . So I said "Gee I don't know, who's gonna sign?" So Henry pops up, "Well, I'll sign." And then I was kinda feeling identifiable and said, "Well if you're gonna sign, then I'll sign."

In any event, the house was purchased. Things did not, however, progress according to plan, at least not Peg's plan:

> I had no idea, Harry, that this was gonna turn out the way it did. I don't blame anybody. I just was so totally naive about it. I had this vision of oh we were all going to live in a loving community, and we were going to be examples for the poor. I can still see the picture in my head, of the house with my geraniums in all the flower boxes and everything and it would be so uplifting for people who lived around it. Envision that, and you wind up with people knocking out windows and fighting.

The house opened in March, serving a meal and allowing people to sleep wherever they could find a spot. Soon the house was packed, with people sleeping in closets and on the back porches. In August, Henry went to Europe for a month, leaving Peg in charge of the house.

Matters came to a head one day when Peg took a young woman to the hospital for what she found out was an overdose. ("I was so naive.") While at the hospital she got a call from the house saying that someone was running around with a gun. "I come back from the hospital to find one person just draped over the car, and there was nobody hurt but there was a gun floating around. I didn't know what the hell was going on. We had police all over the place. So I couldn't go on with it because I was afraid that people would get hurt."

The next day, after talking to several people who were staunch supporters of the house, she told the guests they had to leave.

> They weren't the people who had caused all the problems. Those people had already left the scene. Now, I'm left with a bunch of old men really. I can't keep them. I cannot keep them because I know I cannot take the risk. But what in the hell are you gonna do? I pack them all in my car. I drive them down to the Salvation Army. Before I got back they were out on their way to wherever they'd go. They didn't come here. They knew the house was closed. So, that was bad enough. It killed me, because I felt at that time like the innocents took the brunt of the whole thing. And yet I couldn't just let that go on. I was afraid for people's health. It became so clear to me that this is now a really dangerous situation that I just couldn't go on with it— any way.

As it turned out, she didn't throw everyone out. When she returned to the house from taking some men to the Salvation Army, she found an older man still there.

> I was heading upstairs and I bumped into Karl. . . . It's August. He's got a heavy black overcoat over his arm. Now, he starts to stand up, shake my hand, "Thanks a lot, Peg." I said, "Where are you going, Karl?" "Oh, I'm going to go back to the weeds. I'll be all right." Now here's an innocent, a total innocent. I'm throwing him out, and he's thanking me for throwing him out. Now I start crying, but I didn't cry while I was talking to him. But I invited him to stay. I said, "Karl, why don't you stay with us, you know, as a family, with us," and he did stay.

Three other men stayed as well, one because he kept coming back:

> So now comes Ronald, the little black man. He just wouldn't go. . . . He didn't put up any fuss. He walked out the door but then he'd come back during the night and sleep on the porch. Now how many nights can you . . . stand it, right? Knowing Ronald was on the porch. I mean he's there every night. That's how it went for awhile, 'til they came back.

On Henry's return from Europe, the house began letting people in again. Soon, Peg left for nine months in California. Gary left on a cross-country trip to visit other Catholic Worker houses. Henry was left running the house with his girlfriend. In March 1975, Al, a former classmate of Henry's, moved in to help out "temporarily" and stayed for three years. When Gary returned from his trip, he moved into the house briefly. At that point, as he recalls it, hospitality was still limited—only a dozen or so people were staying there. He pushed to expand hospitality and soon the meal was more open and more people had moved in.

> We were working on the whole idea of still there was no staff. We're all in this together. When I got back from traveling, I didn't have any job. I was broke. I was begging for money. And we had this thing that everyone lived in the house, that it was our house, and that we would make decisions together. We had house meetings to determine how the house was gonna run. But Don and some other people who were living there at the time were kind of undermining the whole thing anyway.

Things began to get "crazy" at the house again, with people threatening others with guns and knives, others getting robbed and rolled. As one Worker put it: "There were so many stories you couldn't tell who was connin' you and who wasn't. You know, people were saying 'Oh, we're getting ripped off.' . . . There were so many stories from everyone you talked to." A particular problem according to several of the Workers at the time was Don, a young man who was pimping his girlfriend and intimidating others in the house. One Worker recalls:

> He tried to intimidate everybody, and he slugged Henry and gave him a black eye. You know, he knew he wouldn't hit him back. He probably knew me better than I knew myself. He probably knew if he hit me I'd slug him or something. And anyway he was just as intimidating as hell. We felt like we were handcuffed in terms of getting rid of him—what he would do to the house and all this other stuff. Finally, I remember calling the cops on him and eventually we got him out. But it was a real big hassle to get him out.

Another Worker remembers telling Don and his girlfriend to leave and driving them to Rhode Island, where they had family. The Workers stopped for an ice-cream cone on the way back, and by the time they had returned, the couple was sitting on the porch waiting for them.

Peg returned from California during this period and was aghast that the house had deteriorated once again after she had invested so much energy in cleaning it up only a year previously. She remembers the low point as being one night when she and Henry were sleeping on the first floor and heard windows breaking upstairs: "Essentially, we were so overwhelmed by everything that we just kept waking up to the windows crashing and didn't have the energy to even go up and try to put a stop to it. It was that bad."

Gradually, the core group of Workers came to the decision that something drastic had to be done again and asked for a meeting of Workers and outside supporters, a meeting that led to the second decision to close the house. Ironically, two of the Workers remember this second closing as one of the high points in the history of the Mustard Seed. One recalls: "That was the first time that we really prayed together as a group. And spoke, prayed and spoke. We always had weekly meetings, or every two weeks we met, but here we prayed, we spoke, we closed the house." The other remembers:

> There are two times that I felt that we really raised ourselves to better heights outside of our own picayune personalities. One of them was when the house was overrun by different people. We all met, we talked, we prayed, and we came up with a nonviolent decision for action. Also that meeting was one where we met outside the house. We had to, because the house was overrun anyway. And actually most of the people who were there were—whatever you want to call them—chosen community members or something. Not a whole lot of hospitality [guests] or not even a lot of—I don't know what name you would call them now—a lot of live-in community people. We prayed, we agreed, we identified the problem, and we came up with a creative solution which was Henry's creative idea.

The plan was to stage a nonviolent occupation of the house by the live-in Workers and the outside supporters, to tell the guests they had to leave, and to help them find places to go.

> We backed each other up, and we mustered our forces. I mean people who didn't even live there, but who were very much involved . . . all moved in. Whoever could, came. Even if they had jobs, they came at night. And that worked. There was very little hostility toward any of us. They knew anyway. They knew that life couldn't go on like that. They knew. In fact some of them said so, I think to Henry, what assholes that we had been for putting up with all of that for that long.

In short, the closing was seen as a nonviolent action to reclaim the house from a group of violent guests who had been terrorizing everyone. However, the closing was also a hard thing to do, as reflected by one of the Workers:

> Only a core group of folks stayed. And it was then that we decided that the physical structure of the Mustard Seed had limits, that we couldn't be in the business of taking in thirty or fifty people, that we ourselves had limits. We had to get our sleep. We had to be secure in doing this work. We couldn't be about the business of replacing win-

dows all the time. It was expensive. And it was from that time that we really set limits.

And that was hard for Henry and for Gary to admit that. You know, when they opened the Mustard Seed, it was like their response to what was going on in Southeast Asia. And they had sort of the mentality of "save the world," "save the city," "everybody that the other agencies can't take care of, come to the Mustard Seed, come to the storefront." So that was a painful kind of thing—that we can't be all things to all people. You know, we have limits.

After the closing, the house focused on providing a daily meal open to all plus limited overnight hospitality to a few. In an article a few months later (Moynihan 1976), a Worker was quoted as saying, "We only accept people who have some sort of plan"—that is, a plan to leave soon. This marked a significant change from the early years, in which the house had been primarily a "crashpad."

During 1976, the three "focal people" at the house were Peg, Henry, and Sally, an alcoholic who had come to the Seed for a place to stay and who had become a part of the community. In 1977 two persons arrived who would play important roles in the Seed: Tom (the current director of hospitality) and Mary (the daughter of the founder of an early Worker house, who lived at the house for the next three and a half years).

The time was one of hopes and plans. A shelter for women was begun with the aid of some of the Workers. But the main dream was to make the Mustard Seed the nucleus of a Catholic Worker "village" in the inner city, in which a number of houses in the neighborhood would be inhabited by people involved with the Worker on some level. In early 1978 the first step toward this dream was taken when the Seed purchased the house at 9 Merrick Street, practically in the Seed's backyard. There was hope of buying a large abandoned building next to the Seed as well. This hope was never realized.

Meanwhile, tensions were developing within the community, fostered by interpersonal conflict. The house split into two camps. Peg and Sally left before 1979. Some new Workers came for awhile. With the arrival of Clare in the early 1980s, Mary left the house and moved to an apartment across the street.

Henry, exhausted by the demands of the work, took a cross-country trip in the spring of 1982. Accompanied by a guest, he traveled to a number of Worker houses and farms. Upon his return, he decided to leave the house permanently, placing it in the hands of Sally. She and Tom, who also had originally come for shelter, became the principle figures in the house. The house thus passed into the control of the homeless. Sally and Tom were, however, unique individuals.

Sally was a powerfully built woman in her early forties, with short black hair and a commanding voice. A veteran of the streets, she had been born in Worcester and had led a rather colorful life. In her words:

> I spent half of my life in institutions—hospitals, jails, halfway houses. . . . And then I lived in the streets.
>
> And [I] was a habitual runaway—used to run away from home, with a lot of friends, used to get beat and abused by a brother, and so I used to run away from home, not because I was being abused. I ended up really drinking heavy. And I met plenty of street people and they always bought booze for me. And I was a big girl. I looked sixteen, seventeen when I was twelve years old.
>
> I worked all my life. I worked from the time I was about nine years old at a fruit market as a cashier. I've worked every kind of job there is to work. I was a meatcutter. I worked in shoe shops. I worked in stitching factories. I worked in grocery stores. I worked in plastic factories, gas stations, you name it. I worked on everything there is to do. Worked in machine shops. I can set up a machine, machinery. I can make toilet rolls, drill presses, read blueprints. I can do just about any job there is to do.
>
> I lived down by the railroad tracks down by the Blackstone River. Winter, summer, spring, and fall, with Wolfman and Ernie and Dakota. And then I used to sleep on the floor at Catholic Charities.

She had come to the house in its early days, an alcoholic looking for shelter. She moved onto the back porch at first, but after awhile Peg asked her to move inside and got her a real bed. She has been a part of the house off and on ever since.

Tom was a large, personable, exuberant man. In his own words, he is "a concert pianist, college professor, Catholic Worker, and alcoholic." He came to the house in 1977, a homeless alcoholic who had been divorced, lost his professorship, and lost several jobs since then. He had been living at the Salvation Army. "On the second day of Holy Week 1977 I was given the bed that I am currently laying on in the Mustard Seed." He continued "closet drinking" for several years, but after a confrontation in which Henry told him that the community would no longer tolerate his drinking, he went to a detoxification program and has been sober ever since. He says that in the detox program he realized that he had lost the two things by which he had always defined himself: his memory and his skill with the piano. He embraced the Alcoholics Anonymous approach and turned his life over to God, becoming a well-known member of the local AA community. He also resumed his piano playing.

The 1983 Schism

A crisis occurred about a year after Sally took charge, leading to a schism in the ranks that resulted in virtually no contact for months at a time between community members who lived across the street from each other. Although the schism occurred only a month or so before I arrived, it proved to be the most difficult event to "nail down" in my entire research. The more people to whom I talked about the schism, the further I seemed to get from ascertaining the facts. The following, however, is a tentative reconstruction of the event.

Upon Henry's departure, Sally became "house manager and steward," in charge of the house as a whole and directly in charge of food distribution. Her style was drastically different from that of Henry. Consensual decision-making was abandoned, and Sally assumed all decision-making responsibility. With the help of some old friends from the street, notably a behemoth known as Ernie, she began "clearing house," evicting several members of the community who had been "terrorizing" the other residents, as well as a few with whom she had "had trouble" but who were not violent. She also began cleaning the house in a more physical sense, calling in an exterminator to deal with the roaches. Eventually, angered that the treasurer (a Worker who did not live in the house) would not give her money for things she deemed essential, she started her own Mustard Seed bank account and began depositing donation checks directly into it rather than giving them to the treasurer to deposit in the official account. Sally also resumed drinking.

Clare, a peace activist who worked at the Seed in addition to working a "normal" job, began to criticize the way Sally was running the house and treating the guests. Eventually, some members of the extended community called several meetings, in which they argued that Sally had violated the basic principles of the Catholic Worker and should not be allowed to continue to run the Seed. The attempted coup failed because Sally refused to attend the meetings and several key people (including Henry, who was recruited at long distance by both sides) refused to take the side of the "rebels." Sally continued to run the Seed and the people who had tried to unseat her were cut off from interaction with the house by mutual consent.

The split occurred along several lines, which happened to coincide (as might have been predicted by both Simmel 1955 and Coser 1956). Those most strongly critical of Sally tended to be strongly involved in the peace movement and civil disobedience, college educated, and attracted by the Worker ideology. Those siding with Sally were, for the most part, not active in the peace movement. Many had not completed high school. Most had come to the Seed in search of shelter. Also siding with Sally, however, were several Workers from the old House of Ammon—motivated by a vision of the Catholic Worker that was probably more radically anarchistic than that of Dorothy Day.

What was happening at the Seed violated the peace activists' idea of what a Catholic Worker house should be. For Sally's supporters, events at the Seed were compatible with Worker philosophy. Although there were many nuances to the differences in approach of the two groups, the crux of the matter seemed to be a crucial difference in visions of the Worker, a difference that was not clearly articulated because it was never articulated in the Worker ideology. This is the difference between building community and providing hospitality.

Clearly, Sally's style of hospitality differed from the Worker ideal in certain respects—particularly in terms of rejection of nonviolence. Also clear, however, was that Sally had come a long way toward embracing Worker ideology from the day she had first walked into the Seed as a homeless alcoholic. Less clear, perhaps, was the fact that various aspects of hospitality—particularly the quality of the food— had been improved by Sally.

The question that divided the Seed thus became "Which path is true to the Worker ideal—to unseat Sally because she has violated certain standards or to support Sally as a member of the Worker community who has both strengths and weaknesses?" I will advance my own reflections on this question after describing the house as I found it, a month after the schism.

Physical Description

The Seed was located on Piedmont Street, half a mile from the central business district in a poor, mostly white, neighborhood of wood-frame and brick row-houses. Piedmont Street was Worcester's version of a "red light district." I could easily have conducted an observational study of prostitutes and their tricks from the side window.

The neighborhood was lively in other ways. One evening while in the neighborhood drugstore, I witnessed a battle between two groups of youths swinging baseball bats. Another time there was a drug bust across the street. Fires were not uncommon. One broke out at a house one block over, destroying the upper story.

The Mustard Seed itself was a three-story, gray-shingle, wood-frame house. A handpainted sign, mustard yellow with brown letters, hung on the front porch. The house had three floors, "her floor, his floor, and the dirt floor," as one disaffected former Worker put it. The first floor was used to serve the meals, containing two small dining rooms and a serving room in the back with a counter and a three-basin sink. The floor also housed the room of Mrs. Christ.

The second floor was Tom's floor, an apartment complete in itself, with two private bedrooms, a combination kitchen-living room-bedroom, and two guest bedrooms. Tom's room contained a modern stereo system, bookshelves, an aquarium, and usually his two cats. To the left was Carl's room, dominated by a clutter of books that often threatened to overwhelm his bed. The second-floor back porch contained a refrigerator and a locked storage closet. It served as my bedroom for much of my stay.

The third floor was Sally's floor. It too was a complete apartment, with kitchen, bedrooms, and the chapel. The back porch was used for parties, dope smoking, and for sleeping out when the weather was good. The third floor was home to between four and six members of the human community as well as four dogs, two guinea pigs, and up to seven cats.

The Catholic Worker presence in the neighborhood extended beyond the house on Piedmont Street. Diagonally across the back yard was 9 Merrick Street. It had at one time housed Seed Workers, but currently housed several members of the Seed community, one former Worker who had left during the schism, and several Native Americans who reportedly ran a prostitution business. Farther down Merrick Street was Mark's apartment, the place where most Workers went when they needed to get away from the tensions of the Seed. Across Piedmont Street was an apartment shared by former Workers who had split with the Seed during the schism but were still actively involved in the peace movement and in some distribution of food in the neighborhood.

Organization

The organization of the Seed differed markedly from that of the other houses. There was never any doubt that Sally ran the show. There were no meetings of Workers or community. Decisions were made by Sally after consulting individually with others in the community. Since, as is true at every Worker house, organization is never truly separate from the persons who occupy the roles, the stories of some of the community members reveal something of the nature of the community.

Carl was the person in charge of the clothing room. In his mid-thirties, he had been a resident of the neighborhood when the first Mustard Seed was started; when he lost his apartment, he came to the house for shelter. Born with a slight physical defect, he was the peacemaker in the house—the one who tried to patch up differences within the community—as well as the one who seemed most interested in Catholic Worker philosophy on an intellectual level.

Mrs. Christ was perhaps the most memorable of the people at the Seed. A strikingly handsome woman of about fifty, she was a former mental patient who had lived in the house during her childhood (before it became a Worker house). Upon release from the mental hospital, she lived in an abandoned building for quite some time, coming to the house for meals. Eventually she was persuaded to stay and became the sole occupant of the first floor (the bulk of which, except for her room, consisted of the dining rooms). She was fond of colorful clothes and robes, to which she affixed strips of masking tape on which she had written small messages such as "hershe fish" and "I'm in the military." The door and walls of her room were also decorated with a multitude of similar aphorisms and phrases. Among my favorites was "Clostafobia." She was likely to greet a newcomer either with the most gracious hospitality or with shouts of "You murdered my babies! You stabbed me in the stomach and my babies are bleeding!"

Mrs. Christ contributed both warmth and humor to the house. Once when Sally had some friends over, Mrs. Christ climbed up to the third floor and introduced herself very politely as "Cleopatra Christ, but you can call me Patty." Sometimes she would ask one of us to say, "Fly away, Mrs. Christ." If we did so, a beatific look would settle on her face as she stared off into space. Some of the old-time Workers claimed that she was the most well integrated into the neighborhood of anyone in the Seed. Everyone knew her, and she even did some work in a local restaurant in exchange for cigarettes and food. For all her apparent insanity, she was amazingly perceptive and capable of seeing behind people's acts.

Stewart was in his sixties, a tall, rangy man who looked like a farmer, quite pleasant except for the occasional times he came home roaring drunk. He was in charge of taking out the garbage, but his most apparent role was dog herder. You could set your clock by their evening stroll in the yard because it was invariably punctuated by furious barking at the nearest passerby and Stewart's shouts of "Christie, Bruno, shut up!"

He never tired of talking about the cross-country trip he had taken a year earlier with Henry, visiting numerous Worker houses. He spoke fondly of the hope that he would go again. The trip marked the high point of his past few decades, as much because someone had taken the personal interest to ask him along as for the sights he had seen. The importance of this trip to his self-esteem bore ample witness to the power of the personalist approach to affect someone's life—not in an efficient, measurable manner, but in giving a person a genuine feeling that someone cared about him or her personally.

Three young men—Jim, Little Jim, and Harold—lived on the third floor, essentially as Sally's "wards." Jim was a muscular man in his early twenties who Sally had taken under her wing a year or so earlier and for whom the Seed represented the most important thing in his life. Their relationship was stormy—Sally threw Jim out of the house several times during my stay, but he always managed to get back in her good graces within a few days. Little Jim had first come to the House of Ammon as a young runaway and had stayed at the Seed several times. Harold had lived at the Seed previously and moved back in several weeks before I left.

Another regular resident of the third floor was Lynn, a burly woman who was a close friend of Sally's. Although she was not regarded as an official member of the community, she was a constant presence at the house and participated in the work. Her presence was a stormy one, punctuated by several violent outbursts after which Sally would usually throw her out "for the last time." The outbursts were usually caused by a combination of alcohol and the ever-present rivalry between herself and Jim for Sally's attention.

The community structure was a crucial element of the organization of the house. Unlike the other Worker houses, the Seed had a community into which members could be admitted only by a formal process. An ex-Worker describes the procedure for entering the community as it existed in the late 1970s:

> People would come into hospitality and we'd say, you can stay for four or five nights and that's it. Many of those people would put out the feelers—"Wow! I really want to be a Catholic Worker." And several people did absorb into the community that way. If people really expressed a need or a desire to stay around for awhile and did say I'd really like to join this community, we'd have meetings about it. We would let people know that was an option if they did kind of say that. An awful lot was on intuitive feelings about people. You can get a clear sense of where someone's at after being with them for awhile. Plus you leave in your mind that about forty-five to sixty percent of their behavior is on good behavior. In other words, they're playing the ropes before you get in. So a lot of it was intuitive and just kind of sensing where someone was at.
>
> But then we would have meetings. Talk about it, talk about people's feelings about the folks. . . . Have the person come to the meeting and kind of express where they're at and then kind of have a—we said consensus, but people didn't understand what really consensus is—but we'd kind of take a consensus agreement about having the person join the community. And it wasn't really a majority vote. If anybody had real strong feelings they would be listened to and try to figure out whether or not they should be allowed in.

Despite the consensus procedure, most community members felt that the real decisions were made by the two or three "core" Workers. However, as one Worker remembers, "Pete [an alcoholic community member] would say 'give 'em the deep six!' And that had a lot of weight. When Pete said that, you knew something was going on."

There were about a dozen community members. Given Sally's policy of no meetings, it was unclear how new members would be formally inducted. When I asked Sally about the community, her reply envisioned a much broader vision: "Like I consider you a community member while you are here. Because you are here not just doing a paper, not just walking around interviewing people, but doing it. To me that constitutes a community member, a part of the family."

There remained, however, a sharp distinction between guests and community members. A month or so after I had left, I got a call from Tom about one of his hospitality guests, a former mental patient who had been quite congenial and helpful but who had stayed for the absolute maximum of three months. Tom called to ask me if I knew of a place for him because, in order to stay longer, he would have to join the community and he was too "off the wall" to be voted in. Thus, community membership remained a formal part of the organization of the Mustard Seed.

Another aspect of house organization was a marked division of labor, almost absent in the other houses. Sally was house director and steward. As director, she was the official outside spokesperson for the house, made all major decisions, and was the only person allowed to interfere with the duties of others in the house. As steward, she was directly in charge of food donations, preparation, and distribution. Tom was director of hospitality. As such, he made all decisions about who would stay on the hospitality floor, for how long, and by what rules they would abide. Carl was in charge of clothing—only he could give clothes to the guests.

These three persons controlled the three major aspects of hospitality. However, nearly every member of the community was responsible for some regular task. Jim did the third-floor laundry. Stewart took out the garbage. Mrs. Christ cleaned the first-floor bathroom daily. Pete took charge of the front yard.

The task of each person was not only his or her duty; it was also his or her turf, jealously guarded against encroachment. One's task was also one's claim to community, the reciprocity that entitled one to room and board. Enfringement on another's task could easily be interpreted as an attack on their right to be in the community.

Thus, unlike other Worker houses, where anybody might give out clothes or food, or take out the garbage, people in the Mustard Seed did not do another's task without permission. If someone asked for clothes, they would be referred to Carl. If they asked for food, they would be referred to Sally. If they wanted to spend the night, they had to see Tom.

This division of labor was justified in terms of equity rather than competence. Since only one person was in charge of a function, a greedy guest could not get more than his or her share by going from person to person. Tom observed: "Yes, she [Sally] gives out the food. She doesn't have anything to do with my hospitality on the second floor, and I don't give out food on the third. It's not a matter of competence. It's a question of equity. Someone like Larry will ask her for a bag of food one day, and then me the next. He's a manipulator."

Thus, while in New York City or Rochester someone could amass clothes by asking different people in succession, the Mustard Seed arrangement for the most part precluded this type of manipulation.

Exceptions to this division of labor were rare. Usually they met with at least a reprimand, as I quickly found out when I gave a bag of food to someone who came to the door.

The major exception to the division of labor was the role of Sally, who, as house manager, could intervene in the work of either Tom or Carl when she felt it necessary to do so. Thus, on several occasions she discussed with Tom problems that she saw arising from one of his hospitality guests and at times urged or even demanded that he ask a guest to leave. Similarly, if she felt Carl was letting too many clothes pile up, she would intervene and clear out the clothing room. Just before I left, Carl turned over the clothing room duties to another community member. Although no one would say so, it seemed clear that this had been done at the insistence of Sally.

Another exception was due to a crosscutting division of authority. Both Tom and Sally controlled certain functions. Yet they were also uniquely in charge of separate floors. Because of this, Tom could dispense food from the second floor, and Sally could dispense hospitality on the third floor to people Tom didn't want or had no room for.

The division of authority on the basis of floors superceded all other organization of authority. Tom rarely ventured to the third floor. Sally made only brief visits to the second, usually to confer with Tom. They recognized each other's autonomy with respect to floor almost as absolute. For example, at one point Sally had thrown Jim out of the house. He went to Tom, who allowed him to stay on his floor. Although Sally fumed, she would not violate the autonomy of Tom's floor to enforce her ruling. Jim was reinstated within a couple of days, so it was not possible to see how the situation would have been resolved in the long run.

In many respects, the upper floors resembled nothing so much as medieval fiefdoms. Those living on each floor lived in the house at the discretion of the person in charge of the floor and could be expelled by that person. Thus, each person was in effect "sponsored" in the house by either Tom or Sally. This was true for both hospitality guests and community members. (The only exception to this rule was Carl, who lived on the second floor, but spent most of his waking hours on the third and so felt tied primarily to Sally). Thus, each inhabitant of a floor was personally bonded to the person in charge of the floor. In Tom's case, the persons in this relation were his hospitality guests. In Sally's, they were either community members or guests.

The Seed also had an "on-the-house" mode of organization for the daily meal. One member of the community signed up to "do the house" each day. Doing the house involved opening the front door at 4:30, letting the guests in, providing them with several gallons of iced tea or other beverages, being present until the end of the meal, keeping order, helping those serving the meal, and cleaning up afterward.

Tom did the house every Friday. Pete did it every Sunday. Most other evenings were divided among myself, Carl, David, and Jim. Sally did not do the house while I was there, saying that she was taking advantage of my presence to get a break.

Although superficially similar to the on-the-house structure in New York City, authority of the person on the house at the Seed was far more limited. In matters of food (other than the meal itself), clothing, and shelter, the person on the house could only refer the guest to the appropriate person. If that person was unavailable and had not appointed a temporary fill-in, nothing could be done.

Two roles in the division of labor were filled by people living outside the house: treasurer and chaplain. Both exercised considerable influence over Sally, due in part to their position and in part to the fact that they had supported her during the schism. Both were veterans of the House of Ammon.

Mark Jaworski was the treasurer, a mild-mannered, hardworking plumber in his thirties who lived two blocks away. He also did many of the repair jobs in the house. Father Barry Peters was the chaplain. A fiery preacher and avid singer, his Friday masses at the house were among the most moving I have ever attended. (I particularly remember that he closed the Mass not with the traditional "The Mass is ended, go in peace," but with "Go in peace. The Mass goes on.") In his role as chaplain, he was the major person to whom Sally turned in crisis.

Also important, at least in terms of informal moral influence on Sally's decisions were Peg and Jean, two roommates who were Sally's confidants. They lived about a mile from the Seed, but came over once or twice a week. Peg was one of the founders of the house. Jean had volunteered at the house quite a bit but had never lived there. They maintained an extra room in their apartment which could be used by Workers who needed a break.

Finally, although gone for over a year and living across the continent, Henry still constituted a force in the authority structure of the house. Sally often remarked to me that "if Henry asks me to leave, I would." At times she indicated that this was due to his charismatic authority—the moral influence he had had on her. At other times, however, she referred to a more rational-legal basis for his alleged authority over her—he was still the owner of the house.

Typifications of People

The way people were typified at the Seed differed substantially from the patterns at the other houses, primarily because of the importance of community membership. The most crucial distinction at the Seed was not Worker versus guest or "in the house" versus "out of the house," but membership in the community. Community members had to be voted in formally. Thus, community membership was a category rather than an ideal type. Membership was somewhat like tenure—once you were in, you were in for life unless your behavior became truly outrageous. (And the definition of outrageous was pretty broad. The community contained people who were physically violent, actively drinking alcoholics, and one person who often complained that babies were peeing out of her eye sockets.)

Community membership was the major status distinction at the Seed. It did not matter whether you were ideologically committed to the Catholic Worker or if you were even coherent—if you had been voted into the community, you were entitled to a place in one of the houses and this entitlement could not be denied without great effort. Again, I mean this literally. Several years ago, Henry reportedly paid one man $500 to get him to leave. Sally and her allies had also removed several community members with threats of physical violence.

Three major types contrasted with community members. The first was the guests. In terms of social origins, there was little distinction between guests and community members, since the community members all had come to the house as guests.

As at the other houses, meal guests were distinct from hospitality guests. At the Mustard Seed, the meal guests were primarily white, and nearly a third were women. Many lived in rooms or apartments in the neighborhood and used the house as a neighborhood social center as well as a source of food. Hospitality guests were the four men in the hospitality beds on the second floor. These were roughly typed into either extended-stay or short-term, with the extended-stay guests being men who Tom thought had a chance to rehabilitate themselves, and the short-term guests being those who received only a night or two.

Another type was the member of the "extended community,"

which ranged from Barry and Mark, who were intimately involved in the house and without whose support the house would undoubtedly have collapsed, to the volunteers and church groups who cooked and served meals regularly, to those who brought in donations.

The final type consisted of those persons who had been part of the extended community but who had actively tried to unseat Sally as house director and who now had little or no contact with the house. These tended to be the peace activists of the community, mostly in their thirties.

Although community membership constituted a category, the other three groupings were ideal types. In particular, the distinction between extended community and those who had rebelled against Sally was not clear-cut. A number of people had tried to stay neutral during the struggle. Clearly, for Sally, one was no longer part of the extended community if one had sided with the "rebels." Speaking of one ex-Worker, she told me, "That's why he's still welcome around here. He didn't side with them across the street."

The 1983 schism heightened what was probably a preexisting tendency to classify those involved in the work in terms of Peter Maurin's distinction between Workers and Scholars. Although Maurin had spoken of a hope that in the Catholic Worker, "the scholars must become workers so the workers may be scholars" (Maurin, 1977, 27), the Mustard Seed residents regarded worker and scholar as a basic distinction between people. The fact that all of those who had opposed Sally were college educated, while relatively few of her supporters were, heightened this dichotomy. For Sally in particular, "scholars" were suspect, because it was the scholars who had tried to unseat her: "Those College Joes—they don't like my methods. I got backstabbed and criticized and denounced because of my methods, but I've made the place right. I'm serving meals and giving out clothes. My way works. Their's didn't, not Peg's, not Henry's."

The day I arrived, she told me, "You'll be working mostly with Tom. He's a Ph.D., too, and you two'll be able to communicate better." A few days later she reassured me, "You're gonna fit in. I can read people. You're not like those other Ph.D.s—College Joes I call 'em. You don't talk down to people." Nevertheless, I had the feeling that I was under suspicion of being a scholar throughout my stay.

This transformation of the worker-scholar distinction into another term for class war is not unique to the Mustard Seed. Dorothy Day recounts a similar interpretation at the Staten Island "farming commune" in the 1930s (Day 1963, 43–44).

Other Catholic Worker terms for denoting relationship to the house were also employed, but had less importance at the Seed at this point in its history. There were friends of the house, although these were not as distinct a group as at other houses. More important were friends of the individual community members, who could be granted special privileges. Even the term Worker, although used frequently, did not carry as much weight as community member. Several people made it clear to me that not all community members were Catholic Workers, although only Mrs. Christ actively repudiated the label: "I'm not a Catholic Worker. I'm the military."

Deviant categories were used here as at the other houses. Guests were classified as alcoholics, drug addicts, crazies, etc. The one exception was Tom, who often characterized guests in a clinical manner, utilizing the AA definition of alcoholic as "addictive personality" and taking care to distinguish among psychiatric categories. In this, he was perhaps "the exception that proves the rule." He was the only Worker in any of the houses who had any great interest in clinical diagnostic categories.

Hospitality

Although the organization of the house differed significantly from the other houses, the life of the house did focus on the three main activities of hospitality: food, shelter, and clothing. There were, however, some intriguing differences in how these were carried out in practice.

Food

Monday through Saturday, the house opened at 4:30 P.M. for people to come in, sit down, and chat while waiting for the 6:00 meal. On Sunday, a brunch was served at 11:00 A.M. During the summer, we usually put iced tea or fruit punch in a five gallon pot in the middle dining room, from which people could dip as much as they wanted. Occasionally we would also put out snacks.

The two dining rooms had an assortment of tables, benches, and chairs. Two of the tables in the front room were homemade—sheets of plywood with wooden legs. Benches lined these tables. The other table in that room was a huge old dining room model, and it was flanked by the seat from an old van and a wooden bench.

Most of the early arrivals lived in nearby apartments. They used the same seat every day and felt that this was "their" place. They gave the house the atmosphere of an old-time general store. Jokes and insults were bandied about freely. If a pretty young woman happened to walk in, she would often be greeted with whistles and soft-spoken comments of the sort that would inflame any feminist. Over the next hour and a half, people trickled in until the place was packed.

By 6:00, there were anywhere from 60 to 250 people waiting to be served. Usually, the meal was served cafeteria-style by a group from a parish or other organization in the city. Four or five servers would line up behind the serving counter. The person on the house would go into the middle dining room, ask everyone to rise, and begin the Lord's Prayer. Afterward, the prayer leader would announce who had cooked the meal, who was serving it, and perhaps make some other announcements.

Some guests would take their plates outside and eat on the picnic table or porch, or leaning against the fence. Even before everyone had received their first serving, others were moving to the back of the line to get seconds. Almost everyone returned their dishes and silverware to the counter. Although the time before the meal was leisurely, most people ate quickly: everyone was usually out of the building well before 7:00.

The meal differed from that in other houses in one crucial respect—it was usually prepared outside of the house by a church group, which then brought it in and served it with the assistance of the community member who was on the house. Most groups signed up to do one day a month. Over two-thirds of the days were covered by such groups, the remainder being covered by the Workers themselves.

Most of the groups were responsible for a regular day of the month. Some had been doing this regularly for four or five years, but several new groups began while I was there. Not all groups were Catholic. One spot was done by an ecumenical coalition of churches. Another spot was done by a PTA group. Still another was done regularly by one woman (with help from the Workers). A charismatic Christian, she often preceded the meal with a brief sermon to the assembled multitude about the miracles Christ had wrought in her life and offered to pray with anyone who so desired after the meal. She had few takers.

The groups were quite self-sufficient, relying on the person on the house to keep order if there was any trouble, but able to set up and serve without assistance. Experienced groups were quite proud of their ability to conduct the meal themselves.

Most groups remained behind the counter the whole time, keeping personal contact with guests to a minimum. The main exceptions were the leaders of the more experienced groups, who circulated among the guests and knew a number of the regulars by name. This was particularly true of the two or three groups that served family style rather than cafeteria style. They would instruct the guests to remain in their seats while four or five group members would carry the plates to the tables. This apparently was the older procedure at the Seed, but had been largely abandoned due to the crowding.

The quality of the food varied, although I would say it was good to excellent. Most groups brought a casserole or chicken, along with salad, vegetable, desert, and drink. One church group regularly brought several hams and turkey rolls, and gave each person thick slices of each. The guests knew the differences between groups and were eager to know who was serving. I didn't consider it important at first, but a guest soon set me straight: "It may not mean anything to you, but it does to us. Some groups are good, some not so good. We know who the good ones are. It's important for us to know who's coming. Or, if the house is cooking, whether it's Sally or Tom. I'm not saying who's better, but it matters."

A few minutes later Sally came down and the guests asked her who's coming. She replied, "Donna and Jane." One of the guests said "Oh, the green-bean people," and explained to me, "They bring the best green beans. They're great." There was a murmur of agreement. The ham and turkey group was generally ranked as one of the best. They always served during the last week of the month, and the crowd often reached 250. I've seen the line reach out the door, down the driveway, and almost to the corner.

A couple of the groups were usually accompanied by priests, who often said Mass in the dining rooms after the meal. One of the tables was converted into an altar and the servers plus perhaps a half dozen of the guests and Workers attended. Most of the servers viewed these Masses as a return to primitive forms of Christian worship—held simply, attended by rich and poor alike, located in a house rather than an ornate church.

Most crucial to the atmosphere of the meal, however, were the guests themselves. In contrast to the other houses that I visited, the meal guests at the Seed were predominantly white, and many were not homeless. Many persons who had rooms or apartments nearby came for the meal, and about a dozen of these—about equally split between men and women—formed a core that unofficially set the norms of conduct in the dining rooms.

The dining room had a feeling of conviviality. On walking in, one had a feel that this was a neighborhood hangout and that people knew each other and looked forward to meeting each other here. There was an atmosphere of play—three of the men liked to do the Three Stooges routine of slapping each other on the head, to everyone's delight. The guests themselves enforced certain norms. The "regulars" knew who was greedy and would keep an eagle eye on such characters as soon as they walked in the door. One such "greedy character" was Gary, a tall, rail thin former mental patient. One day he came in and began wandering around. Howard, the self-appointed guardian of the place, yelled at him repeatedly to sit down. I came down with a tray of finger sandwiches and began passing them around. When I got to Gary, three or four people yelled out, "Just take one, Gary!" Later, when he tried to take someone else's seat, he was again reprimanded by several guests. If guests didn't like something but didn't want to interfere personally, they would mention it to the person on the house.

The atmosphere of the dining room was more convivial than in the other houses, for a number of reasons. In the New York house, there was no "drop-in" time before the meal, so everyone got down to the business of eating rather quickly. Rochester had a drop-in time before the meal, but the atmosphere there was more individualistic. Men came in singly or in twos or threes, but rarely did I feel a sense of community among them. I suspect that the explanation lies primarily in the fact that in Worcester there was a core of neighborhood people who set the tone, while in Rochester most of the guests were homeless men who tended to stick to themselves and often spent the time before the meal sleeping in a chair or couch. Also, there were more women at the Seed—often a third of the guests were women, in contrast to 5 percent or less at the other houses. Finally, the fact that the Workers themselves had been homeless may have encouraged guests to define the Seed as a neighborhood hangout.

This neighborhood identity created one problem that was practically unknown at the other houses—what to do with unaccompanied children. The neighborhood abounded in children who roamed about with little adult supervision. About half a dozen kids from a "three-decker" house behind the Seed were almost always present. The Seed had adopted a rule of not serving unaccompanied children;

however, this rule was challenged and renegotiated repeatedly while I was there, particularly by two urchins named Pedro and Pete, about eleven years old. Pedro in particular would come in nearly every day. The first time I asked him to leave he did so, but climbed back in through an open window. Occasionally we would relent and let him stay awhile, but invariably when we did he would end up shoving an older guest or stealing something from someone. Eventually, we came up with the tactic of feeding the kids on the side porch, but this also led to a great deal of confusion.

Occasionally, an adult guest would take charge of an unaccompanied youngster. Once, Jimmy, a five-year-old neighbor, came in and I told him to leave. A tall young woman said she would look after him. She told him to go to the bathroom and wash his hands, which he did immediately. Then she held his hand while they went through the line and sat with him while he ate. He beamed the whole time, ecstatic at the individual attention. I noted in my journal: "The generosity of our guests often exceeds our own. These poor kids respond to the slightest individual attention." Often, however, the tactic of letting a guest volunteer to supervise a child didn't work out so well, particularly when the guest had been drinking.

There were occasional acts or threats of violence at the meals. It was one such threat that gave me insight into one of the roots of the schism. For weeks, I had heard Sally talk about those "College Joes" who had criticized her "tactics." Then, one day, a guest who had been barred for life was rumored to be in the neighborhood while I was on the house. Hearing the rumor, Jim grabbed a baseball bat and said he would keep an eye out for him. I went upstairs and informed Sally that Jim was looking pretty menacing with the bat, to which she replied accusingly, "Those are my tactics. What's the matter, don't you like my tactics?" (This was one of those great moments in participant observation when the beleaguered researcher finally grasps the meaning of a phrase she or he has been hearing for weeks.) Not wanting to be confused with a College Joe, I returned downstairs, hoping that the guest would not arrive. He did, but with Carl's help, the incident was resolved without violence.

Since most of the meals were prepared outside the house, there was often more food donated than could be used, particularly in the summer when garden produce was frequently donated. Since there was no need to save this food for future meals, it was given out to neighbors. On days when Sally went to the Food Bank, there were often a dozen or more neighbors, many Spanish-speaking, who came to the door to see Sally and get a box. In addition, Sally and other third-floor Workers had families to which they took boxes of food. Several boxes went to Peg and Jean, who distributed them in their neighborhood.

There were several times when the supply of fruits and vegetables exceeded what was needed both for the meal and for the neighbors. When this happened, the food was loaded into the trunk of a car and taken to a public housing project. I accompanied Peg and Jean on one such foray. We loaded the trunk with half a dozen large boxes stuffed with broccoli, beans, cucumbers, and zucchini and drove to the largest public housing project in the city, several acres of garden-style apartments punctuated by stripped down hulks of cars and fire-scarred dumpsters. We stopped at a parking lot where some people were hanging out. We felt a bit of trepidation, aware that our act of "charity" could well injure people's pride. As Peg said, "It's so hard for people to accept food like this."

Peg walked over to the group and asked if they wanted vegetables. A young Spanish woman came over to the car. A few others followed, tentatively, at a distance. None appeared to speak English very well. Jean said, "This is from the Mustard Seed, the Catholic Worker." At the word Catholic, the woman's face lit up and she said to the others, "Iglesia, iglesia." This seemed to give us the seal of approval, and people began asking what the vegetables were. We had forgotten to bring bags, so they just took whatever they could carry in their hands. Several kids excitedly grabbed cukes and zukes. We gave the first woman a whole box of green beans—since people couldn't carry them—and asked her to distribute them. We then drove to another parking lot and repeated the process, this time careful to emphasize that we were from the church (*iglesia*).

Our last stop in the project was at the apartment of an older woman who had called Sally several times asking for food. I carried what was left of the vegetables into a small apartment crowded with knickknacks. The lady was confined to a wheelchair. She thanked me profusely for the paltry gift, then told me she used to come to the Seed, but three years ago had had a massive heart attack. She could hardly walk across her apartment and couldn't even wheel her own wheelchair because of her heart condition. She said she couldn't get any supplies without paying someone gas money. I stayed and talked a few minutes. She said, "If you have any extra, remember me. Especially tomatoes. I'll make some tomato jelly and send you down some." She asked me to pray for her.

The meals and food distribution were all under Sally's control. She organized the schedule of groups coming in and persons on the house. She had responsibility to cook if someone else hadn't covered the day. Food was not to be given out the door without her OK.

Shelter

The second floor was the locus for overnight hospitality. There were four hospitality beds (two of which were actually couches). As the director of hospitality, Tom made all decisions as to who could sleep in the hospitality beds, for how long, and under what conditions they would be asked to leave. Anyone asking for shelter was referred to Tom.

Beds were offered for a maximum of two months, although the stay could be shorter, depending on the person's needs and Tom's evaluation of what would benefit them and the house. The four beds were given out on a first-come, first-served basis unless Tom had reason to believe that the guest would be disruptive. Almost every stranger who asked was given a bed if there was a vacancy. If Tom knew the person, however, he based his decision on his perception of how disruptive the person was.

For instance, one morning, Joe, a stocky, fortyish fellow who looks like a hardened, poverty-stricken version of Lou Costello, came up to Tom's room to ask for shelter. I walked by as Tom was telling him, "So it doesn't look like it's for you." Joe shrugged as if unconvinced, said "I guess not," and left. I asked Tom what had happened, and he told me, "Joe was looking to be a permanent resident here. I told him that wasn't possible." Later he expanded his explanation. "You understand why I refused hospitality to Joe. On the basis of seven years' experience with him, I know it wouldn't work out. I knew him back in detox. It would be like having a rock of granite here," referring to Joe's rather obstinate disposition. At other times, however, I saw Tom welcome into shelter men who looked to me to be just as unpromising candidates as Joe. These, however, were newcomers, to whom he was willing to give the benefit of the doubt.

Tom's view of hospitality included rehabilitation. He decried the years that the Seed had been a "flophouse." Although he would offer a night or two of shelter to someone passing through town, he expected longer-term guests to use the opportunity to search for a job or otherwise work themselves back into "normal society." He gave frequent pep talks and often used his rather considerable network of AA connections to get his guests appointments at agencies or news of job possibilities.

Longer-term guests were expected to pitch in with the work of the house if they did not have a job. If they were not helping out, they were expected to be out of the house between 9:00 A.M. and 4:30 P.M. Tom often gave longer-term guests a key to the house once he had come to trust them.

Since guests were often allowed to stay for up to two months, relatively few men passed through hospitality during my sojourn. Six men stayed for at least a month. Perhaps a dozen others stayed for briefer periods, sometimes a single night. The stories of some of the longer-term guests give insight into the nature of shelter at the Mustard Seed.

James was a stocky, ebony-skinned African who had been an administrator in his homeland but had come to the United States to go to college. After graduating, he applied to graduate programs in business administration. Although he was accepted into one program, he was not offered financial aid, so he came to Worcester to stay with a friend and look for work. When he arrived, he found that the friend had moved. After exhausting his money staying at a hotel, he found the Mustard Seed and Tom told him he could move in while he looked for work. James was in his forties and reluctant to return to Africa for reasons he chose not to discuss.

He was cheerful but at times seemed bemused by the customs of this country. He went out daily to look for work, dressed in white shirt and often a suit. For weeks, he trudged back disappointed. Occasionally a lead would appear, then evaporate. Tom called various contacts looking for jobs and wrote several letters of recommendation. (Tom often referred to himself as Doctor because of his Ph.Ds, and James always called him Dr. Tommy. We thought he was using this name jokingly until Tom got the first call for a reference from "Dr. Tommy" from a prospective employer.)

James never seemed to understand the Seed or its rules. Although he was told that guests were not allowed to drink even outside the house, he came back frequently after a day of job hunting and told Tom and myself that he had had a few beers at a local bar. Nothing was ever said to him about this since he did not have a drinking problem.

A few weeks before I left, James got a job as a busboy at a fancy downtown restaurant. He was practically ecstatic, and Tom shared his enthusiasm, telling him that he could easily work up to waiter, where he could earn good money. The enthusiasm dimmed, however, as he realized he would be working only part-time. Nonetheless, James persevered, and by the time I left he was preparing to move into a rooming house. Tom called him the "success story" of my stay.

Mike arrived a few days after me, a lanky Vietnam vet, about thirty-five with black hair and an affinity for narcotics, a man who never seemed able to "get back into society" after his return from the war. He was an amiable guy, with a "yuk, yuk" kind of laugh. He was unemployed but not looking for work too actively because of an arm injury. Tom often let him stay around the house during the day and in return he washed dishes, chopped vegetables for the Sunday brunch, and did some general cleanup work. In the evenings, Mike and I would often play chess.

Mike's downfall began with the arrival of Dan, who had a construction job but asked for shelter while he saved up for a place of his own. Mike and Dan quickly became buddies and would go out together for the evening when Dan returned from work. They had a mutual interest in marijuana and cocaine, which Dan's income enabled them to acquire, with the result that they began returning to the Seed at increasingly later hours in increasingly debilitated states. Tom gave them a warning that he would ask them to leave if they kept indulging. The warning went unheeded, and Tom eventually told them that they had three days to leave. They took the ultimatum rather nonchalantly. When I asked Dan if he had a place lined up, he replied, "No, I've got a possibility. I've been in this situation before." The situation was painful for Tom and myself, since we had become fond of Mike and viewed the situation in terms of his corruption by Dan, although knowing full well that his sobriety during his first few weeks had been due more to a lack of funds than to a desire to reform.

Greg was a boyishly handsome man of thirty-five who stopped at the Seed on his way to Boston, where he planned to meet with Edward Kennedy to arrange a marriage to his niece Caroline. Although he had never met Caroline, he had found a church that he felt was the ideal site for such a wedding. We used every available opportunity to gently dissuade him from this plan, fearing for his safety if he should make his intentions known. He ended up staying at the Seed for several months.

He was a gentle person, although he did tell me that he had once been arrested for hitting his stepfather when the latter refused to let him enter the house.

> I knew it was a crime. But it was aggravated assault, in the sense that I was aggravated, not in the sense that I struck him repeatedly. I only

struck him once, in the mouth. They said I was on drugs or something. I hadn't had anything to eat in days. I had traveled across the
country for the last four days, from Kansas City. I was sleeping in the
weeds. He told me, "You're no part of this family." And the courts
accepted that.

The story was told with great pain.

Greg was gifted with great vision. He could look at a place and
envision something that should be done there. He would always be
talking about a parking lot that he thought would make a beautiful
church, or a restaurant that he proposed to change into an art gallery.
"But," he would sigh, "nobody would listen to me." He told me that
he had been in foster care. "My father, whether in fact or in mind, was
in an Air Force bomber squadron. When he died, my mother gave us
to people to take care of. We were abused. My sister was raped when
she was seven." He spent some time in a mental hospital. When he
mentioned a doctor, I asked him if he was a psychiatrist. "Well, he
had the credentials. I think he was a drunk my sister picked up in
the park. . . . These psychiatrists—they think they've risen above the
culture that produces us all and then they speak from their transcen-
dence." Greg spent much of his time at the Seed cleaning windows.
He worked diligently, taking the whole window out of the frame so
he could clean the outside. By the time I left, he had cleaned every
window in the house.

I became quite friendly with a number of the guests at the Mustard Seed—far more so than at the other houses. This was in part due
to the fact that guests often stayed longer than in the other houses.
But it was also due to the intimacy of the hospitality floor and to the
guests themselves.

The long-term guests were mostly young men in their twenties or
thirties, rather articulate and fairly well educated, and not yet totally
addicted to alcohol and drugs. All were homeless, and some had been
so for years; however, most were able to contemplate a return to
society. In short, they were closer to my own social class than most
guests at other houses.

The setting for hospitality was more "homey" than in the other
houses. Those on the floor often had breakfast together. Occasionally
Tom would cook a special supper for his guests, which heightened
the feeling of solidarity. Since the third floor was usually off limits
to guests, guests spent most of their time in the house on the second
floor. As a result of all this, a spirit of community developed among
the long-term guests, Tom, and myself. In the other houses, guests

would think of themselves as individuals or at times as pairs, but only at the Seed did I get a feeling of solidarity among guests as group.

The hospitality of the Mustard Seed was not limited to the second floor. Sally could grant hospitality on her floor, although those who stayed on the third floor usually participated in the work of the house.

Some persons associated with the house gave hospitality in their own homes. Mark had guests regularly. Tom said of him, "Sometimes he takes people in there—people who are all strung out—people we won't take here now." William was a former mental patient and an old-time frequenter of the Seed who was capable of carrying on monologues for hours on end. When he lost his place, Mark let him stay in his apartment for a couple of days. His incessant chatter, however, proved difficult to live with, and so Mark announced, "I'm all Williamed out." He did, however, tell William he could sleep in his van until he found another place. Mark's apartment was thus a House of Hospitality in its own right.

Finally, the community of the Seed granted hospitality to each other in a more profound sense than was true at the other houses. All members of the community were in need of shelter. None had resources to procure shelter for themselves on a permanent basis outside of the house. In a very real sense, then, everyone at the house was in need of hospitality and gave it to each other.

Clothing

Clothing distribution was performed exclusively by Carl. The process bore a superficial resemblance to the procedures at the New York City house; however, the limitation of responsibility to one person created profound differences. Clothing donations were stored in a large enclosed front porch, where unsorted clothes were piled almost to the ceiling. The porch was padlocked, and only Carl had a key.

Every weekday before the house opened, Carl would come down and put some of the clothes neatly on three tables—two for men and one for women. As people came in, they could sort through these clothes and take what they wanted. There were no limits placed on how much any one person could take, but once the clothes Carl had laid out were gone, that was the end of it for the day.

Carl did take requests and get people clothes in emergencies. However, he frequently declared, "My sole responsibility is to have clothes out on the tables. Any personal requests for articles is done on my own personal choice." Once I got so frustrated at not being able to get coats for two men who lacked them on a chilly day that I jimmied open a window in the clothing room and climbed through to get two jackets that had been in plain view.

The other distinctive aspect of the Seed's approach to clothing was that there was an abundance of clothing donations. Although there was no institutional source of clothing, an amazing number of clothes arrived almost daily. At one point, Sally, frustrated at the disorder of the clothing room, instituted a massive cleanup, clearing out the porch and taking two van loads of clothes to the Salvation Army. Soon, however, clothes again began to accumulate.

Carl came under a great deal of criticism for his handling of the clothing room—not because he was stingy, but because he was disorganized, letting good clothes lie around rather than searching for them and putting them out. He responded, "People say I'm lazy, but I tell them I do the clothing room. I don't do a good job of it, but nobody ever has. Since I've done it, three people have tried to do it and none of them could take it."

Style

The style of hospitality differed in a number of ways from the other houses. Other than the non-nonviolent style that has already been discussed, the two most important differences were more parties and more reciprocity between hosts and guests.

Every Friday, Mass was said in the chapel by Father Peters about 7:30 P.M., followed by a party in the third-floor kitchen. Mass was generally attended by the third-floor Workers, myself, Carl, Mark, and perhaps half a dozen meal guests.

Sally spent most Friday afternoons preparing for the party with the assistance of one or more of the third-floor Workers. By Mass time, the huge kitchen table was piled high with cakes, cookies, donuts, ice cream, and whatever else had been donated that week. After Mass, everyone sat around the table, drinking coffee, eating the pastries, and talking. Mrs. Christ would often join us for the party, although never for Mass. There were always mounds of leftovers, which the meal guests divided among themselves and took with them.

Sally always made it a point to fill the table to overflowing. One day, as she was discussing the schism with me, she explained why this was so important. She noted that "they" had criticized her for wasting food at these parties. Somewhat paraphrased, her explanation was:

> What they don't understand is that, to a poor person, dignity is being able to leave something on the table after you've eaten your fill. I

know because I am poor. That's why I always make sure there's more
than enough on the table. I want there to be plenty left over—it
makes people feel good. Besides, none of it goes to waste. I give it all
out to the people who come.

These parties were frequently converted into special-occasion parties, often on the spur of the moment. If someone had had a birthday
that week, the party became a birthday party. One became my going-
away party.

There were three major picnics that summer, all held in the front
yard. These picnics had the atmosphere of a huge backyard barbecue.
The first was on the Fourth of July, complete with hot dogs, potato
salad, bean salad, watermelon, ice cream, and punch. Two picnic
tables were brought in, and nearly all the benches and chairs from
the dining rooms were moved into the front yard. Around a hundred
people came. It was a time to get to know people. After helping serve,
I sat on a bench with a quiet older man who had been coming to the
Seed for years. He told me about his days as a traveling salesman and
of a trip he had taken his daughter on, which "she remembered all
her life."

I missed the second picnic, but the third was an even larger affair,
staged by a church group from out of town. They brought their own
grills and served hot dogs, corn, salad, and soda. About 150 attended,
and, apart from one argument about someone cutting in line, the
event was quite peaceful. One of the dissident Workers from across
the street even came over for awhile.

Hospitality also involved advocacy and visiting at jails and hospitals, as at the other houses. Such advocacy was often done for
people who were old drinking buddies. Wolfman, an old companion of Sally's from her days on the streets, drove up one day from
California in a huge step van adorned with a Confederate flag. He
was arrested the next day on a six-year-old warrant, largely because
his van, which was large enough to house a motorcycle and to sleep
Wolfman and his girlfriend, was a bit conspicuous sitting in front of
the Seed. Sally spent the next two days going to court, trying to bail
him out, getting his van towed to a safe place, storing his belongings,
and helping his girlfriend get back to California. This was not ideologically motivated hospitality as much as the age-old reciprocity of
the poor—taking care of one's friends because they've taken care of
you in the past and may do so in the future (Stack 1974; Addams
1965; Day 1939).

The style of hospitality at the Seed differed from that of the other houses. It was certainly less nonviolent, and also less concerned with such niceties as flowers on the tables, salt and pepper shakers, and matching plates. Some persons, while on the house, even refused to provide toilet paper for the bathroom because "they just mess the place up with it." However, it was also sometimes more unstintingly generous, less calculated, and more "natural" in the sense that the hospitality was provided by people who were genuinely a part of the neighborhood, who would probably be living in similar conditions regardless of their ideological convictions. The other Worker houses provided a hospitality that was clearly more spontaneous, natural, and personal than that provided by social-service agencies. Yet even those houses appeared somewhat rationalized compared to the Seed.

Reciprocity was a crucial aspect of this style of hospitality. At all Worker houses, guests are allowed to reciprocate for hospitality by helping in the work of the house—mopping floors, washing dishes, serving meals. However, the norm of personalist responsibility generally precludes asking a guest to help. Adherence to this norm varies both among and within houses. Thus, Workers in Rochester did not hesitate to ask guests to mop the floor on occasions. At the Mustard Seed, however, the Workers regularly encouraged guests to help out, justifying this practice by the aphorism that "work is a gift." And, many guests at the Seed seemed happy at the opportunities to repay the hospitality offered them.

Only once do I remember a guest explaining his motives for "helping out" in terms of ingratiating himself to the Workers—"This oughta make so-and-so happy." Usually, the explanation was in terms of repayment of favors. Occasionally, a guest would explain, "I'd rather be washing dishes here. It beats drinking, which is what I'd be doing if I weren't here."

One evening, Billy, a mildly retarded man whose frequent offers of help were not usually received with enthusiasm because of his tendency to do a poor job and talk your ear off while doing it, showed up at the side door with one of the house dogs in tow, explaining that he had found her wandering in a park a mile away. Stewart had been looking for her frantically for most of the day and was overjoyed to see her again. Billy went away glowing with pride at having done something useful, something for which he could be sincerely thanked. This opportunity to reciprocate may have been a greater gift to him than were the numerous meals he had received.

Tensions in Hospitality

My stay at the Mustard Seed was the most morally demanding aspect of the entire research project. I saw there some of the most heartening interactions I have ever seen. I also saw some aspects that were deeply disturbing. That tensions abounded at the Seed should be obvious. It is precisely these tensions, however, which can lead to some real insights into the nature of Catholic Worker hospitality. The two that seem most important were the tensions in the decision-making process and the related tension between giving hospitality and building community.

"A Ridiculous Form of Consensus"

For the first decade, consensus was the formal process for making decisions. Everyone I interviewed agreed that there had been a serious effort to implement this collective process, but that in practice it had been flawed. One of the main figures in the house called it "a ridiculous form of consensus." All agreed that the important decisions were actually made by the two or three ideologically committed people who had assumed major responsibility for the house. The people involved advanced several reasons for the breakdown in the consensus process. Intriguingly, many of their explanations paralleled findings from sociological studies of other organizations that had attempted such processes. The majority of the problems concerned the delineation of the group that would make the decisions—a major problem due to the Worker's rejection of concepts of formal membership.

Initially, decisions were made collectively by those who had been instrumental in starting the house plus several others who had become involved in supporting the effort. A rift developed, however, over the issue of whether those living outside the house should have a say equal to those living in the house. One person who was not living in the house at the time traced the rift to the time of the second house closing.

> And this group of people [those who had helped to close the house] became the decision-making group and they were to make decisions about what the house was gonna look like and what it was gonna be like. That was fine while the house was closed, but when the house started up and was running again, then you had all this hassle about in-house people and out-house people, and in-house people should have the last word because they have to put up with the most bull-

shit. What eventually happened was that the people who didn't live
there . . . felt like why should I even give my opinion or put in any
energy because . . . [I] can only be a part of it to a certain point. . . .

I think in-house people would listen to out-of-house people, but
it was more than that that needed to happen. There needed to be decisions made. So you'd say who's gonna be on the house? So some of
the in-house people would be on the house and some of the out-of-
the-house people would be on the house. . . . But as decisions came
closer to how the house should work, who should live at the house
and who shouldn't, what time it opens and what time it closes—
things that really do affect in-house people more— . . . you could
see where the in-house people didn't want them [the out-of-house
people] to have a say.

A Worker who had been living in the house recalled the problem
in much the same terms:

I had problems with that kind of situation [collective decision
making] because you had people who were living there and as far as
I could see were committed to being there for a long time. But I had
the problem of—if we were all going to be making decisions but yet
only some of us were going to be implementing them. I think I may
have lost some help, some people, by taking that attitude.

One problem for her was that the out-of-house people outnum-
bered the in-house people by roughly three to one, leaving the in-
house people bearing the brunt of the work but having relatively
little say in the decision making. This type of problem has been noted
elsewhere, particularly with respect to a rift between part-time volunteers and paid staff in egalitarian cooperatives (Newman 1980,
153–54).

Gradually, the collective decision-making process evolved to include primarily those who were living in the house on a long-term
basis. This involved both an expansion and contraction of the definition of the decision-making group. The "extended community"
members came to have less say, but the long-term guests became formally included in the decision-making group. This change appears
to have been both a response to the in-house versus out-of-house
rift and an attempt to extend the egalitarianism inherent in Catholic
Worker ideology explicitly to the decision-making arena.

It was at this point that the community structure peculiar to the
Seed apparently arose. The official community included both live-in
Workers and long-term guests who had been accepted formally into
the community. Membership in the community meant equal partici-

pation in the consensual process. This formalization of the decision-making process, however, created several problems that undermined the consensual approach.

The majority of persons in the Seed community were not ideologically committed Catholic Workers but were, rather, persons who had come in need of shelter, some of whom had spent years in mental hospitals, others of whom were actively drinking alcoholics. Thus, the very nature of the persons involved in the process created problems.

First, most of the members of the community preferred the traditional hierarchical model of decision making. Thus, those who were committed to a collective decision-making process found it necessary to impose their will on the majority simply to maintain a collective process. Quite simply, how does one maintain a collective process when most of the participants want leaders? One Worker recalls: "Most of the people who come are really searching for a mother or father who will tell them what to do. A lot of times just from their own needs and from their own fears and insecurity . . . they want someone to answer the questions for them or tell them what the questions are."

Joyce Rothschild-Whitt, in her seminal article on collectivist organizations (1979, 521), notes in a similar vein: "Due to prior experiences, many people are not very well-suited for participatory democracy. This is an important constraint on its development."

Second, the majority of community members neither knew how collective decision making worked, nor felt self-confident enough to really believe they had a say. One Worker recalled:

> There was a certain amount of a triad of people who would make the major decisions in the house but there was an awful lot of working at trying to get people to a place where they would really join in on decisions. "Well, what do you think? What would you do in this situation?" . . . I could remember people living there three years and it would take six months for them to even get to a place of even thinking that they might even be able to say something about it. I mean, "My opinion matters? I can say something about it?" And then a year and a half or two years beyond that before they say "Well, yeah, this is what I think you should do. Why don't you try to go about doing this." There were several people [for whom] that just never happened.

A person who was an actively drinking guest at the time expressed a similar opinion in terms of maturity: "Decision making was nonexistent really for the first two years of my life here because Peg and Henry were in the neighborhood. When one or the other of them were here, it was always possible to say, 'Well it's your house, you decide.' And because of that we were abdicating what was in fact our responsibility as adults." There was also a conflict between commitment to a collective decision-making process and adherence to Worker ideology. Since most of the community was not ideologically committed, the only way the Seed could adhere to Worker principles was for the ideologically committed persons to insist on maintaining these principles against the will of the majority. One cannot have a true consensual process while still adhering to an ideology if the vast majority of those involved in consensus are not committed to the ideology. At the Mustard Seed, adherence to ideology took precedence over consensus. One Worker recalls: "Ideally, you're telling people they have an equal say in how things are gonna be run, but yet they don't because if their say is one that disagrees with the idealistic notion, then their say is overruled."

A problem related to the inclusion of guests into the decision-making process was that, according to all concerned, nearly everyone in the community, Workers and guests alike, was "damaged goods," with either chemical dependencies or emotional problems. One Worker recalls:

> Most of us who were in the community at the time came with, as we all do, an awful lot of baggage, but several of us were active, addicted people to either drugs or alcohol. I'm an alcoholic. I'm recovering . . . but I went through my last years of drinking at the Seed, and I was a closet drinker, you know, really. At the Seed you had to be. Or a parking-lot drinker. I'd go out and get a six-pack and drink it up the street and then come back home. I was trying to become sober at the time, but I wasn't being really honest. . . .
> Tom was drinking at the time. Carl was drinking at the time. Steve was drinking at the time. Bertha, thank God, didn't drink. She sort of took care of the rest of us. Sally was drinking at the time. Peg and Henry didn't have chemical addictions, dependencies of any sort. Thank God. Most people were either psychologically or chemically having some real problems, and then the people coming into hospitality were—many of them, most of them—emotionally, mentally unstable to begin with. So there's a lot of interpersonal deceits going on, and a lot of illusions people were living, a lot of dishonesty. And so it was very complex to try to be in community with each other when most of those with addictions were not even being honest and saying "Hey, I'm having a real problem here guys. I need some help."

A final problem with consensus was that although everyone may acquiesce to the decision, not all would be motivated to carry it out. This problem was heightened by the Worker notion of personal responsibility—that no one should be forced to act; one should act only from their own personal sense of responsibility. One Worker recalled a particularly galling incident:

> At that point cleanliness was not a priority, but we had this meeting about it, and to some degree by consensus [decided] that this Saturday would be a cleanup day. And so no one disagreed with that, according to the consensus, but many—not many, but some—sort of acquiesced to it. So now you have this day of cleanup and you've got some people who are really interested in doing it, and others who have acquiesced but undermine the energies. . . .
>
> You have this group of people who have agreed by the consensus process to do thus and so, but you have a majority of them whose heart isn't in it. Now, from hindsight, and a little more maturity, I would say that if I wanted to do it and I had two or three people with me who wanted to do it, we'd get together and do it.

Interestingly, her solution to this dilemma lay in taking personal responsibility—doing what you felt needed doing without trying to get community consensus about it.

The upshot of these dilemmas was that, although the collective decision-making process was maintained, the real power lay in the hands of the three or four ideologically committed Workers. One Worker recalls: "I'd say most of the decisions . . . go on with two or three or four people who were in the major place of responsibility in the house just really talking on the side. You know, an awful lot happened that way. But we tried. We fought against having . . . the three or four of us be the people who made the decisions." Peg recalls: "It was ridiculous because the decision making really boiled down to Henry and I. And after I left, it was more ridiculous for awhile. Because you had people who were given the impression that they really had a lot of power and say in the community, and yet they didn't."

The analysis of the problems with the consensual decision-making process by the Workers and guests themselves was remarkably similar to that advanced by social scientists, such as Rothschild-Whitt and Newman, who have addressed the problem. In essence, the explanations were of two types. The first was the "type-of-person" theory— that the problem lay in the fact that the vast majority of those involved were not amenable to collective decision making because of their lack of experience with anything but hierarchical models and because of their addictive and emotional problems. The second type of explanation lay in the inherent structural tension in what the Mustard Seed was trying to do. Consensus is impractical without some definition of the boundaries of the group. In particular, it is almost impossible to utilize consensus without some restriction of the group in terms of their commitment to both the ideology of collective decision making and the basic initial ideology of the group.

With the departure of Henry and the return of Sally in 1982, all efforts at consensual decision making were dropped. This was usually explained in terms of Sally's personality—her mistrust of meetings and her strong-willed approach to leadership, which brooked no dissension. Several people, however, also advanced the explanation that the community members had tired of the efforts at consensus and were ready for a powerful leader.

> Henry's last year was just one of total agonizing. He was usually agonizing, but it was just [a] total, burned out kind of indecision, inability to make any kind of a decision whatsoever. So the house was in one sense up for grabs because the other people who were still living there, none of whom were really feeling in a place [of] "Well, I'll take the anchor, I'll steer the ship for awhile." . . .
>
> But Sally . . . was there at the time. Because of her personality and her nature, she just fit right in and was very comfortable and people were comfortable with having her particular way of organizing responsibility.

The rapid abandonment of consensus after Henry's departure can be interpreted in terms of Kai Erikson's notion of "axes of variation" (1976, 81–82):

> Cultural forms help determine how a people will think and act and feel, but they also help determine what a people will imagine. . . . Whenever people devote a good deal of emotional energy to celebrating a certain virtue, say, or honoring a certain ideal, they are sure to give thought to its counterpart. . . . Thus the idea and its counterpart become natural partners in the cultural order of things setting up what I will call an *axis of variation.*"

People respond to change by shifting along the axis—often radically—from the culturally approved ideal to its opposite. This is, in effect, what happened at the Seed. After nearly a decade of trying to achieve a real consensual process, consensus was dropped precipitiously when Henry left and was replaced with its opposite—virtually one-person rule. At least one result of trying to inculcate collective decision making as a value among people accustomed to hierarchy was perhaps to strengthen their commitment to the hierarchical model, a commitment that had probably been quite vague to begin with.

Giving Hospitality versus Building Community

As I noted previously, the crucial question in the 1983 schism was the Catholic Worker vision of hospitality. Which path was true to the Worker ideal—to unseat Sally because she had violated certain standards, or to support Sally as a member of the Worker community who had both strengths and weaknesses? Those who did not withdraw support from Sally tended to talk about the Worker as community, while those who withdrew support emphasized the provision of hospitality. These differences point to a tension within the Catholic Worker vision that has not been clearly articulated.

The Worker sees itself as both building community and providing hospitality, with very little distinction made between the two. Sociologically, however, the two are distinct. A community requires a relatively well-defined group. New members are inducted in some manner, but, by definition, the community is not all-inclusive. There is always some line, however ambiguous, between the in-group and the out-group. Within the community, all members share some basic rights and responsibilities, although the community may lean toward either egalitarianism or hierarchy. Hospitality, on the other hand, is open to all. Whoever comes to the door is accepted as a guest. However, there is always an imbalance of power between host and guest. Thus, the hospitality model entails a power difference within the house, but no clear lines of distinction between those residing in the house and those outside; the community model entails a distinction between insiders and outsiders, but can diminish the power distinctions within the group.

The Catholic Worker has merged the notions of building an egalitarian community and providing hospitality. Guests can become members of the community, and, therefore, hosts. The Seed has merely taken this to an extreme in which the only remaining hosts are guests.

Conflicts inevitably arise from this mixing of community and hospitality because the guest/community member/host often does not thoroughly internalize the Worker philosophy of hospitality. She or he may reject certain aspects, particularly nonviolence. Nonetheless, as an "equal" community member, she or he cannot be denied the opportunity to play the role of host. Thus, by demanding that persons not be "screened" for their commitment to the ideology, the ideology places itself at risk. This was the situation in which the Seed found itself in 1983. Reactions to this situation depended on whether one's vision of the Worker tended toward building community or toward providing hospitality.

Those who supported Sally tended to speak of her role as a combination of host and guest. If she were at times derelict in her duties as host, one must never forget that in the larger scheme of the Seed, she was also guest. Moreover, she was a member of the community, a member of the family, and must be treated as such, rather than as a host. One told me, "About Sally's drinking, we try to deal with it like she's a member of the family. We don't just throw her out, we try to work with her about it." In short, although Sally had assumed the role of host, she was not to be treated solely in terms of this role.

These persons also tended to talk about the Worker in terms of building a community that included all classes, a community that gave a meaningful, responsible role to persons who were almost universally denied such a role in larger society. Thus, the House of Ammon veterans supported Sally. As noted earlier, the House of Ammon, according to Father Peters, was originally an attempt at building community rather than at hospitality. A former Worker at the Seed noted:

> [In the beginning] I was interested in making a community of people
> who weren't otherwise going to survive on the outside. Like making
> meaningful work, which in fact did happen. Even though some
> people criticize Sally and the community, I myself don't. Where are
> those people gonna go and work—just starting—work full-time at
> a job? They're never gonna get hired. They're never gonna do any
> kind of meaningful work, and it's true that no matter how much they
> fight, at least they have somebody to fight with.

The Catholic Worker, in this view, was not intended to be a community of pristine middle-class people giving charity to the poor, but rather a community in which both upper and lower classes shared together—a community that included people who weren't able to make it in "normal society" and that gave them a chance to make a genuine contribution. And this had happened at the Seed. In this view, the beauty of the house consisted in the fact that it was now run entirely by people who had come in search of shelter, most of whom would not be able to hold down a "normal" job, but who, as a community, were capable of keeping the house running. The community of individuals could perform a meaningful task, crucial to the survival of many homeless folk in the city, even though it was questionable whether more than one or two of them would have been capable of holding down a full-time job.

Thus, the importance of the Seed lay not only in what it did for guests, but in what it did for members of the community. In a very real sense, the people running the Seed were giving hospitality not only to the guests, but also to each other—"at least they have somebody to fight with."

Underlying this approach was Father Peters's vision of the Catholic Worker as a group of penitents. All Catholic Workers are repentant sinners. This is their basic unifying characteristic—regardless of whether they came initially in need of shelter or for ideological reasons. As he said, "That's the only reason I can be in the Worker. I am a penitent."

Those who opposed Sally emphasized almost exclusively her role as host. Although she had had the status of guest, once she assumed the role of host—indeed, the role of house director—she had to be evaluated in terms of her performance as host. Anything less would be a disservice to the homeless who came to the Seed for food and shelter. By assuming leadership of the Seed she had abandoned any claim to be treated as a guest. If she did not meet the requirements of the role of host, she should be removed from that role.

These persons did not, however, ignore the topic of community when talking about the history of the Seed. All talked about the Seed as a community that throughout its history had consisted primarily of the "broken." However, in discussing recent history, the emphasis was always on the notion that the standard of hospitality and nonviolence had fallen so low that the Seed was hardly Catholic Worker in its current form. As we shall see in the next chapter, however, this tension between hospitality and community building was not unique to the Mustard Seed, but was really reflected in all three of the houses.

7

Personalist Hospitality versus Professional Service

The basic elements of hospitality in the three houses I have examined were quite similar. All held meals that were free to anyone who came in the door. All gave shelter to a limited number of guests, choosing those guests by informal interviews without the "benefit" of intake forms. All distributed free clothing (and all disliked this aspect of hospitality more than any other). All three were also involved to a greater or lesser extent with less formal types of hospitality and with the other corporal Works of Mercy, especially visiting the sick, visiting the imprisoned, and burying the dead.

Nonetheless, there were profound differences. The New York City house was faced with the severe problem of trying to maintain openness to all in the face of the overwhelming number of homeless and impoverished persons in New York City. The Rochester house had become partially bureaucratized, at least to the extent that it had a board of directors. The Worcester house was now being run by formerly homeless persons.

Despite these differences, all three houses enacted a model of personalist hospitality that stood in sharp contrast to the nearly ubiquitous model of professional service that has come to dominate not only aid to the homeless but almost every long-term attempt of human beings to help one another in modern society.

In this chapter, I will argue that the Worker houses succeeded to a remarkable degree in implementing the ideology of personalism. This successful implementation was not attributable solely to their possession of such an ideology. Rather, it was a function of their project, their definition of the situation as one of hospitality. Contrasting this project with the more traditional project of rehabilitation, I will argue that hospitality permits a typification of persons that is ideal typical rather than categorical, thus allowing the guest to be apprehended in more personal fullness.

Is Catholic Worker Hospitality Personalist?

The first question that must be addressed is whether Catholic Worker hospitality is truly personalist in practice. Certainly, in the minds of Catholic Workers, hospitality is intimately connected to the notion of personalism. Most Catholic Workers would connect "personalist" with "hospitality" in much the same way as social workers would connect "professional" with "social work."

In the language of policy analysis, we might ask, "How is the philosophy of personalism implemented?" Or, in the language of ethnomethodology, "How do Catholic Workers do personalism?" This latter way of phrasing the problem may be more accurate, for personalism is far more something that Catholic Workers do than ideas they believe. Many Workers can give only rudimentary descriptions of the philosophy of personalism, yet their daily interaction with guests illuminates personalism quite eloquently.

In order to do this, we must launch a two-pronged analysis. First, we must determine how Catholic Workers currently use the term personalism (as opposed to how the term was used in the early literature of the movement). Second, we must determine what role the notion of personalism plays in the day-to-day practice of providing hospitality to the homeless.

Contemporary Usage of the Term "Personalism"

Half a century after the founding of the movement, Workers still use the term personalism in much the same ways it was used in the early days. There are several interrelated meanings given to the term by Workers who I interviewed.

The first meaning of personalism is an affirmation of the innate value of the person. Although this was the basic notion of European personalism, most Workers do not advance this as their first definition of the term. Those who do are usually the few who have read Mounier or Berdyaev.

> More important than systems and more important than government and more important than laws and more important than the police and the welfare office and more important than the institution of the Church . . . is the power or the reality or the experience of the person.

That's more important than any kind of label, any kind of permit, any kind of racial barrier, any kind of economic system.

Personalist responsibility [is] primarily a respect for each individual person and a great respect for the fact that most of us are very wounded people. We're wounded healers and we're the healing wounded.

The second, and most frequently advanced, meaning of personalism is personal responsibility. This is meant in two senses. First, one must take personal responsibility for others:

Personalism means taking a personal responsibility and not letting "human services" up to the "impersonal" care of the state. This attitude is possible in a one-to-many situation.

[It is] the acceptance of a personal responsibility for social justice, for Christian charity, for the Works of Mercy, whether they be the spiritual Works of Mercy or the corporal Works of Mercy. But it's not making a contribution to the Community Chest, and that doesn't mean that we shouldn't contribute to the Community Chest. It means that we don't satisfy our obligations as Christians by that; we have a personal responsibility to do what we can in addition to contributing money. It's a matter of doing something, of feeding a hungry person, of taking care of someone, visiting the sick, visiting those in jail.

This interpretation of personal responsibility is applied to daily routine, as when one Worker complained to another about some overflowing garbage bags, evoking the response, "If you see something that needs done, do it. Take personal responsibility." At times, Workers acknowledge sadly that personal responsibility can give way to routinization, as was reflected when a New York Worker reminisced about changes in the house schedule: "We used to have only two shifts on the house a day. When we had the soupline seven days a week, we didn't sign up anyone to be on the line. [Now one person signs up to take overall responsibility for each soupline.] People just showed up and did the work. I guess we were more responsible then." Another implication of personal responsibility is that others should be allowed the freedom to choose whether or not to take responsibility.

Personalist responsibility is the idea that . . . given their difficulties and weaknesses, if people are given a basis of love, support, and security—like in a community—and their needs are met, eventually they'll heal to a place where they'll be able to be self-reliant and able to rule their own life, rule their own fitting in. So organization and structure and all the rest of that were open, open-ended.

Using this latter meaning, some Workers argue that personalism is another, perhaps gentler, term for anarchism: "But now I've restricted my anarchism. Personalism is the word I'd use now," "Personalism . . . is the Catholic Worker word for anarchy."

A third meaning for personalism is personal, I–Thou style of interaction, treating the other as a person rather than as a social role. "I think that the most important thing we do here is chatting with people. It's important to give people a name, to know people's names because you don't have a name out there, on the streets."

A common theme in New York City and the Mustard Seed was that the increase in numbers on the soupline in recent years had hurt this aspect of personalism. The first quotation comes from a Worker in New York, the second from a dinner guest in Worcester:

> There didn't use to be so many people in the line. We used to serve maybe a hundred or a hundred and fifty. There would be more time for people to sit around. You got to know the people more. I shouldn't make it sound so utopian, but now it's just numbers. There isn't the personalism. It used to be a place to sit around.

> That's the group from Harvard. It used to be they would come in early and set up and Susan would have lots of time to come over and talk with us. We'd be sitting here at this table, and she'd come over and talk with us. But lately, it's been so hectic she has to spend all her time setting up the dinner. . . . There's a lot more [coming to the meal] than there was a year ago.

This face-to-face interaction develops personal friendship despite the fact that the social distance between host and guest is never completely erased.

> I think there always will be [a distinction between host and guest] . . . but I think there can be a movement toward more inclusion. And it's not artificially developed. I think it grows with the engagement of person to person, friend to friend, stranger to friend, . . . I think that's pretty different from a social action program. . . . You spend time with people. Someone says, "Well, I'm having a problem with the house today; it's driving me crazy." And we talk, we might go out and have a beer or sit down or go for a walk or go to some meeting together and then—I don't know—just naturally relationships go when people befriend one another. Well, I'm not denying the very varying histories of say the college student who comes to work at St. Joseph's House and the person who comes from a history of chronic alcoholism . . . but I think there's still the opportunity to engage and befriend.

A related, although rarely used, connotation depicts personalism as individualized attention in somewhat the same sense as is meant in "individualized education"—tailoring one's response to the individual needs of the other.

> It's treating each person individually according to his or her needs. . . . It's just to treat people on a human level, as an individual, and not say "all of you who come to us can only stay here for three days." Some people need less; some people need more. So if everybody's treated on the level like everybody's alike, that's not personalism. Personalism is like taking this guy and giving him the time he needs. . . .
>
> We've had a variety of systems [in the clothing room] over the last few years and all of them had their drawbacks. We tried letting five persons in for five minutes each, then we tried letting someone in as someone else left, but found that some people stayed forever. The men didn't like this system [where each is accompanied by a Worker] at first, but now they appreciate its order. Also, it's more personal; each staff member gives one person individual attention.

A final meaning of personalism is that it is a means for social change. This meaning takes two forms, one related to personal responsibility and one to personal interaction.

> Well I guess one thing that attracted me to [the Catholic Worker] since I was dealing so much with facts and figures about . . . the environment . . . and nuclear energy problems and realizing how bad things were, . . . I guess I was attracted by the personalism of the Catholic Worker. . . . Somehow that if we look for those simple things, the Works of Mercy first, that everything would work out OK somehow. And that would have effects of course on the environment too and the world in general, if we took care of each other as best we could. I guess I was attracted by that and have been working at that—trying, having a hard time with that since then.

> I believe that change comes from face-to-face interaction. Like Larry Rosebaugh. He was arrested at the Pantex plant at Amarillo and when the bishop talked to him he experienced a conversion. Larry did the same with [Bishop] Hunthausen. And it was the same with [Bishop] Gumbleton, . . . a meeting with Vietnam war resisters changed him.
>
> I'm not too interested in national elections. Dorothy never voted in a national election. She felt you make changes by personal relations. She'd vote in state and local elections where you could see the man face-to-face. It's a question of where you put your energies.

The Problem of "Doing" an Ideology

Clearly, the Worker remains as verbally committed to personalism today as it did fifty years ago. One must ask, however, whether this ideology is reflected in practice. The sociological studies that have demonstrated that ideology is often violated in practice are too numerous to count (e.g., Selznick 1966; Bell 1968). Particularly relevant is Jaber Gubrium's (1975) study of a nursing home he calls Murray Manor.

Gubrium's account of the ideology of the top staff is remarkably similar to Worker personalism:

> To top staff, good clientele care is care that is individually oriented. This means that the needs of the patient or resident are believed to come before institutional expedients. If a choice must be made between a care policy that would hinder the least able patient's well-being and having no policy at all, top staff considers it best to opt for no policy. "No client is worth sacrificing for the institution" (44).

The administrator of the home emphasized the importance of personal interaction: "I think the real essence of professionalism is to know who you're working with" (45).

Despite this "profession of faith," Gubrium observes that the top staff rarely interact with the patients and that, when they do so, the interaction is quite perfunctory.

> On most occasions (with the exception of death), when members of top staff are on the floors, they have little or nothing to do with patients and residents as persons. They do greet them; they smile; they may ask perfunctorily about their health—but all this occurs "in passing."
>
> "Passing" never takes serious account of others' wishes to talk or gestures that signify a desire to exchange personal cares. It can only afford the openings and closings of encounters. Those who pass others are "busy" people with work that "simply must be done." When it is on the floors, top staff deals with clients "individually" by passing while it gets on with its administrative work (54).

Gubrium uses the administrator as an example of how patients are dealt with "in passing":

> Patients or residents whom he encounters are dealt with in a highly stylized way. As he proceeds down a hall or as they walk by him, he offers exaggerated greetings to each one; "Hello–o, Mr. Canfield!" "Well, Margaret! Nice to see you today!" He often perfunctorily in-

quires about their health, and each inquiry is much the same as the next: "How are you, today?" "You're looking just fine, I see!" "How's that leg now?" He then signals closure with statements of approval or encouragement, depending on what those who have passed by have said: "Good! Good!" . . . "Well, everyone has his ups-and-downs. I'm sure it will improve." The intonation of these statements suggests that they are the *last* ones that will be offered (55–56).

Clearly, then, a personalist ideology does not guarantee an approach to service in which "clients" are treated as persons in actual interactions with "staff." One must ask whether the Catholic Workers do in fact interact with guests in a way that is substantially in keeping with personalist philosophy. Before doing this, however, it is necessary to interject a brief comment about the sociological approach to such matters.

The answer to the above question is almost preordained by the fact that I am doing sociological analysis. Sociology is preeminently a debunking discipline—sociological analyses are designed to show that supposedly altruistic actions are in fact based on self-interest and can be explained by social forces. An analysis that concludes that actions are motivated by altruism is suspect—either the analyst was not critical enough or she or he is biased in some way.

More importantly, perhaps, the answer to the question is preordained precisely because, as Schutz has demonstrated, social science by definition cannot treat the I–Thou relationship. One cannot describe or analyze the apprehension of the other's stream of consciousness without utilizing ideal types, and it is precisely this use of ideal types that destroys the direct apprehension of the other. Sociology is suited to deal with the typical, with the routinized, rather than with the unique, the irreplicable. In doing so it contributes to a worldview that assumes that what is real is the typical, the objective.

Thus, by the very fact that I am doing sociological analysis, I am constrained to answer the above question in the negative. And there are some excellent reasons for doing so. Nevertheless, I feel that such an answer is not entirely true to the phenomenon. Therefore, the following analysis will be somewhat more involved than the standard sociological approach to such a question.

Perhaps the best way to approach the question of how faithfully Workers put the ideology of personalism into practice in their hospitality is to address each of the three main meanings of personalism separately: the person as absolute value, personal responsibility, and personal interaction.[1]

The Person as Ultimate Value

Clearly, the person is not consistently treated as the absolute value above all others in the course of Catholic Worker hospitality. At the three houses I observed, individuals are turned away nearly every day because "the house is full," a phrase that can mean either that all the beds are used up or that the social density of the house (in terms of tension, ratio of reliable Workers to troublesome guests, etc.) is as high as is deemed tolerable. Violent individuals and individuals who bring alcohol inside are asked to leave for the good of that abstraction, "the house." There is no question, then, of a literal application of the principle in daily life. Nonetheless, there are a number of indications that the conviction that the person is of infinite worth strongly affects the practice of Worker hospitality in ways that are rarely seen in social-service agencies.

One indication is the way in which troublesome individuals are handled. A frequent practice in social agencies for handling "troublesome individuals" is to exclude them from the premises. This practice was not unknown at the houses, but it was handled quite differently. Of all the houses I have known, Unity Kitchen had the most rigid barring procedures; therefore, it might be useful to describe these briefly as a frame of reference from which to evaluate the systems in the other houses.

At the Kitchen, someone could be barred for either drinking or fighting inside the building. Drinking usually carried a penalty of being barred for a day or two. The penalties for fighting varied greatly—from a few days to a year to "indefinitely" to "for life or until the Second Coming, whichever is later"—depending on the Workers' estimation of seriousness of injury, reason for violence, "who started it," and prior violent incidents. Careful note was made of the date at which the person was allowed to return. This was written in a notebook and reported orally to every Worker. The person was then not allowed inside the building, although he or she was still given food in a brown paper sack, "to go." It should be noted, however, that the barring procedure was used far less frequently at the Kitchen than at the nearby Rescue Mission, which served essentially the same group of persons.[2] The Kitchen averaged roughly ten persons barred at any one time (including the half dozen who were "barred indefinitely"), whereas the Mission averaged seventy.

In the three houses under study, the procedures were far less systematized. The Mustard Seed was the only house that had guests who were barred "indefinitely." Two men had "earned" this status—one for repeated acts of violence (Sally had procured an order of protection on him—the only time I have ever heard of this happening at a Worker house); the other for "abusive behavior." Several persons were put out of the house while I was there, but only for that day.

In Rochester, the approach to barring was quite different from Unity Kitchen. No one was barred indefinitely, even though there were a few guests of whom the staff members were genuinely afraid. Several times while I was there, persons were barred, usually only for the day. There appeared to be no systematic effort to set a definite date for return or to communicate such a date to other Workers—barring was looked upon simply as giving everyone a "cooling-out time," and persons were allowed back in whenever the situation seemed to have "cooled out."

In New York City, there was no systematic procedure for barring. The person who was on the house might keep a list in their head of people she or he didn't want to let in, but there was no attempt to ensure that there was any correlation between these lists. The only case in which a collective decision was made to bar someone was after a young man had been involved in several violent or near-violent incidents over a two-week period. It was decided at a weekly scheduling meeting to tell him that he could not come in "for awhile," and persons who were at the meeting tried to tell those who had not been that he should not be allowed in. As it turned out, he was allowed in the very next day by someone who wasn't sure whom they had been talking about.

The point of this discussion is that barring is a very infrequently used procedure in the three houses—used far less than at Unity Kitchen, which used it far less than a comparable social agency. There was, in short, very little a guest could do that would cause the Workers to totally exclude him or her from the hospitality of the house. In New York City and the Mustard Seed, at least, even guests who had slugged or otherwise assaulted Workers were not always barred (according to reliable reports). This approach to barring indicates the effect of personalism on daily practice—the estimate of the value of the person is not great enough to totally preclude barring him or her from community at the house but is great enough to severely restrict the use of the procedure.

The concern with the ultimate value of the person is also revealed in the unspoken norm that any house rule can be violated if there is a real need. The Mustard Seed had an "absolute" limit of two-months stay for a shelter guest; yet two guests stayed for three months. In all houses, the meals were served at specific hours and regular meal guests would not be fed except during those hours; however, if a stranger appeared asking for food, she or he would be fed regardless of the hour. In New York City, no one slept on the first floor—except for the time an elderly black man staggered in drunkenly with a cut above his eye and an editor of the paper pulled a mattress down for him to spend the night. Shelter guests were not supposed to come in drunk at any of the three houses, yet we regularly watched (or even helped) them stagger up the stairs. The list of regular exceptions to the "rules" is endless. This was not carried on surreptitiously. It was generally acknowledged that any rules or norms could be broken in the interest of a person's health or welfare—that, if anything, was the ultimate norm.

Concern with the ultimate worth of the person was also reflected in the agonized deliberations that usually accompanied situations in which the good of one obviously conflicted with the good of many. The most revealing example of this comes not from the three houses but from my experience in the large dormitory at Unity Kitchen, where we were often faced with the situation of having a screaming drunk come in on a freezing night. There are certain people who simply will not sleep when drunk; rather, they will scream or talk loudly to themselves for hours on end, effectively preventing anyone in the dormitory from getting any sleep and often provoking threats from other guests. Clearly, one is faced with the welfare of one versus that of many. The fifty or so other men in the dorm face a tough day on the streets or working for day labor, and the prospect of facing it without a decent sleep is enough to arouse anyone's ire. Yet one can't throw the offender out without running the risk that he will freeze to death. He is too drunk to walk. The Kitchen is the last resort—one knows from prior experience that the Rescue Mission "detox unit" will not take him in this condition, and the police are probably the very ones who have brought him to us. I have spent many hours debating this dilemma, trying all manner of approaches to quiet the man—consoling him, pleading with him, reasoning with him, ordering him to shut up, asking him to shut up as a personal favor, threatening to throw him out—while the rest of the dorm suffered through another sleepless night.

In short, it is clear that Worker houses do not follow literally the personalist approach of valuing the individual above any abstraction or collectivity. However, the principle is embodied in certain social practices by which the tranquility of the house is sacrificed to a considerable extent rather than refuse hospitality to an individual.

Personal Responsibility

The second meaning of personalism is personal responsibility, which has two aspects—taking personal responsibility for helping others and leaving others free to accept or reject personal responsibility.

With respect to the first aspect, the very fact that Catholic Workers have abandoned middle-class environments to live in lice- and rat-infested houses in the middle of dangerous slums without pay in order to feed, shelter, and share the lives of the poor is prima facie evidence that the members of the movement have taken personal responsibility for the poor. I can think of no credible argument to the effect that this aspect of Catholic Worker ideology is compromised in practice.

The notion that hospitality is something that anyone can do (and therefore is everyone's responsibility) also flows from this aspect of personal responsibility. In practice, this has been reflected in the fact that Worker houses do not establish training programs. As one Worker told me, anyone who is young and reasonably healthy can expect to move rapidly into a position of responsibility in the house.

The question of the implementation of the second aspect of personal responsibility is more complex. Worker houses are faithful to this principle in the sense that guests are never dragooned into repaying their hospitality in any way other than by not drinking and fighting in the house. There is no formal requirement that guests help with the work in any of the houses. Nor is there a requirement that guests join in prayer. (The one exception to this is the Mustard Seed, where guests are asked to stand while the Lord's Prayer is said before each meal.) Many guests have told me that they are extremely grateful that the house does not require them to "sing for their supper" (i.e., attend religious services in exchange for a meal) as do so many of the missions (see, e.g., Wiseman 1979, 191–93).

Shelter guests at the houses are usually told that they are free to help if they wish; however, in New York City and Rochester, Workers do not ask them to perform any specific task. Although most shelter guests do help in some way, a number do not. I have never heard a guest criticized by a Worker for not helping out, although such criticisms are sometimes leveled by other guests. Most guests seem glad for the opportunity to reciprocate for their hospitality. This desire for reciprocity in the relationship, coupled with the rewards of companionship entailed in being involved in the work, the prestige of working, and the desire to "keep busy," seems to explain the guests' decisions to "help out." In the Mustard Seed, shelter guests are sometimes asked to perform specific tasks, such as washing the dishes. I saw no evidence of any penalties, however, if they refused.

Meal guests are sometimes asked to help with specific cleanup tasks in both Rochester and the Mustard Seed. In Rochester, if there are not enough servers, guests will be asked if they want to help serve or to mop the floor afterward. At the Mustard Seed, the person on the house usually asks guests to help clean tables, wash dishes, or sweep and mop the floor after the meal. Although I never asked when I was on the house, I usually found that two or three guests would volunteer their services or simply begin helping out.

In short, reciprocity is not required and usually not even expected of the guests. However, the possibility is always open for them to reciprocate for hospitality by helping in the work. The practice of the houses in this regard seems fundamentally faithful to the ideology of personal responsibility. Some of the practical difficulties in this approach are revealed in the reflection of a Worker about the situation at the Mustard Seed before Sally took over from Henry.

> There was absolutely no telling anyone what to do. And it was difficult to come in from wherever and want to help out because people would kind of just say "Well, whatever you see that needs to be done, you know, just whatever you see, you do it." And there was . . . very minimal telling anyone what to do. And so, things would get done primarily by three or four people [who] would break their ass trying to get things done because they didn't want to tell anybody else to do anything. It was very frustrating.
>
> You know, it's one thing to say "personalist responsibility" . . . and then [have a] kind of under-your-breath frustration because you're doing most of the work. Somebody else could do it if they would get up from the table, but you really can't say to them, "Hey, Luke, how would you like to do this or do that." Eventually you do work out a system of that—"Hey, I really need some help with this. Do you want to do this today?" But Henry was on the other extreme of self-reliance—people will come to a place where they will . . . find their niche and they will do what they can.

The notion that one should leave others free to accept or reject personal responsibility implies that there should be no rules. None of the three houses had any written rules. All did have two semiofficial rules—no fighting and no drinking inside the house. These rules, however, were negotiable and were not enforced in any conventional sense. I remember coming back to a soupline in New York City and being told that a fight had broken out earlier. Instead of ejecting the man who started the fight, the Workers simply moved everyone away from him so he could throw punches in the air until he tired of it and resumed his meal. I have already mentioned that in New York City, even when I pressed for a rule about what to do if a shelter guest came in drunk, I was unable to get a response other than "use your common sense."

There were generally several other unwritten rules; in Rochester, for example, guests were not supposed to smoke in the dining room, and in the Mustard Seed guests were not supposed to play radios in the dining room. These rules, however, were treated as problematic. Mustard Seed Workers explained to me at least three times that there was a rule against playing radios in the dining room because past experience had shown that once one person started bringing in a radio, several others would too, and a contest would quickly erupt to see whose radio could overpower the others. The Rochester rule was explained by the fact that the linoleum on the floor was new and that cigarette burns scarred it.

In sum, it would seem that the Worker houses are reasonably faithful to the notion of personal responsibility. Unwritten rules and norms do exist; however, enforcement is negotiable and their very existence is generally treated as problematic even by the Workers.

Personal Interactions

The final major meaning of personalism concerns quality of personal interaction. Here the analysis of whether the Worker has been faithful to the ideology is the most complex of all. Michael Harrington once wrote of his days at the Worker: "I think of Dorothy Day's impossible motto: to see Christ in every man, never to develop a scab, never to become clinical, always to react one to one, even to the most ugly and deformed of people. I couldn't do it at the *Catholic Worker*, at least not for long; I can't do it now" (1977, 86).

Catholic Workers live in constant face-to-face contact with their guests. Many sleep in the same rooms with persons off the street. They use the same bathrooms. They do not have the power to structure their interaction with guests as the director of Murray Manor does—eventually they'll be waiting in line for the bathroom or for a meal together. This ensures I–Thou interaction in at least the superficial sense of face-to-face contact.

But does it ensure I–Thou contact in the deeper sense intended by

Martin Buber, in which two persons address each other as whole persons, attending directly to the other? Committed Catholic Workers make an enormous effort to address guests as whole persons, even when the guest's language is largely unintelligible. Nonetheless, this effort is not always successful, hampered as it is by social, intellectual, and temporal barriers.

One particularly perceptive guest, the former electrical engineer at the New York City house, argued that there was no real I–Thou contact between host and guest. Due to the social and intellectual distance between the two, the Workers often appeared to be listening intently to the guests' words, but their minds were elsewhere.

> This place is poison to me. It's lukewarm. And you know what the Bible says about lukewarm. . . . I see very little of what I'd perceived to be the spirit of Dorothy Day here. . . . Half-heartedness—that's the problem here. Being on a different, more spiritual plane. I did the same thing myself with that lady there [an elderly friend of the house]. She was telling me her life story and I was elsewhere, hearing but not hearing.

His critique was accurate, and yet it was unfair. He was looking for the pure I–Thou interaction and no human interaction could stand before his merciless gaze, as a few of his other statements indicate.

> You meet a man on the street. He extends his hand. How you respond changes the world. And how he responds shapes his life. . . . You can't apply the Golden Rule in this city. The most people do is to ignore each other. I ignore you and you ignore me. There are too many distractions, too much going on here. But then I remember Jesus and the Golden Rule.

Perhaps it is the job of the sociologist to have such a merciless gaze—to conclude that the attempts to achieve personal relations between hosts and guests at the Catholic Worker are as illusory as the attempts at Murray Manor because the pure I–Thou relationship was rarely if ever achieved. I think, however, that this is an unrealistic position. One cannot simply contrast I–Thou with I–It relations and conclude that all relations are impersonal because none are truly personal. Rather, we must, with Simmel (1950, 317–29), view interactions in terms of the degree to which reciprocal knowledge of the other is achieved.

Due to the extreme difficulty in ascertaining whether an interaction is I–Thou or not, it seems best to begin with an investigation of my own interactions with guests. There were numerous times when I did attempt to encounter the guest as a whole person, to empathize, to understand "the radical other." This occurred most frequently when the guest was attempting to articulate sorrow or rage or even joy.

To generalize from my own experience, I would say that one can most fully address the other as person in his or her suffering. It is in sharing the other's sorrow and pain that one truly grasps the other as person. It is in times of sorrow that the other most fully opens himself or herself to you, and it is in times of sorrow that I become most receptive to the complexities and uniqueness of the other. As events "normalize," the relationship also normalizes, becoming more superficial, more concerned with the trivialities of everyday living than with grasping the other at his or her core, although always retaining the memory that that had happened once and could happen again.

If the Catholic Worker house does encourage true personal interaction, it is at least in part because Workers are in a position where people come to them in their sorrow, in their distress, and because the project of hospitality allows Workers to address this distress without the objectifying screen of routine questions to be asked, social security numbers to be discovered, and bureaucratic procedures to be followed.

In all honesty, however, there were many interactions in which I made no attempt to address the other in their full personhood, even when they were begging me to do so. I find it extremely difficult to try to grasp the other in his or her fullness when I can make no sense out of what is being said. It is also quite difficult, even if the sentences are individually coherent, when I have learned from past experience to expect no correlation between this person's accounts and historical reality—or when the person is inebriated. In such situations, I often retain the form of I–Thou interaction—appearing to be listening intently—without truly trying to understand what is being said.

At other times, the reason for my failure to accept the other as a complete person lay within myself or within my definition of the situation—I was tired or distraught, or I felt other responsibilities to be more pressing. I remember responding very coldly to a new guest, who I thought was particularly demanding, until he observed, "You aren't very hospitable here."

My observations suggest that most Workers had similar approaches to interactions. Many were far more open than myself to addressing the guest as a whole person, far less reluctant to place limits on the extent of their interaction. Some were, perhaps, less open than myself. It is important to note, however, that it is common to see a Worker and guest seated together at a table or in a corner, engaged in a lengthy and apparently intense conversation, usually initiated by the guest and concerning the guest's needs or problems. It is also important to note that Workers did not, in Goffman's terms, utilize the "props" that traditionally give one "the upper hand" (e.g., uniforms, desks, offices).

One point that particularly struck me was the honesty of many Workers in their relations with guests. One evening I was sitting downstairs at the New York City house with an experienced Worker who was "on the house." A quite inebriated man who lived down the street came in. Susan got him some tea and he sat down with us, talking incessantly. He kept repeating that he wanted to help us out at the soupline that Friday. I know that I would have told him, "Sure, that's great," just to get rid of him, assuming that in his state he'd never remember it anyway. Susan, however, meticulously refrained from giving him any indication that he could help, even though this meant spending an extra fifteen minutes getting him out the door after he had finished his tea. In our conversation afterward she made it clear that she felt it to be extremely important never to mislead someone, no matter how drunk or crazy they might seem.

Other observer–participants have concluded that the Worker provides an unusual setting for personal interaction. A Catholic missionary who lived at the New York City house for four days a week for a period of several months prior to returning to his work in South America gave a sermon at his "farewell" Mass in which he said in part:

> As a priest, I was supposed to be in the people business. But it wasn't until the Worker that I realized I wasn't dealing with people but with abstractions—with communities, with organizations, but not with people. Here, in the guys who come to the soupline, you deal with people. So I thank first those who are outside the house, those who come in for the soupline. And secondly I thank those in the house for what they have taught me. And here I don't make a distinction between Workers and guests or whatever. Everyone here has taught me things.

In looking at the question of personal interaction between guests and hosts, it seems fruitful to turn to two more limited questions: do "genuine friendships" develop between Workers and guests? and do Workers make efforts to include guests in non–house-related aspects of their lives? Both questions are limited versions of the general question of whether guests are treated as whole persons.

Norman Lifton, a sociologist who conducted participant observation at the New York City house during the 1970s, concluded that true Worker–guest friendships did not occur.

> Generally when Workers speak of the satisfactions they have gained from their interactions with clients, they refer to getting to know them or developing a friendship, though they are not entirely clear what that means to them. More often than not–on the basis of field observations–this is not a "friendship" of equals. It is, rather, caring for someone who is in a more unfortunate or subservient position or feeling sorry for that person. It is roughly equivalent to the sympathy or empathy felt by someone in the "helping" role toward someone in the "sick" role. . . . For there is a disparity in status, and this brings about role distance. In using a word such as "friendship," Catholic Workers may be referring to an ability to banter with them, even feel affection; but it must be remembered that, as caretakers, they wield considerable power over their clients, to the extent of being able to evict them if they become troublesome. Workers reported that there were rewards in being able to communicate with clients or in developing a mutual liking. Again, this is not equivalent to friendship or a relationship of equals. The system of interactional rules involved in such cases is more likely based on relationships characteristic of paternalism (1981, 406–7).

On the basis of my somewhat more extensive experience with the movement, both in terms of time spent and number of houses, I would say that Lifton's conclusions are essentially accurate but also simplistic. My own experience has taught me that the difference in status, education, and power between myself and guests presents an almost insuperable barrier in developing "true friendship."

A particularly vivid example concerns Don, who lived in a small hospitality house in Syracuse with my wife and myself for over a year. I had known Don for some years before that and had an easy-going relationship with him. He was friendly, but not well educated, and a bit slow to pick up on things. While living with him I felt that we had a good relationship, a friendship even, until one day when he came home drunk. He began to verbally "lay into" me, dredging out feelings that he had concealed while sober. He told me how resentful he was that when he and I got together with friends, I would engage in "that goddamn college talk," leaving him out of the conversation. (We didn't discuss Husserl or Parsons, mind you; a conversation about the daily news would often be beyond Don's grasp.) Until that day I had not realized the extent of the cultural difference between us—how easily I could leave him out of the conversation just by talking about issues that involved any abstraction. By not being alert to this problem and not making enough effort to keep conversation at a level in which Don could participate, I had undermined the possibility of real friendship.

Nonetheless, I feel that Lifton's statement is too narrow to encompass the whole movement. His observations about status differences are quite accurate. However, the movement makes some systematic efforts to counter the differences in power, in ways that make genuine friendship possible. At the Mustard Seed, for example, the former guest, Sally, was able to accumulate enough power to withstand an attempt by the "College Joes" to unseat her as house director. The unfortunate schism at that house provides direct evidence that power is not a commodity from which guests are entirely excluded. As another example, the status of "friend of the house" gives the guest a certain amount of power, in the form of vested rights that cannot be legitimately violated by a single Worker. Friends of the house may be thrown out, but not by one Worker. The entire house would have to conclude that the person should be excluded. Friends of the house have little or no power in the sense of the ability to enforce their will on house practices, but they do have power in the sense of the ability to protect themselves and their vested rights in the house.

More directly, I would say that genuine friendships between Workers and guests, although rare, have developed. They may not be life-long friendships; however, these are in general becoming rare in our "temporary society." At the Mustard Seed, I think it safe to say that a genuine friendship developed between Sally (when she was a guest) and Peg and Henry. Repeatedly in her interviews, Sally told me, "Peg and Henry loved me." The tone and demeanor that accompanied this statement indicated that this belief was crucial to her current self-image. It is also important to note that occasional marriages between Workers and guests have occurred.

Friendship, however, is something that can be proven only over time, and so the most appropriate house for which I can evaluate whether friendships developed is not one of the three in this study, but rather the Syracuse community in which I spent seven years. There, genuine, "deep" friendships between Workers and guests were rare, but they did occur.

In sum, deep mutual friendship between Workers and guests is not the norm. However, the social structure of the Worker does not preclude such friendships. Indeed, it may be one of the few structures in America that facilitates friendships between people of such different social backgrounds.

Workers frequently make efforts to include guests in various aspects of their lives—particularly by inviting guests to go to parties, movies, or even their weddings. Once a college student who had volunteered at the Rochester house for the summer invited us to her parents' place for dinner. We invited Johnny, an alcoholic who was on the wagon and living at the house, to come along. Although he was clearly ill at ease eating dinner in an upper-middle-class suburban home, he did feel good at being included as part of the group. Similarly, when I returned to Rochester for John's wedding, Mike was there, decked out in a suit, happy to see even me, his old nemesis. At the Mustard Seed, Henry invited Stewart, an elderly alcoholic member of the community, to travel across country with him for several months, an experience that Stewart constantly talked about. In New York City, a resident of the house was included in an urban homesteading venture with several of the Workers.

Efforts to include guests are not always rewarding, as the following tale from the early days of the Mustard Seed illustrates. One hot summer day, Peg and Sally were going swimming at the house of Jim, a well-to-do friend who had told them they could use the pool anytime as long as they didn't bother anyone. As they were getting ready to leave the Seed, up walked Vera, a middle-aged woman who often came to the meal. Feeling guilty, Peg told her they were going swimming. Vera pleaded to come, saying all she wanted to do was sit by a tree. Peg relented and invited her to come. In her words:

> To make a long story short, before we left . . . she got herself into the swimming pool. She had borrowed from the daughter the kid's father's pajamas to swim with. She went into the house, which we never did, where Jim was trying to write a book. . . . She helped herself to a peanut butter sandwich. She borrowed his slippers to walk out with. She, well naturally, disturbed him talking and tearing about. And finally [she] dropped all her clothes in the middle of the bathroom and went swimming.

They had some explaining to do before they were invited again.

Clearly, efforts were made to escape a "professional" delineation of areas in which interaction with the "client" can occur. One Worker noted the strain this effort could involve, particularly in the early days of a house before norms about involving guests in outside activities have evolved.

> We had to do a lot of kind of figuring out who we were. . . . We [went] through a whole thing of do you have any social life or do you bring along [the guests], because we would get invited to parties. Henry was guilty of this more than the rest of us but you feel like "well, shit, we all live together," and so we used to bring the Mustard Seed people everywhere we went. And it didn't always work out so hot. And it takes a long time until you kind of decide for yourself, "well I'm gonna do this and I'm not gonna do that." And "I'm going here this afternoon and I'm not taking anybody with me." Well, that's when you first start out. All of that is virgin territory, so to speak.

The special role of part-time volunteers should be mentioned. Although most part-time volunteers are satisfied with rather superficial contact with the guests (e.g., the majority of the Mustard Seed food volunteers who never venture beyond the serving counter into the dining room), there are volunteers at each house who establish intensely personal relationships with a few of the guests. These relationships often come to mean quite a bit to the guests precisely because, having a home life outside the skid-row area, these volunteers can invite the guest into a new social circle, an act of trust that Workers often cannot perform since their primary social circle is the Worker house. In addition, part-time volunteers usually do not have as much power over guests as do full-time Workers. Thus, this barrier to friendship is diminished. In short, the part-time volunteers are sometimes in a position to establish deeper friendships with guests than are many of the Workers. In the Syracuse community, the deepest, longest Worker-guest friendship I know of has been between a part-time volunteer and a guest.

In sum, Catholic Worker hospitality does not eliminate the social, intellectual, and political distance between middle-class Workers and homeless guests. There is, however, evidence that Workers do address guests as persons to a remarkable extent given these social, educational, and power differences.

Typification of Persons in Social-Service Agencies

A universal characteristic of social-service agencies is that they categorize persons. This is due not only to the fact that they are bureaucracies, which are notoriously poor at dealing with ideal-typical schemes, but also because of their functions. All social-service agencies perform two functions: people processing and rehabilitation. The former concerns conferring public statuses on people, and the latter concerns changing the behavior of people (Hasenfeld 1977, 60). The people-processing function entails categorization of clients—the statuses conferred are discrete entities. In Jeffrey Prottas's (1979) terminology, citizens must be transformed into clients—placed into a category—so that they can be matched to one or more of the services provided by the agency. Thus, by the nature of their functions, all social-service agencies develop a categorization scheme for their clients.

> To provide service to a citizen a bureaucracy must first reduce that citizen and that citizen's demands into a simple and patterned package of processible attributes. Bureaucracies cannot deal with the complexities and ambiguities that go into a complete human being; rather they must categorize a person in terms of a limited subset of attributes or characteristics. Only in this way can a person be sufficiently simplified to be processed by a bureaucracy (Prottas 1979, 85).

The categorization of clients is performed by what have been called "street-level bureaucrats," the members of the bureaucracy who deal directly with the clients on a face-to-face basis (e.g., doctors, nurses, social workers, emergency-room clerks, police, teachers). According to Prottas and Lipsky, a major function of such organizational roles is to transform the person into a category usable by the agency for determining the benefits for which the client is eligible (although in many cases the street-level bureaucrats may also have the function of providing the benefit or service themselves). "The agency for which the bureaucrat works provides a 'menu' of categories; it is for the street-level bureaucrat to distribute clients among them. Each category has two interrelated defining elements: the eligibility rules and the benefit rules" (Prottas 1979, 123).

The menu of categories that the agency provides reflects the agency's "theory of office" (Kelly 1984, 3–4) and thus the agency's interests as well as ideology.

> Since the typologies which agents use are provided by the organizations within which they work, the typologies are heavily influenced by the organization. In particular, typologies and their use reflect and are sensitive to organizational goals and functions. . . . They also reflect the goals and viewpoints of the agents themselves (Drass and Spencer 1987).

Rubington and Weinberg argue that these theories and categories have important implications for how the client is treated:

> Not only do these theories help in categorizing the people who have come to the official attention of the agency but they also help in specifying which agents should do what and when, how, and why such action should be taken in the course of the client's career in the agency. . . . In effect, an etiquette of agency-client relations obtains. And clients often do not receive services until their behavior corresponds with the category into which the agents have assigned them (1987, 102).

Prottas argues that the person does not exist for the agency until she or he has been transformed into a processable client. One illustration he used for this point is particularly vivid. An alcoholic was brought into an emergency room with a head injury.

> For some reason the police then left. The clerk . . . never signed him in. Three minutes after the police left the client was without a bureaucratic identity . . . [but] his arrival mode entitled him to be where he was. He was therefore not an interloper and could not be asked to leave. . . . In ten minutes he was up and pushing his way out through the emergency doors. He was at all times in full view of every passing doctor and nurse. At this point I decided to intervene and so told a doctor that a patient was escaping. He said he was in pediatrics and hence it wasn't his patient; a second doctor said he wasn't his patient either and so the client staggered into the street unimpeded. . . . So because of the conflicting clues of his location, arrival mode, and appearance, he was without a category and hence "untreatable." . . . A client was unprocessable, even unrecognizable, because no street-level bureaucrat had translated his obvious but complex human characteristics into usable organizational ones (Prottas 1979, 82).

Even when they are imposed properly, these categorization schemes can have deleterious effects in and of themselves, as demonstrated by Michael Lipsky.

> People come to street-level bureaucracies as unique individuals with different life experiences, personalities, and current circumstances. In their encounters with bureaucracies they are transformed into clients, identifiably located in a very small number of categories, treated as if, and treating themselves as if, they fit standardized definitions of units consigned to specific bureaucratic slots. The processing of *people* into *clients,* assigning them to categories for treatment by bureaucrats, and treating them in terms of those categories, is a social process. Client

characteristics do not exist outside of the process that gives rise to them. An important part of this process is the way people learn to treat themselves as if they were categorical entities (1980, 59).

Interactions with clients are ordinarily structured so that street-level bureaucrats control their content, timing, and pace. . . . In a study of two legal services offices the following were observed. Interviews are structured by routines developed to expedite the collection of information. Lawyers first ask clients questions designed to complete a general intake form, then ask questions designed to complete another, more detailed form. . . . The dominance of the forms restricts the search process to those categories anticipated by the format. . . . Clients are observed to make repeated efforts to tell their stories in their own ways, consistent with a nondirective information search process. However, lawyers continually talk them down by insisting on conducting the interview according to the established format. . . .
　　Thus we have the ingredients for another self-fulfilling prophecy. In the expectation that most clients will fall into previously defined categories, bureaucracies follow search procedures based on that expectation. Having constricted the kinds of information they receive, street-level bureaucracies find confimation that, indeed, clients tend to fall into certain well-defined categories (1980, 120–22).

Numerous studies of individual agencies lend support to Lipsky's analysis of the depersonalizing effects of agency procedures. Rosenhan, in his study of twelve mental hospitals into which he had infiltrated "pseudopatient" observers, graphically describes the depersonalization both witnessed and experienced by the observers.

At times, depersonalization reached such proportions that pseudo-patients had the sense that they were invisible, or at least unworthy of account. . . . On the ward, attendants delivered verbal and occasional physical abuse to patients in the presence of other observing patients, some of whom (the pseudopatients) were writing it all down. Abusive behavior terminated quite abruptly, however, when other staff members were known to be coming. Staff are credible witnesses. Patients are not (1975, 68; see also Goffman [1961]; Wiseman [1970]).

The contrast between Lipsky's analysis of street-level bureaucracies and my analysis of the Catholic Worker could not be more striking. The Worker has no categorization scheme, thus leaving the individual Workers free to interact with the client without a standardized scheme into which to fit him or her. The Worker has no intake forms. In the vast majority of instances I have seen, guests tell their story their own way. They are interrupted occasionally by questions from the Worker; however, it is often the guest who structures the interaction.

However, the effect of categorization schemes on the behavior of street-level bureaucrats is not as simple as would appear from the above analysis. Street-level bureaucrats do not simply fit clients into the categories provided by the agency using the rules prescribed by the agency. According to Prottas, this is so for two reasons. First, the rules provided by the agency are too numerous, too complex, and often too contradictory to be followed legalistically. (Indeed, any attempt to do so would completely disrupt the functioning of the agency.) Second,

> The formal client categories are inadequate for the street-level bureaucrat. Those categories define the way the organization distributes its financial resources . . . and the way the time and skills of its employees will be used. But the time and energy of the street-level bureaucrat is but one part of what the agency distributes and not necessarily the most important; for the street-level bureaucrat, however, it *is* the most important. It follows that the criteria on which street-level bureaucrats evaluate clients differ from that of the agency (Prottas 1979, 133).

Sudnow's famous study of "normal crimes," for example, found that DA's did not simply utilize the bureaucratic categories for crimes given them by statute. Rather, they created ideal types of crimes utilizing not only information about the act performed but also about the client's characteristics and other factors irrelevant to the official definition. This study might suggest that the restrictive character of categories has been overstated in my discussion. However, it should be noted that the subjects in question then utilized their ideal-typical "normal crimes" to determine how to categorize the accused according to the official scheme. Thus, ideal-typical notions came into play but served simply to alter the category into which a person was placed.

Similarly, Lang (1981) and Peyrot (1982) both found that screening workers in mental-health agencies typed prospective clients as suitable or unsuitable for treatment based not only on diagnostic categories, but on their perception of the client's cooperativeness and willingness to "accept responsibility."

Scheff proposed a theoretical scheme that delineates three stages in how agency personnel use diagnostic categories:

In the beginning, a new staff member would have only theory and little experience to guide him and would find that his handling of clients is time-consuming and that his diagnoses tend to be inaccurate. As he learns the conceptual packages, he becomes more proficient and more rapid in his work, so that effectiveness increases. The crucial point comes after the time in which he has mastered the diagnostic packages, when the question becomes, is his perceptiveness of client situations and placement opportunities going to remain at his stereotypic level . . . or is he going to go on to begin to use these stereotypes as hypotheses for guiding further investigation on his part (1965, 144)?

Scheff, then, says that categorization schemes can become the basis for more thorough understanding of the client. The extent to which this actually happens, however, remains to be seen.

Finally, Roth, in a study of moral attributions in a hospital emergency room, demonstrates that ideal-typical schemes do exist in bureaucratic services. Specifically, emergency-room personnel make moral as well as physical evaluations of patients. Although Roth talks of these moral evaluations in terms of categories, his description of the actual process of typification seems more in line with ideal typification, as shown in the case of the drunk, a particularly apt example for comparison with the Catholic Worker:

Take, for example, patients who are labeled as drunks. They are more consistently treated as undeserving than any other category of patient. They are frequently handled as if they were baggage when they are brought in by police; those with lacerations are often roughly treated by physicians; they are usually treated only for drunkenness and obvious surgical repair without being examined for other pathology; no one believes their stories; their statements are ridiculed; they are treated in an abusive or jocular manner; they are ignored for long periods of time. . . . Emergency-ward personnel frequently comment on how they hate to take care of drunks. . . . But how do we know he is drunk? By the way he is treated (1977, 503).

Thus, the existence of an organizational scheme for categorizing clients does not preclude the development of subsidiary, informal schemes of typification that come to be used by service providers in their day-to-day operation. This is because, as noted by both Prottas (1979) and Drass and Spencer (1987), the typification schemes actually used also reflect the agents' own interests.

Although the agency's categorization scheme is not the sole determinant of how street-level bureaucrats typify their clients, its importance should not be overlooked for two reasons. First, whatever the unsanctioned criteria the street-level bureaucrats use for categorizing clients, they must ultimately place them into one of the categories provided by the agency. Second, the official categorization scheme always has some effect on the thinking of employees, as revealed in a study by Jehenson of a psychiatric hospital. He noted that psychiatrists even applied their psychiatric scheme to their colleagues (1973, 232–43).

It seems safe to assume that all social-service agencies have moral ideal-typification schemes for clients that exist alongside the official categorization schemes. This does not, I think, change the basic character of the argument for the effect of categorization schemes on interaction between worker and client.

In sum, sociological studies of professional social-service agencies indicate that the ubiquitous presence of a system of categorization of clients decreases the possibility of worker–client interactions in which the client is treated as a whole person.[3] Many of these studies (e.g., Roth 1977; Prottas 1979) have singled out homeless alcoholics—the "prototypical" Catholic Worker guests—as the group that is most dehumanized both by the formal categorization schemes and by the informal moral typologies utilized by agency workers. In a later section, I will argue that the Catholic Worker model of personalist hospitality appears to have overcome this problem to some degree, in part at least because its project of hospitality excludes categorization schemes in favor of ideal-typical ones. The Worker has adopted some very specific strategies aimed at maximizing the likelihood of personal interactions between hosts and guests. Categories are avoided, as are case records and technical jargon for describing guests. This leads to a use of biographical ideal types for guests. Past history is not sought out, so that the biographical ideal types will be based primarily on the results of face-to-face interaction with guests. All of these strategies run counter to the practices of professional social agencies.

In order to compare in a more exact manner the practice of Catholic Worker houses with the rehabilitation approach of street-level bureaucracy described above, however, it is necessary to consider the rather esoteric phenomenological sociology of Alfred Schutz.[4] I will summarize relevant aspects of Schutz's theory, add some concepts that I feel extend the theory, and then show how it can be applied to compare hospitality and rehabilitation.

The Phenomenology of Typification

For Schutz, the world we perceive is not simply "what's out there." Rather, what we perceive is affected by what is relevant to us. What is relevant is largely determined by our project—by what we intend to do.[5]

Schutz argues that we perceive everything in terms of typifications, that is, we assign everything we see to a type:

> The factual world of our experience . . . is experienced from the outset as a typical one. Objects are experienced as trees, animals, and the like, and more specifically as oaks, firs, maples, or rattlesnakes, sparrows, dogs. . . . If we see a dog, that is, if we recognize an object as being an animal and more precisely as a dog, we anticipate a certain behavior on the part of this dog, a typical (not individual) way of eating, of running, of playing, of jumping, and so on (Schutz 1970, 116).

Thus, in typifying, we select out certain characteristics on the basis of their relevance for whatever project we have in mind and decide that those are "the same as" characteristics of other objects of the same type. It is important to note that how we typify something is affected by our project—what we plan to do—as well as by the thing itself. Thus, if I want to build something, I would type a hammer as a tool, but if I wanted to hit someone, I might type that same hammer as a weapon.

The most common mechanism for typification is language. By naming something, we place it into a type. Our tendency to typify objects extends to human beings; here, however, because we are encountering other streams of consciousness, the process becomes more complex. It becomes crucial whether or not we are in face-to-face contact with the other person.

Schutz places the distinction between face-to-face and more abstract interactions at the center of his analysis of social relations. He distinguishes two primary types of social relations: the We-relation and the They-relation. The We-relation occurs when two persons grasp each other in their fullness as persons and, for some period of time, "grow old together" by sharing the same experiences in face-to-face interaction.[6]

> As I watch you, I shall see that you are oriented to me, that you are seeking the subjective meaning of my words, my actions, and what I have in mind insofar as you are concerned. And I will in turn take

account of the fact that you are thus oriented to me, and this will influence both my intentions with respect to you and how I act toward you. This again you will see, I will see that you have seen it, and so on. This interlocking of glances, this thousand-faceted mirroring of each other, is one of the unique characteristics of the face to face situation. We may say that it is a constitutive characteristic of this particular social relationship (Schutz 1967, 170).

The We-relation exists only as long as each person remains fully attuned to the consciousness of the other. As soon as one steps back and reflects on the other (i.e., typifies the other), the relation is broken.

While I am directly experiencing you and talking with you, the whole complicated substructure of my own interpretation of you escapes my attention. . . . However, I can at any given time change all this and bring these acts within the focus of my gaze. For instance, I may ask, "Have I understood you correctly?" . . . The moment I raise such questions, I have abandoned my simple and direct awareness of the other person, my immediate grasp of him in all his subjective particularity. . . . I no longer experience my fellow man in the sense of sharing his life with him; instead I "think about him." . . . The more I reflect the more my partner becomes transformed into a mere object of thought (Schutz 1967, 140–41, 167).

The We-relation, then, exists only as a limiting concept (Schutz 1967, 164). We cannot interact even face-to-face with another without in some way typifying him or her (e.g., typifying as a him or a her). Nonetheless, orientations toward other persons exist along a continuum of anonymity. Some utilize the fullness of being of the other to a greater extent than others.

At the other extreme stands the They-relation, which occurs when two persons relate to each other, not as conscious persons, but as types; that is, when each constructs the other as a social type and interacts on the basis of his or her assumptions about that type of person. All interactions that are not face-to-face are They-relations, even if they occur between persons who have known each other for years. This is because it is only in the face-to-face situation that one can immediately grasp the other's consciousness, that one can experience the other's stream of consciousness. Once the other leaves one's visual field, one can think of him or her only as a type constructed from one's past experiences with him or her. One no longer experiences the person as she or he actually is, but as he or she was in the past.

The We-relation is the primary social realm, on which all sociality is based. For one can construct types of persons with whom one is not directly interacting only by drawing on one's experiences from prior face-to-face interactions (either with that person or with other persons) and generalizing these experiences into a type.

Schutz and Luckmann distinguish two basic kinds of types of persons: personal types and functionary types (Schutz and Luckmann 1970, 82).[7]

A personal type is a mental model, if you will, of an individual person, created by generalizing from experiences you have had with that person (or tales you have been told about him or her). I have such a model, for instance, of my friend Joe—a simplified image of how he acts in certain situations, of his views, and so on. I utilize this model to think of Joe when I am not in face-to-face interaction with him. Thus, if I hear a tale about him I can say, "Yes, I can see Joe doing that," meaning that the action fits my image of Joe, or "I can't believe he'd do a thing like that," when the action doesn't fit my image of him.

Functionary types, on the other hand, are types created by generalizing from the actions of several persons. A functionary type is a model of "the type of person who would do such a thing." It is closely related to the traditional sociological notion of social role (the behavior we expect of someone in a given status). Examples of functionary types would include post-office worker, alcoholic, sociologist, and bag lady. As Schutz and Luckmann note, "In contrast to the personal, the functionary type is relatively anonymous" (1970, 82).

In short, a personal type is created by generalizing from past actions of a person to establish how the person usually acts in certain situations. A functionary type is created by generalizing from a number of persons who share a characteristic to establish how a person who has that characteristic usually acts in certain situations.[8] Personal types, then, are longitudinal, requiring familiarity with the personal history of an individual. Functionary types are cross-sectional, requiring familiarity (either direct or indirect) with a number of persons who share a characteristic or perform a certain type of action. For example, if you have seen your friend Joe repeatedly respond to racial epithets by decking the person who said them, you might create a personal type: "Joe is a person who tends to punch out bigots." On the other hand, if you are told that Donna is an alcoholic, you might refuse to give her a drink because you apply to her the functionary type: "Alcoholics should never take the first drink."

Other things equal, the more face-to-face experience one has with a person the more concrete is one's type of the person (i.e., the more it is based on the actual experience of the person). The more a type is based on general concepts, the more anonymous it is. Thus, for example, the postal worker who handles the letter I mailed today is a rather anonymous type to me, constructed out of general knowledge of the functions of postal workers. "My friend Joe," however, is a far more concrete type, based primarily on my experiences with him rather than my general knowledge of the social roles he may play. This continuum between concrete and anonymous types is of crucial importance, for, as Shutz observes:

> The more anonymous my partner, the less direct and personal the relationship and the more conceptualized must my dealings with him be. And the more I conceptualize my partner, the less can I regard him as a free agent. When I am face to face with someone, I immediately grasp him as a spontaneous and freely acting being: His future action is as yet open and undecided, and I can only hazard a guess as to what he is going to do. The *ideal type,* on the other hand, is, when rightly conceived, without any freedom; he cannot transcend his type without ceasing to be a contemporary and becoming a consociate of mine (1967, 219–20).

According to Schutz's analysis, then, we form ideal types of every person with whom we have interacted, since there is no one with whom we are in continous face-to-face interaction. There are, however, important differences in the anonymity of the ideal types we construct. Those that are most anonymous, most conceptual, are least able to represent the person as a free agent, as a thou. For, as Schutz implies but does not address explicitly, the type we form of a person affects our face-to-face interaction with her or him. An implication of Schutz's analysis seems to be that the more conceptualized the ideal type one applies to a person, the more difficult it is to engage in a thou relation with that person, precisely because our typifications affect face-to-face interaction.[9]

There is, I believe, another important distinction we can make with respect to typologies of other persons. This is the distinction between categories and ideal types, where by categories I mean discrete types—those that have clear-cut rules for inclusion and are mutually exclusive (i.e., one cannot belong to both of two mutually exclusive categories—one cannot be a man and a woman). Ideal types, on the other hand, are models that are useful for conceptualizing the similarities and differences among people but that are not discrete.[10]

Examples of categories of persons would include male, female, client, staff, military, civilian. Examples of ideal types would include genius, above-average intelligence, rich, poor, pretty, homely. The distinction is really the degree of ambiguity that we permit in our typifications: categories permit no ambiguity, while ideal types permit a considerable amount of it.

Returning to Schutz's notions, it is easy to see that a personal type must be an ideal type. One knows from experience that the model one has created of an individual is a simplification—that the person is not totally subsumed in the model but can act in ways quite divergent from it. Functionary types, on the other hand, can be either ideal types or categorizations. Post-office employee, for instance, is a category—one is either employed by the post office or one isn't. Schizophrenic is an ideal type (although some would claim that the "new, improved" DSM-III [the Diagnostic and Statistical Manual of the APA] has magically transformed it into a category by providing "clear-cut" diagnostic rules.[11])

Thus, for Schutz, we inevitably typify persons with whom we interact (as well as persons we imagine or hear about). However, there are differences in the anonymity of the types that we use. Generally speaking, the least anonymous types are personal types, based on our historical encounters with another. These are followed by functionary ideal types and, finally, by categories. The more anonymous the type we apply to the person, the further we are from being able to grasp that person in his or her fullness. Furthermore, Schutz has made it clear that the typifications we employ are affected by our project—what we conceive of ourselves as wanting to do (or, equivalently, our definition of the situation).

Applying this theory to the models of professional rehabilitation and personalist hospitality leads me to the following analysis. The project of rehabilitation necessitates the categorization of persons so that they can be matched with treatments or other benefits. This hinders, indeed almost precludes, the establishment of a We-relation between staff and client. Indeed, as soon as a street-level bureaucrat begins to ask the standard questions on an intake form (e.g., "What is your social-security number?"), she or he has stepped back from the thou orientation in order to classify the person. The interviewer is essentially incapable of grasping the other in his or her fullness since she or he is constantly engaged in stepping back and categorizing rather than attending to the other's stream of consciousness.

The project of hospitality, on the other hand, does not demand categorization, and hence allows the host to utilize personal types and functionary ideal types to think about guests. This allows the host to come close to the We-relation with the guest. Indeed, as Nouwen (1975) argues, one of the primary characteristics of the host role is openness to the guest.

Thus, I would argue that it is the project of hospitality, rather than the ideology of personalism per se, that enables Catholic Workers to more closely approximate the We-relation than is common in professional service agencies. It is the project, or definition of the situation, that plays a more important role than ideology in influencing the quality of interaction among persons. This point is perhaps best illustrated by an encounter I had while working at Unity Kitchen. I will describe it as I recorded it a few years after the fact:

> She appeared one winter afternoon at the 11:30 lunch line, looking like a middle-class housewife of about forty, except that she had no coat and was wearing sandals. I remember her going up to some of the guys who were standing there drunk and saying, "Praise God, brothers." When lunch was over she stayed behind. I asked her if I could help her. She told me she had come from the Hotel Syracuse, that God had told her to walk in this direction and she would get the help she needed. She needed a place to stay. I got her shoes and a coat, and then had to convince her not to give them away according to the biblical mandate.
>
> I drove her to the Salvation Army Women's Shelter, where we waited for an interviewer. . . . After awhile we went in to a small office where a young woman interviewed us. She asked Sister Allen, "What's your name?" "Sister Allen." "Last Name?" "Allen. A-L-L-E-N." "First name?" "Sister." "Don't you have another first name?" "No, just Sister." "Social-security number?" "I don't have one, but I'm baptized." "Marital status?" "I'm a mother." "Are you single, married, widowed, divorced?" "I'm a mother." "What is your means of support?" "God provides." "Do you have any future plans?" "To do God's will."
>
> About the middle of the interview, the worker gave me that knowing look social workers give each other when they're dealing with someone crazy. I refused to return the look. Immediately, she asked me, "You're from Unity Kitchen?" "Yes." "Are you a worker there?" She eventually decided she couldn't help Sister, so we left.

From the perspective of the intake worker, Sister was simply another crazy applicant so out of touch that she couldn't answer simple questions. From my perspective, however, two entirely different conversations were going on, and it was the interviewer who was missing the point. In every case, Sister had given an answer that was relevant but that deliberately didn't fit into the intake worker's categories. The exchange about her social-security number was particularly intriguing. From the perspective of a branch of popular theology that says that the social-security number is the "sign of the beast," the intake worker had asked Sister, "Do you have the sign of the beast?" and Sister had responded, "No, but I have the sign of the Christian." That Sister understood it in such a way was indicated by the fact that, after we left Catholic Charities (where we went through an exact replication of the Emergency Assistance interview, a state form used by both agencies), she asked me, "Why are these Christian organizations asking for my social-security number?"

In short, the categories employed by the intake workers from the start prevented them from achieving a deeper understanding of Sister Allen, an understanding that was at least open to me because I was operating out of a hospitality model.

Typification of Persons in Catholic Worker Hospitality

This theoretical argument can be used to extend the earlier analyses of the schemes the three houses used for typifying persons. In terms of the above argument, the schemes described in the observational chapters were functionary ideal-typical schemes. All three of the houses, in other words, constructed ideal types of persons based on their relationship to the house, moral characteristics, and deviant characteristics. The types used in these schemes were, with the single exception of "community member" in the Mustard Seed, ideal types rather than categories.

What was not as obvious in the observational chapters was the importance of personal ideal types. At all three houses, Workers placed great importance on the ideal type they constructed for each person based on their past experiences with him or her. These personal ideal types were integral to the functioning of the house.

When I was being initiated into the houses, I was always told that "the important thing is to get to know the people." At a Worker house, it is not considered important to know that Leo is a paranoid schizophrenic and that paranoid schizophrenics tend to act in a certain way. It is important to know that when Leo gets upset he tends to start throwing punches. Ideal types are created for each person based not on his or her similarities with other persons but on his or her typical past actions. A Catholic Worker must learn, not diagnostic categories, but rather these personal ideal types. In a very real sense, one's experience at one Worker house is only marginally transferable to another house. Although it is important to know how to work with "drunks," it is far more important to know the actual persons who come to the house. One must build up one's personal ideal types primarily through personal interaction with the guests. In the rather haphazard "training" one receives, one is not taught very much about types of guests, but is told the stories of individual guests so that one knows how to interact with them. Thus, one's initiation as a Worker emphasizes personal ideal types.

An additional source for personal ideal types (of both guests and hosts) is oral tradition. When Workers gather to relax, conversation often turns toward stories about the guests, particularly the old-time guests. One hears outlandish tales—about Jerry, a harmless deinstitutionalized man who was hunted down by the FBI and incarcerated for a year because he had written a letter deemed threatening to the president, or about Mrs. Christ:

> She's always calling the police and telling them that somebody just shot her and killed her babies. So don't be surprised if the police come rushing in some day because of a call from her. I almost got arrested once that way. There was this guy on the third floor, and I didn't want them to arrest him. Maybe I should have let them—he drove us all bananas. They got a call from Mrs. Christ that there was a murderer on the third floor, so they were rushing up and I was trying to slow them down. I came this close to getting arrested.

This sharing of anecdotes about the guests functions in some ways like the case records of social agencies—it gives the newcomer a chance to expand his or her personal ideal types beyond the results of personal interaction. One can learn that Big John, a very gentle guest, had once torn the house apart, or that Timmy, who is occasionally violent and rarely coherent, had once been responsible enough to be "on the house."

However, this oral tradition differs from case records in two crucial ways. First, it is not available to all "staff," as are case records. Thus, the discrediting aspects of a guest's personal history are not an "open book" for anyone who wants to read it (see Goffman 1961, 155–60, for an account of this aspect of case records). One hears a person's oral history only if someone decides to share it.

Second, the oral histories are not limited to negative, discrediting incidents in a person's life, as are case records (Goffman 1961,

155–60). The oral histories are selective—they tend to concentrate on the unusual, the interesting, the stories that give one an idea of how to "handle" someone if there is trouble. However, they are not confined to discrediting accounts. The tradition also contains stories that indicate which guests can be relied on, which guests have unusual virtues, which guests have unusual skills, which guests are unusually compassionate. One learns that one of the craziest guys in the house regularly used to wash the blistered, bleeding feet of a filthy, smelly, lice-ridden alcoholic, who even the charitable Catholic Workers were reluctant to touch. One learns of one of the more feared characters that, "He didn't abuse the house. In fact, he was one of the few people who didn't abuse the house." Thus, the oral tradition is selective, but not in the same way as case records. The tradition does not function to demonstrate that the person is sick or ill. Rather, it functions to provide interesting and perhaps humorous stories and to help newer Workers build their personal ideal types of guests (and other Workers) so that they will know how to handle future situations.

The oral tradition about guests is not utilized to place guests in categories (as a case record is used, for example, to place a mental patient into the category of paranoid schizophrenic). Rather, the oral tradition tends to emphasize the uniqueness of the individual. Stories are told about persons, not about types of persons.

An intriguing feature of the Worker's use of the personal ideal type is that it is constructed primarily on the basis of experience with the person after she or he has come in contact with the house. A strong norm at Worker houses is that a guest should not be questioned about his or her past. One Worker told me: "As Catholic Workers, we don't inquire into a guest's background. If they volunteer information, fine, but I don't pry. . . . That's the way I was trained in the Catholic Worker."

Thus, there is a systematic effort to avoid inquiring into a guest's past life. The data for constructing the personal ideal type are confined to the period in which there has been face-to-face interaction between the guest and Workers at the house plus whatever previous personal information the guest has volunteered and any information that might have become known accidentally.

In short, the prevalence of personal ideal types and of functionary ideal-typical schemes suggests that the project of hospitality did indeed allow for more concrete, less anonymous typifications of guests than is normal for professional service agencies. One can argue further that the creation of We-relations is further enhanced by the way in which Catholic Worker hospitality differs from the traditional hospitality model.

Giving Hospitality versus Building Community

As mentioned in Chapter 3, Worker hospitality operates on a much longer time-frame than does traditional hospitality. Guests often remain, not for hours or days, but for weeks or months. This increased duration of hospitality has resulted in an almost unconscious merging of hospitality with a very different type of relationship—building community.

At its heart, the Worker approach to hospitality is an uneasy blend of two distinct models of social relationship: building community between social unequals and providing hospitality. These two models are alternative approaches to dealing with outsiders. In building community with outsiders one invites them to become part of the group. The community group, however, cannot be indefinite—boundaries must be drawn between community members and those who are still outsiders. When one is dealing with a larger number of outsiders than can be accommodated in the group, a selection process must occur. This process divides outsiders into two groups: those now in the community and those still outside. Ideally, the community model implies equality for all members. This very equality between members, however, generates inequality between those who were originally outsiders and those who remain outsiders, an inequality that the new members of the group have a strong interest in maintaining. Thus, the model of building community between social unequals entails the creation of inequality among those originally of lower status.

In contrast, the hospitality model, as delineated in the early chapters of this study, does not offer group membership to outsiders. It maintains a distinction between host and guest but thereby does not necessitate differentiation among guests. Although there is extended face-to-face interaction between host and guest, the model does not call for strict equality (although allowing for the possibility of role reversal).

These two models combine to create four classifications: (1) host–community member, (2) host–outsider, (3) guest–community member, and (4) guest–outsider. Persons falling into numbers 1 and 4 present no problems for a merging of the two models. Since there is in the Catholic Worker no group corresponding to number 2, number 3 becomes our main concern: those who are treated as community members by one model but as guests by the other. These are the residents of St. Joseph's in New York City, the current community members of the Mustard Seed, the "disenfranchised staff" of Rochester. As has been seen in each of the ethnographies, the persons in these situations present some of the most perplexing problems faced by the houses.

Since the conflict between the two models is never made explicit, the situations in which these persons should properly be considered guest or community member are usually not articulated. Their ambiguous status leads to role conflict for themselves and often generates strains that reverberate throughout the house (e.g., Mike's conflicts in Rochester, Sally's rise to house director at the Mustard Seed, Gene's attempt at "taking over" in New York City).

The houses themselves may respond to this strain by moving toward one model at the expense of the other. Thus, Rochester moved quickly from the community-building approach of Patrick Grady to the hospitality–service approach of Barb as soon as she took over. The house had moved so far toward one end of the spectrum that the debate was phrased in terms of community versus service. The Mustard Seed had moved toward community to the extent that former guests had the power to take over operation of the house. The New York City house remained somewhere in the middle, as, perhaps, befits the "flagship" of the movement. Thus, its major tensions often took the form of conflicting status distinctions between Worker versus resident (guest) and in-the-house versus on-the-line (community member versus outsider).

There is little doubt that this attempt to utilize two conflicting models without articulating their differences takes its toll—on the guests, on the Workers, and often on the house as a social group. However, it is precisely the existence of such an unarticulated duality of models that facilitates the personalist approach to hospitality of the Worker. What makes it particularly difficult to objectify guests is, first, that there are two alternative roles available to the poor who come to the house and, second, that the differences between these roles are not articulated. One cannot simply cast the other into the role of guest or community member. Each person must negotiate his or her own combination of these roles. This negotiation allows for a maximization of appreciation of the guest as a full person. In effect, the tensions resulting from the conflicting roles impede the objectification of the person into a single social role (e.g., guest).

Thus, the dual project of Catholic Worker hospitality is directly related to its personalist philosophy. Because the person is valued, Workers want both to treat the poor stranger as an equal (the community model) and to receive all who come (the hospitality model). It is the negotiation of the tensions between the two models that helps Workers to grasp the poor stranger as person rather than as social role.

Organizational Supports for Personalist Hospitality

The Catholic Worker has been reasonably successful in doing personalist hospitality, in translating the ideology of personalism into day-to-day practice. This is particularly true in comparison to social-service agencies, which may have an official ideology quite similar to personalism. I have tried to demonstrate that this is due, in part at least, to the nature of their project of hospitality. It is due also, however, to a number of social and institutional processes that have facilitated the practice of hospitality. I will delineate several.

The first is the Worker's approach to division of labor. There is no class of Worker that is not required to spend large amounts of time in face-to-face interaction with the guests. In Rochester, all Workers, including the house director, were expected to serve the meal and be present whenever the house was open five days a week. In New York City, all Workers, including the editor of the paper, signed up to be "on the house" several times a week. In Worcester, Workers also volunteered to be "on the house." Thus, even the "top staff" of a Worker house had periods of ten, twenty, or more hours a week when their primary responsibility was to be in face-to-face contact with the guests.

Another factor is that Workers live in the house with the guests. Catholic Worker hospitality is truly hospitality—it is taking guests into one's home. It is difficult to interact only "in passing" with someone with whom you are sharing kitchen, bedroom, and shower. The multiplication of contexts for interpersonal interaction entailed in living together precludes the possibility of Workers structuring all interactions between themselves and guests. Further, living together entails a certain equality, as one Worker at the Mustard Seed noted:

> If you're separated by the chasm of coin, of money; if they think
> "that's all well and good for him, he's only putting in his forty hours
> a week, he's gonna drive away from here in a forty-thousand-dollar

sports car" [then we are not equal]. Oh no. I don't have very far to go—just from the first floor to the second floor. This is my home. I don't live elsewhere. I don't live in Holden or Paxton. This is what makes us different.

Third, the Worker offers little that can be considered material incentive to anyone who has the ability to maintain a home of his or her own. Indeed, it offers material disincentives—crowded living conditions, cockroaches, mice, rats, lice, no air-conditioning, uncertain heat. Therefore, it attracts two types of people: those who come because they believe strongly in the Worker ideology, and those who have been homeless. In the first instance, people adhere to the personalist approach because it is their primary reason for being there. In the second, people are used to dealing with the homeless personally, as equals, because they have been homeless themselves.

Fourth, the Worker rejects anything that even remotely resembles bureaucratic procedure. In a very real sense, the Worker does not have a concrete positive model of personalist hospitality. Rather, it has two antimodels: bureaucracy and professionalism. There is a great dispute within the movement about what constitutes personalist hospitality. There is no question, however, that any procedure that resembles bureaucracy is contrary to personalist hospitality. Bureaucracy is avoided because it requires categorization of persons, advocates impersonal treatment, and necessitates rules that tend to act either as hindrances to helping persons with the myriad of problems they arrive with or as handy excuses for refusing to respond to human need. Professionalism is rejected for essentially the same reasons, coupled with the belief that hospitality is a nonprofessional activity—something that anyone can do and that requires no training or education.

Fifth, the Worker eschews any funding from organizations. This type of funding has been shown by Newman (1980) to push nontraditional organizations into more bureaucratic forms because bureaucratic funding agencies feel uncomfortable dealing with other types of organizations.

Finally, personalist hospitality is facilitated precisely because it uses a model of hospitality rather than one of rehabilitation or people processing. One can respond to the other as person because one is interested neither in changing the other in a specific direction nor in determining a new status for that person; both of these processes require attention to selected aspects of the person only.

Implications for Aiding the Homeless

Catholic Worker hospitality is an alternative to the professional model to aiding the homeless that has been proven over half a century. It seems unlikely that enough people will choose to embrace the rigors of Worker life to make it a viable approach to ending the problem of homelessness. However, the Worker example has made important contributions to addressing the problem. It has received some attention in recent studies (e.g., Hope and Young 1986). It has also been a strong influence on the two advocacy organizations most responsible for bringing homelessness to American attention in the 1980s: the Community for Creative Nonviolence (see Rader 1986) and the Coalition for the Homeless (for which many New York City Workers have volunteered their time).

The Catholic Worker approach has some general implications for aid to the homeless. Most important, it identifies hospitality as a project that must be separated conceptually from rehabilitation. By utilizing the roles of guest and host rather than client and therapist, hospitality creates an atmosphere in which the homeless person can be received graciously, in a noninstrumental way. To the extent that homelessness is a problem of disaffiliation (Bahr 1973), perhaps the only solution is the creation of communities that will welcome the homeless as full persons rather than clients and thus to some extent empower them rather than treat them. For those persons whose homelessness is due to the strain between our society's achievement ideology and the limited access to the ladder of success (Merton 1968), it may be that only nonbureaucratized communities can provide a place of welcome.

For the Catholic Worker, the real therapy needs to be performed on society rather than on the individual homeless person. To "cure" the problem of homelessness, we need a massive increase in low-income housing, a massive increase in community-based residential services for the deinstitutionalized, a massive commitment to improved income maintenance and health benefits, and a massive demilitarization of society, at the very least. Ultimately, we need to become more cooperative, both as persons and as a society.

Although the Catholic Worker advocates both anarchism and personal responsibility, Workers have become forceful advocates of government intervention on behalf of the poor and homeless as well as increased efforts by individuals. This somewhat paradoxical position is usually explained in terms of the overwhelming needs of the homeless—given the philosophy of personalism, one cannot allow one's ideology to impede efforts to help those in need, and government is the one organization that has the power and resources to make a major immediate impact on the situation of the homeless. There is no danger, even with massive government aid, of the Catholic Worker finding itself without work. No matter how many bureaucratic, professional, categorical programs are established, there will always be those who fall between the cracks—or gaping chasms. Thus, there will always be a need for personalist hospitality. In this respect, as probably in no other, the Worker approach would agree with Charles Murray, who states in his "law of imperfect selection" that "any objective rule that defines eligibility for a social transfer program will irrationally exclude some persons" (1984, 211).

One implication that goes beyond specific statements of the Worker is that hospitality should be kept organizationally separate from rehabilitation efforts. Too often, it seems, programs are established to provide hospitality but, because staff become concerned that "we aren't doing enough to solve the problem," a rehabilitation component is added (see Torrey 1988 for an example of this type of thinking). Gradually, this rehabilitation component comes to be the major focus of the organization and hospitality is relegated to the status of an "ancillary service." With rehabilitation come professionals, and with professionals comes professional dominance (Chamberlin 1978). Acceptance of the rehabilitation program often becomes a condition for receiving hospitality, a rule that inevitably excludes many in need of shelter. Furthermore, the rehabilitation program inevitably entails categorization, which inhibits the personal approach of hospitality. Thus, hospitality inevitably suffers when it is linked to rehabilitation. The two projects should be organizationally separate, at least to the extent that every city has some group doing hospitality which is not tied to therapy.

A problem that is commonly cited in efforts to aid the homeless as well as other devalued populations is that of warehousing—keeping people in institutions under inhuman conditions without attempts to rehabilitate them. This problem can, in a sense, be traced to the lack of recognition of hospitality as an alternative to rehabilitation. Given the current professional mindset, if one cannot rehabilitate a devalued person, there is nothing one can do for him or her. Thus, they are simply warehoused, with little or no effort to welcome them—or even to treat them as human beyond providing the bare minimum of food, clothing, and shelter. Were hospitality more widely recognized as a viable project, there would be more one could do for the unrehabilitatable—one could welcome them as fellow persons.

This problem leads to a broader problem in our rational outlook on the world, a problem that Henri Nouwen has defined as the difference between efficacy and fruitfulness. In the rational mindset, our actions are geared toward effectiveness—we set goals and determine the most effective means to achieve those goals. This mode of acting is entirely mechanistic. Nouwen argues that there is another, more organic way to work toward goals—to attempt to be fruitful. In this mode, we do not assume that the best way to achieve a goal is to work rationally toward it. Rather, we attempt to live virtuously and to adhere to values, trusting that God will utilize our efforts in ways we could never predict—in effect trusting that our efforts will bear fruit in ways we did not plan, even if they are not productive in the modern sense. Hospitality, then, is an approach to homelessness that attempts to be fruitful rather than effective. Hospitality implicitly acknowledges the limits of rationality in our relationships to others, a topic to which I will turn in the final chapter.

8

Societal Implications
of the Catholic Worker

In an interview with Robert Coles, Dorothy Day stated: "We are not here to prove that our technique of working with the poor is useful, or to prove that we are able to be effective humanitarians" (Coles 1987, 97). Clearly, to view the Worker as simply an alternative approach to solving the problems of homelessness and poverty misses its significance. The ultimate goals of the Worker are both spiritual and social.

The Worker is a Christian movement, one that attempts to live and proclaim the Gospel of Jesus Christ: "We are here to bear witness to our Lord" (Day, in Coles 1987, 97). This witnessing is done both by example and by the newspapers, although always with a care never to impose preaching on those in need of hospitality. Prayer is a crucial part of Worker life:

> We are *not* another Community Fund group, anxious to help people with some bread and butter and a cup of coffee or tea. We feed the hungry, yes; we try to shelter the homeless and give them clothes, if we have some, but there is a strong faith at work; we pray. If an outsider who comes to visit doesn't pay attention to our praying and what that means, then he'll miss the whole point of things (Day, in Coles 1987, 97).

Although all Workers do not share Dorothy Day's religious views, prayer did play a role in all of the houses I studied—a role that I downplayed both because my interest lay in hospitality and because sociological methods are not well suited to addressing issues of spirituality. (I could imagine designing a study to test the effects of a house's prayer life on the quality of its hospitality; however, I think it would pose some rather insurmountable measurement problems.)

The social aim of the Worker movement is best expressed by combining two oft-repeated slogans—"to build a new society within the shell of the old, a society in which it is easier for persons to be good." The first part gives the means; the second, the end.

"A society in which it is easier for persons to be good" means a society that is structured in such a way that moral decisions are not as painful as they often are in contemporary society. Society would be evaluated not on its gross national product, but on whether it is structured in a way that makes moral action less difficult. Such a goal entails a conception of what "the good" is; for the Worker, the "good" is defined by Christian personalist values and virtues. The notion of structuring society to enhance a predetermined "good" is difficult to advance in this age of pluralism and cultural relativism: who is to determine what the "good" is? However, it must be realized that the practical result of forgoing such an attempt is to continue with a society in which profit and consumption are the absolute values. To deny that we can achieve any other common conception of the good is to admit that acquisitive materialism is the only ideology we are willing to impose on others.

"Creating a new society within the shell of the old" is where hospitality comes in. The Worker does not attempt to create the new society from the top down—by either government action or the creation of a large nongovernmental organization. Rather, change is to be accomplished through the action of small groups of persons creating communities that affirm different virtues and different projects than those affirmed by conventional society. Only in small communities can a way of life be created that allows for I–Thou relationships, that eschews bureaucratic and professional ways of relating to others. These small communities will, hopefully, be fruitful; by their example, they may inspire more communities with similar goals.

From a rational perspective, such an approach seems doomed to failure. The only rational way to cause change is to formulate a goal and then establish the most powerful and efficient organization possible to achieve that goal. However, although the Worker approach is irrational, it may not be illogical in the long run. The Workers' decision not to create a formal organization may be one reason that the movement has persisted at its project of personalist hospitality for over half a century in the face of society-wide pressures toward professionalization and bureaucratization. Numerous studies have indicated that bureaucratic organizations created to achieve a goal normally go through a process of goal displacement, often in the interests of organizational maintenance (e.g., Selznick 1966). This might be an inherent aspect of the rational approach, for the following reason. Any time one wishes to specify a goal precisely, particularly a social goal, one necessarily misspecifies it. Our actual goals are always a bit more ambiguous than our specified goals. Therefore, rational action toward a specified goal always leads one in a slightly different direction than action toward the original goal would lead. (Donald Campbell refers to the effect of using measured progress toward goals for evaluation as "the corrupting effect of quantitative indicators" [1979, 84]). Action that is not rationally planned, but is oriented toward an ambiguous, unspecified goal, might have wide variations from the "straight-line" course. However, one could argue that those deviations would tend to be random—not leading away from the original goal over the long run—while the rational deviations would be systematic, since they are aimed at a misspecified goal. In short, the personalist approach may facilitate greater faithfulness to goals.

The Catholic Worker does not have an overall rational plan for social change. As Dorothy Day said, "We haven't figured out what we should do down to the punctuation marks" (in Coles 1987, 101). The small communities approach, however, harkens back to Jesus' parabolic images of the growth of the Kingdom of God (e.g., the mustard seed, the leaven). There are also secular social theorists who have advocated such a decentralized approach to social change as the only way to create a just society (e.g., Kropotkin 1914, 1972; Sharp 1980).

Having said all this, it still seems unlikely, barring divine intervention, that the Catholic Worker is going to reverse the centuries-old trend toward rationalization. However, one must not make the other mistake of assuming that rationalization is necessarily an irreversible juggernaut. Sociologists of religion had for decades confidently predicted the steady increase of secularization until the religious revivals of the 1970s and 1980s sent them into theoretical disarray. The "progress" of trends such as rationalization and secularization may be even more problematic in the future if people come to doubt their beneficence. The Worker can serve as an example from which those of us who are dubious about the benefits of rationalization can profitably draw.

In reclaiming an area of activity—hospitality for the homeless—from the professionals and affirming it as something that anyone can do, the Worker provides a model of how we can empower our lives. (Actually, it isn't really reclaiming the area—the Worker was there when most professions ignored the problem.) Although some activities can be improved somewhat through the application of rational methods by experts, it is also true that many activities can be performed quite adequately by laypersons and require no training other than general socialization. (One is reminded here of Simon's [1945] notion of "satisficing"—selecting an alternative that "gets the job done" rather than searching rigorously for the "best" approach.) To the extent that we can "stake out" more such areas of activity as not requiring professional help, I believe we are empowering ourselves as humans. We can do more than the professionals want us to think we can do.

The Worker experience points to a larger area of activity that may be incompatible with technique and rationalization—interpersonal relationships. Interpersonal relationships are not amenable to technique, first, because the human person is not reducible to discrete, measurable characteristics. Since the rational, technocratic approach requires measurability, it will inevitably fall short when applied to human persons. The professional approach can never grasp a person in his or her fullness; it can only present a carnival-mirror image— a distortion that emphasizes some aspects of the person and ignores others.

Second, technical training is designed to enhance the rationality of action, that is, training teaches one the best means to achieve a goal in a certain situation. When one is dealing with another person, however, one is not acting but interacting. In interaction, we must constantly assess how the other is responding to our actions and reformulate our actions in light of that response (Mead 1934; Blumer 1969). Can any training in how to interact with another person cover all the possibilities without gross oversimplification? Or does such technical training simply give the trainee categories into which to place responses—categories that may cause him or her to miss an essential aspect of the other's response?

This is not to assert that professional help is never helpful. Professional insights may be useful in revealing those aspects of our behavior that are determined. However, what we do is, at least to some extent, a matter of choice and therefore not open to professional scrutiny. We should not abandon the arena of human relationships to professionalism. We must be open to the insights professionals can bring. But we must be aware that professionals can be blinded to certain aspects of human reality by their disciplinary framework and that their insights may be less valid than those of a person who is untrained but knows the "client." We must not be intimidated into abandoning our insights into others in the face of professional authority. Stanley notes that it is we who give to professionals the authority to interpret human experience. He argues that we should "become deeply aware of the universal continuities between expert and ordinary modes of interpreting the world" (1978, 97–98). Both lay and professional knowledge are socially constructed. Neither is absolute. An excellent example of asserting one's own insight over and against professional wisdom is the claim of some persons who live with severely disabled persons that their friend or relative comprehends far more than the professionals feel is possible (Bogdan and Taylor 1989, 140). The laypersons might be wrong; but so might the professionals.

Furthermore, in the very process of training someone in techniques of interaction, we practically preclude the possibility of real, personal, I–Thou interaction. To the extent that I–Thou interaction is necessary for the development of well-rounded persons, the attempt to rationalize interpersonal skills is deleterious to that development.

Thus, we need to call into question our assumption that applying rationality to interpersonal relations is a positive trend. Given my extension of Schutz's analysis, it appears that a rational approach to interpersonal relations inevitably leads to the creation of more anonymous "types" or categories of persons, which in turn diminishes our capacity to accept the other as a whole person. Interpersonal relationships, perhaps, should not be rationalized because such rationalization leads to depersonalization. The increased efficiency gained by rationalization is not an unmitigated good—indeed, as Rubenstein so effectively argues, it was precisely this rationalization of relationships that facilitated the Holocaust. The bureaucratic "ethic" of impersonality—of keeping one's personal feelings from interfering in the performance of one's duties—was essential to the task of systematically murdering six million human beings: "It was only possible to overcome the moral barrier that had in the past prevented the systematic riddance of surplus populations when the project was taken out of the hands of bullies and hoodlums and delegated to bureaucrats" (1975, 27).

While we may not want to eliminate entirely rationalization and technique from our society, we may wish to target interpersonal relations as an area in which we should attempt to eliminate the hegemony of technique and reassert our abilities as persons. We should explore the possibility that reaching out in love to others is more helpful than the impersonal application of scientific technique. Indeed, we should question whether the person is a proper object for technique at all.

The Worker example can also help us to reformulate the problem of altruism versus self-interest. In the first place, it raises the question of what altruism is. Many analyses of this problem identify altruism with concern for the larger society (e.g., Margolis 1982).[1] Personalism raises another possibility—that altruism is actually concern, not for one's society, but for the other as person. Berdyaev (1944) clearly demonstrated that concern for the other can often conflict with concern for society.

Second, the Worker can help us to question the "common wisdom," which asserts that all actions are traceable to "enlightened self-interest." The truth of such an assertion is inherently unknowable because one can never finally determine the reasons for a given action. One can always posit a self-interested reason for any action; however, one can also posit an altruistic reason for any action. Just as there are certain cases where the altruistic reason seems farfetched; so there are others where the self-interested reason seems equally farfetched. Michalowski argues that the notion of self-interest as human nature is a self-fulfilling prophecy that stems from modern capitalist society:

> Capitalist societies are based on competitive social relations. In such societies the view that individuals are essentially self-seeking and acquisitive is consistent with people's experiences since observable behaviors are more often competitive than altruistic. The problem is that when we generalize from immediate observable behavior in one form of society to all humans, we in effect *create nature in the image of our social system*. This social construction of "nature" provides in turn a strong ideological justification for capitalism. If humans are inherently self-seeking, then competitive social relations are inevitable because they are natural rather than the alterable cultural creations of human beings. . . . Moreover, if individuals perceive competitive relations as inevitable, they are more likely to behave competitively themselves (1985, 48).

Maurin stated essentially the same idea in simpler language:

> Business men say
>   that because everybody is selfish,
> business must therefore be based on selfishness.
> But when business is based on selfishness
>   everybody is busy becoming more selfish.

And when everybody is busy
  becoming more selfish,
we have classes and clashes.
Business cannot set its house in order
  because business men are
moved by selfish motives.
Business men create problems,
  they do not solve them.

(1977, 5)

Bellah *et al.* (1985) document very disturbingly how, under the influence of the therapeutic movement, United States citizens tend to interpret their actions in terms of self-fulfillment. Dorothy Day's thoughts on this topic are revealing: "If I were indulging myself here, feeding these lost souls to make myself feel better or in pursuit of my own little dream, I would be guilty, once more, of the worst sin possible, the sin of pride" (in Coles 1987, 95). The Catholic Worker example can help us to question, first, whether all action is self-interested and, second, whether altruism consists in sacrificing for the larger society or in sacrificing for the good of other persons.

In *Habits of the Heart*, Robert Bellah and his coauthors declared: "Perhaps the truth lies in what most of the world outside the modern West has always believed, namely that there are practices of life, good in themselves, that are inherently fulfilling" (1985, 295). I believe that hospitality is one of those practices and that there is a pressing need to reclaim it as a form of sociation. More generally, we must recognize that loving personal interaction with others is an essential component of any meaningful life and we should structure our society, not to maximize our material standard of living, but to enable us to create the kind of loving personal relationships that will enable us to develop fully as persons.

Notes

Chapter 1

1. The ideal-typical stranger-as-guest is not identical to the type of stranger discussed by either Simmel (1971) or Schutz (1971) in their essays of the same name. Simmel's prototypical stranger is the trader, who comes and stays for awhile, but may move on, and is never assimilated to the culture. Schutz's is the immigrant, who wishes to be "permanently accepted or at least tolerated by the group which he approaches" (1971, 91). Levine's (1985, 73–88) analysis of types of strangers is useful here, distinguishing strangers by two characteristics: the stranger's interest in the host community (visit, residence, or membership), and the host's response to the stranger (friendliness or antagonism).
2. Parsons is analyzing the role of the physician in terms of his five pattern variables: universalism versus particularism, achievement versus ascription, specificity versus diffuseness, affective neutrality versus affectivity, and collectivity-orientation versus self-orientation. A more complete discussion is contained in Murray (1987, 29–32).

Chapter 2

1. The most comprehensive cross-cultural description of hospitality practices I know of is the series of articles on hospitality in *The Encyclopedia of Religion and Ethics*, vol. 7 (1925).
2. I use "myth" in the sense of a story that a culture uses to interpret its experience. This definition makes no judgment as to the historicity of the story. Thus, I include here a number of myths from the Judeo–Christian tradition that I believe are based on historical incidents.
3. See Connolly and Anderson (1987) for a fascinating description of the first contact between Europeans and New Guinea highlanders in the 1930s, based on diaries, photographs, films, and interviews with both

261

European and native survivors some fifty years later. For ceremonies used for strangers, see Van Gennep (1960, 26ff.) and Hamilton-Grierson (1925).

4. See Sahlins 1972; Hamilton-Grierson 1925, 1980; Bodley 1983. Murray 1987 contains a chapter summarizing anthropological research on the topic.

5. These three Gospels are commonly held by historical biblical critics to be the most accurate record of the words of Jesus. Mark is held to be the earliest of the three, and Matthew and Luke are thought to have been written independently using two common sources—Mark and a hypothetical collection of sayings of Jesus known as Q—as well as each evangelist's own sources. I will not address the question of which sayings are genuine—there is precious little agreement among scholars about this point. I will instead follow Theissen's argument that this question makes little difference for interpreting the effect of the tradition on early Christianity since the early Christians either shaped their lives around the tradition if it was genuine or shaped the tradition around their lives if it was created by them. Either eventuality results in a correlation between the tradition and practice (Theissen 1977, 3–4).

6. One argument (suggested to me by a Baptist preacher) about this passage is that it refers to "the judgment of the nations," rather than of individuals. Walter Wink (1986, 96) responds that there is a shift from a neuter to a masculine pronoun when "they" are separated, and that this shift indicates that individuals will be held responsible for the actions of their nations in feeding the hungry. I personally prefer the simpler interpretation of Furfey (1969, 35–36) that the passage refers to the judgment of individuals for their actions. The other explanations seem a bit esoteric.

7. This was quite a contrast from the laws of the early American colonies, which prescribed penalties for sheltering strangers without notifying the authorities, as documented in Rothman (1971, 20–25) and Trattner (1974, 19).

8. The only exception of which I am aware is Greifer (1945), who argued that hospitality had advanced in the transition from primitive to early Hebrew culture. His argument focuses on accounts of hostile reactions to strangers in some primitive societies and is, I think, outdated in light of more recent anthropological research and theory.

Chapter 3

1. For history and general treatment of the movement, see Miller (1973), Piehl (1982), Day (1939, 1963), Vishnewski (1984), Coles and Erikson (1973), and Coy (1988). For the newspaper, see Roberts (1984). For pacifism, see LeBrun (1973). For accounts of the New York house, see Ellis (1978), Lifton (1981), and Aronica (1987). For Dorothy Day, see

Day (1952, 1970, 1983), Miller (1982), Coles (1987), and Forest (1986). For Peter Maurin, see Maurin (1977), Ellis (1981), Sheehan (1959), and Novitsky (1976). For the philosophy of the movement, see Sandberg (1979).

2. Although it was specifically theological, European personalism developed in the same intellectual world that fostered phenomenological sociology. Further, many personalist ideas are congruent with the symbolic interactionist perspective in sociology. The process of becoming a person, as described by Berdyaev, bears some resemblance to Mead's (1934) description of the development of the self. Personalist descriptions of the importance of transpersonal values in becoming a person resemble Weber's description of becoming a personality, as summarized by Brubaker (1984, 96–97). In contrast, the French personalists considered themselves to be the intellectual adversaries of Durkheim and his disciples. Basic writings of the movement include Mounier (1938, 1952, 1954); Berdyaev (1944, 1960); Maritain (1966, 1968, 1971). For Mounier's role in the movement, see Hellman (1981) and Cantin (1973). For the effect of the movement on Pope John Paul II, see Hellman (1980–1981).

3. The list of types of almsgiving presented by Augustine in the *Enchiridion* must have been a source for the eventual codification of the Works of Mercy. Significantly, it does not make a division between corporal and spiritual works. Neither does it include anything that might be interpreted as the seventh work of either type—burying the dead or praying for the living and the dead. There are, however, some interesting additional works listed: "Not only, then, the man who gives food to the hungry, drink to the thirsty, clothing to the naked, hospitality to the stranger, shelter to the fugitive, who visits the sick and the imprisoned, ransoms the captive, assists the weak, leads the blind, comforts the sorrowful, heals the sick, puts the wanderer on the right path, gives advice to the perplexed, and supplies the wants of the needy—not this man only, but the man who pardons the sinner also gives alms; and the man who corrects with blows, or restrains by any kind of discipline one over whom he has power, and who at the same time forgives from the heart the sin by which he was injured or prays that it may be forgiven, is also a giver of alms, not only in that he forgives, or prays for forgiveness of the sin, but also in that he rebukes and corrects the sinner: for in this, too, he shows mercy" (1961, 85).

Catholics traditionally claim a biblical basis for the Works of Mercy. The first six corporal works clearly are derived from Jesus' discourse on the Last Judgment (Matt. 25). The other eight, however, are drawn from more diverse biblical sources (see Guyot 1947, 56–58). With the exception of the first six, there seems to be little biblical basis for this particular listing.

4. After completing observation of the three houses, I visited the Catholic

Worker Archives at Marquette University for one week, collecting materials pertaining to the histories of the individual houses and to the Worker philosophy of hospitality. Data were analyzed in the manner recommended by Taylor and Bogdan (1984).

Chapter 4

1. Aronica confirms the unsystematic nature of the training: "The Catholic Worker movement does not have a policy manual. . . . The investigation revealed that there has never been, nor is there at present, a formal procedure such as a 'formation program' utilized by the Catholic Worker movement to socialize or incorporate new members" (1987, 157). Her interpretation, however, differs from mine. She argues that: "The problem, however, lies not so much in the absence of ideology as it does in the group's need for the proper mechanisms to insure adequate transmission of the vision. It is my belief that the means have not been established to promote the charisma of the movement's founders. . . . If the spirit or vision is not passed on to the membership, the Catholic Worker runs the risk of becoming just another one of the many facilities which offers services to the indigent; simply another social service agency" (1987, 150).

   I would argue that the imposition of a formal training program would do exactly what Aronica feared—turn the Worker into "another social service agency." I was not disturbed by the training method used in the New York City house because it was quite similar to what I had found in other houses. Aronica, on the other hand, appears implicitly to compare it with the formation programs of religious orders and finds it lacking on those terms.

2. Aronica (1987) delineates five types of persons: authorities, volunteers, aspirants, residents, and transients. Her typology substantially agrees with my own—differences probably reflect our theoretical interests rather than differences in observation. She distinguishes more types of Workers, while I distinguish more types of guests. Although she refers to these types as categories, she does not directly address the question of whether these "categories" may actually be ideal types. The very fact that we came up with slightly differing typologies may point to the ideal-typical nature of such designations.

3. This last comment refers to two residents who are traditionally given small sums of money—less than a dollar—every evening.

Chapter 5

1. There may have been one other house that incorporated. A December 1937 article in *Blackfriars* about the Wigan (England) House of Hospi-

tality lists three committee members, including a chair, treasurer, and secretary (Walsh *et al.*, 1937).

2. This is not to say that at Unity Kitchen we did not affirm our guests' worth—we did. But the staff at St. Joseph's articulated it more directly than I usually did. Several other factors probably contributed to the lower levels of violence at St. Joe's, including the more stringent expectations the staff had of guests' behavior and the fact that some of the staff were women.

Chapter 7

1. The fourth meaning—personalism as a means of social change—is beyond the scope of this study. There are, however, several obvious avenues for addressing it, for example, the influence on religious and political leaders of face-to-face interaction with those arrested for antinuclear civil disobedience and the role of Michael Harrington's experience at the New York Worker on the writing of *The Other America* and the subsequent influence of that book on the War on Poverty.

2. The Mission also served employed alcoholics in a residential program. I am assuming that these did not form a significant percentage of those barred.

3. There have been rehabilitation agencies that have made conscious efforts to eliminate categorization. Wiley (1988) describes attempts at "role blurring" by a holistic mental health therapeutic community. The ensuing problems could be interpreted as evidence that such an attempt runs counter to the rehabilitation model. Lang (1981) concludes that the psychiatric framework led workers to restrict service to "good" clients even in a community mental-health center with the stated goal of serving those most in need.

4. The utility of Schutz's notion of typification for describing the categorization of persons in mental-health agencies has been recognized by both Jehenson (1973) and Peyrot (1982).

5. Actually, Schutz and Luckmann (1973) list three types of "relevance structures": thematic, interpretational, and motivational. Projects of action are one of the two types of motivational relevance, corresponding to "in order to" motives. The notion of relevance structures closely parallels the better known symbolic interactionist notion of definition of the situation as described in Blumer (1969). Given the pragmatist definition of meaning employed by Mead (1934), it seems safe to conclude that one's project is a major part of one's definition of the situation.

6. It is possible for only one person to be attending to the other in such a way. Schutz calls this the Thou-relation. The We-relation, then, is a reciprocal Thou-relation.

7. Discussion of personal types is complicated by the fact that Schutz gives

at least four extended treatments of the topic (1962, 19–27; 1967, 163–207; 1971, 41–56; Schutz and Luckmann 1973, 61–87) and that there are subtle differences among the treatments. Particularly problematic is his use of the term "personal types."

Schutz distinguishes between personal types and course-of-action types, where the former is "the ideal type of another person who is expressing or has expressed himself in a certain way" (1967, 187), and the latter is an ideal type "of the expressive process itself" (1967, 187). Personal types are derived from course-of-action types: "By referring a course of action type to the underlying typical motives of the actor we arrive at the construction of a personal type" (1971, 25). However, once we have constructed a personal type, we can deduce acts from it (1967, 188).

Schutz and Luckmann also distinguish between personal (or characterological) types and functionary (or functional or habitual) types, where personal types are "derived from immediate experience of a fellow-man, at first or second hand," and functionary types "grasp contemporaries only in reference to certain typical functions" (1973, 82).

Schutz seems to be inconsistent with respect to whether functionary types are a subtype of personal types or are to be distinguished from personal types. I shall assume that personal and functionary types are distinct, leaving me with three "types of types": course-of-action (e.g., fighting fires), functionary (e.g., fire chief), and personal (e.g., Joe, the fire chief).

8. Schutz would here speak of generalizing from the actions of a number of persons rather than generalizing from their characteristics. I think, however, that the same logic would apply.

9. Schutz divides the social world into several realms: the realm of consociates, which consists of those with whom I am currently in a We-relation; the realm of contemporaries, which consists of those living in the present with whom I have only a They-relation; the realm of predecessors; and the realm of successors. The latter three realms, of course, all consist of persons with whom one is in a They-relation.

There is some transition between the realm of consociates and that of contemporaries. A telephone conversation may be viewed as a transition between the realms. The person at the other end is not fully a consociate since one cannot observe him and pick up all the signs necessary to determine his subjective meanings; however, neither is he merely a contemporary at that point.

The world of contemporaries does, however, stand in contrast to the world of consociates. The contrast lies primarily in the fact that contemporaries can only be grasped as ideal types, either characterological or habitual, while consociates are grasped as conscious, acting persons. There is, however, a continuum here also.

10. In defining ideal types in this way, I am creating a synthetic definition of

the term, dependent upon, but distinct from, the usages of both Weber and Schutz. Weber (1949) defines ideal type as a methodological tool of the social scientist, useful for clarifying the logically important properties of phenomena but not equivalent to categorization. Schutz employs the term as a tool of the "average person" rather than a scientific methodology and does not exclude the possibility that ideal types can be categories. My own use of the term agrees with Schutz that it is a tool of average persons and with Weber that it is distinct from categorization. When discussing Schutz's term "ideal type" above, therefore, I have tried to use simply the term "type," reserving "ideal type" for my own definition.

11. Mirowsky and Ross (1989) demonstrate that the DSM-III categories are not valid—indeed, that "mental disorders" are not categories in any logical sense of the term. They propose that the categories were created for several reasons: because the medical tradition dictates that diseases be discrete entities, because of the demands of bureaucratic insurance and funding agencies for categorical diseases, and because categories are necessary to apply the therapeutic model.

Chapter 8

1. The view of altruism as orientation toward society is particularly prevalent in sociology, probably due to the influence of Durkheim and Parsons. In Parsons's discussion of pattern variables, he contrasts collectivity-orientation and self-orientation. There is a third possibility—the other-orientation—in which one is oriented neither to oneself nor to one's collectivity but to another individual person.

   To form a dichotomy out of the three orientations, one would have to classify collectivity-orientation as a form of self-orientation, in contrast to other-orientation. The ego is a part of the collectivity and regards the collectivity as an extension of itself. Therefore, orientation toward the collectivity is essentially self-orientation, just as orientation toward one's property—also an extension of self—is self-orientation. The true contrast to self-orientation is other-orientation, not collectivity-orientation. Thus, altruism is best defined as orientation toward the other rather than toward the group.

Bibliography

Addams, Jane. 1910. *Twenty Years at Hull House*. New York: Signet.

———. 1965. *The Social Thought of Jane Addams*. Christopher Lasch ed. Indianapolis: Bobbs-Merrill.

Aquinas, Thomas. 1975. *Summa Theologiae*. Vol. 34. *Charity*. New York: Blackfriars and McGraw-Hill.

Aronica, Michele R.S.M. 1987. *Beyond Charismatic Leadership: The New York Catholic Worker Movement*. New Brunswick, N.J.: Transaction Press.

Augustine, St. 1961. *The Enchiridion on Faith, Hope, and Love*. Chicago: Henry Regnery Co.

Avila, Charles. 1983. *Ownership: Early Christian Teaching*. Maryknoll, N.Y.: Orbis.

Bahr, Howard. 1973. *Skid Row: An Introduction to Disaffiliation*. New York: Oxford University Press.

Bailey, Roy, and Mike Brake, eds. 1975. *Radical Social Work*. New York: Pantheon.

Bau, Ignatius. 1986. *This Ground is Holy: Church Sanctuary and Central American Refugees*. New York: Paulist.

Bell, Inge Powell. 1968. *CORE and the Strategy of Nonviolence*. New York: Random House.

Bellah, Robert, Richard Madsen, William Sullivan, Ann Swidler, and Steven Tipton. 1985. *Habits of the Heart: Individualism and Commitment in American Life*. Berkeley: University of California Press.

Bendix, Reinhard. 1962. *Max Weber: An Intellectual Portrait*. Garden City, N.Y.: Anchor.

Benedict, St. 1975. *The Rule of St. Benedict*. Anthony C. Meisel and M. L. del Mastro, eds. Garden City, N.Y.: Image.

Berdyaev, Nikolai. 1944. *Slavery and Freedom*. New York: Scribners.

———. 1960. *The Destiny of Man*. New York: Harper.

Berger, Bennett. 1981. *The Survival of a Counterculture*. Berkeley: University of California Press.

Bishop, Jonathan. 1982. *The Covenant: A Reading*. Springfield, Ill.: Templegate.

Blau, Peter. 1964. *Exchange and Power in Social Life*. New York: John Wiley and Sons.

Blumer, Herbert. 1969. *Symbolic Interactionism*. Englewood Cliffs, N.J.: Prentice-Hall.

Bodley, John. 1983. *Anthropology and Contemporary Human Problems*. 2nd ed. Palo Alto, Calif.: Mayfield.

Bogdan, Robert, and Steven Taylor. 1989. "Relationships with Severely Disabled People: The Social Construction of Humanness." *Social Problems* 36: 135–48.

Bonet-Maury, G. 1925. "Hospitality: Christian." *Encyclopedia of Religion and Ethics*. Vol. 7. New York: Charles Scribner's Sons.

Bornkamm, Gunther. 1969. *Early Christian Experience*. New York: Harper and Row.

Brubaker, Rogers. 1984. *The Limits of Rationality: An Essay on the Social and Moral Thought of Max Weber*. London: Allen and Unwin.

Campbell, Donald T. 1979. "Assessing the Impact of Planned Social Change." *Evaluation and Program Planning* 2: 67–90.

Cantin, Eileen. 1973. *Mounier: A Personalist View of History*. New York: Paulist.

Cassilly, Francis. 1926. *Religion: Doctrine and Practice*. Chicago: Loyola University Press.

Central Intelligence Agency. 1985. *Psychological Operations in Guerrilla Warfare*. New York: Vintage.

Chamberlin, Judy. 1978. *On Our Own: Patient-Controlled Alternatives to the Mental Health System*. New York: McGraw-Hill.

Coffin, Lorane D. 1988. "Hospitality: An Orientation for Benedictine Spirituality." *American Benedictine Review* 39 (no. 1): 50–71.

Cogley, John. 1976. *A Canterbury Tale: Experiences and Reflections, 1916–1976*. New York: Seabury.

Coles, Robert. 1987. *Dorothy Day: A Radical Devotion*. Reading, Mass.: Addison-Wesley.

Coles, Robert, and Jon Erikson. 1973. *A Spectacle Unto the World: The Catholic Worker Movement*. New York: Viking.

Connolly, Bob, and Robin Anderson. 1987. *First Contact*. New York: Penguin.

Conrad, Peter, and Joseph Schneider. 1978. *Deviance and Medicalization: From Badness to Sickness*. St. Louis: Mosby.

Coser, Lewis. 1956. *The Functions of Social Conflict*. New York: Free Press.

Coy, Patrick, ed. 1988. *A Revolution of the Heart*. Philadelphia: Temple University Press.

Cullen, Mike, and Don Ranly. 1972. *A Time to Dance*. Celina, Ohio: Messenger Press.

Davidson, H. R. 1964. *Gods and Myths of Northern Europe*. Baltimore: Penguin.

Day, Dorothy. 1939. *House of Hospitality*. New York: Sheed and Ward.

——— . 1952. *The Long Loneliness*. New York: Harper.

——— . 1963. *Loaves and Fishes*. New York: Harper.

——— . 1970. *Meditations*. Stanley Visnewski, ed. New York: Paulist.

————. 1983. *By Little and Little: The Selected Writings of Dorothy Day*. Robert Ellsberg, ed. New York: Alfred A. Knopf.

Dietrich, Jeff. 1983. *The Reluctant Resister*. Greensboro, N.C.: Unicorn Press.

Dostoyevsky, Fyodor. 1950. *The Brothers Karamazov*. New York: Modern Library.

Drass, Kriss, and Howard Spencer. 1987. "Accounting for Pre-Sentencing Recommendations: Typologies and Probation Officers' Theory of Office." *Social Problems* 34 (no. 3): 277–93.

Duby, Georges. 1988. "Introduction." *A History of Private Life*. Vol. 2: *Revelations of the Medieval World*. Georges Duby, ed. Cambridge, Mass.: Belknap Press of Harvard University Press.

Duby, Georges, Dominique Barthelemy, and Charles de La Rociere. 1988. "Portraits." *A History of Private Life*, Vol. 2: *Revelations of the Medieval World*. Georges Duby, ed. Cambridge, Mass.: Belknap Press of Harvard University Press.

Durkheim, Emile. 1915. *The Elementary Forms of the Religious Life*. New York: Free Press.

————. 1958. *Professional Ethics and Civic Morals*. Glencoe, Ill.: Free Press.

Ellis, Marc. 1978. *A Year at the Catholic Worker*. New York: Paulist.

————. 1981. *Peter Maurin: Prophet in the Twentieth Century*. New York: Paulist.

Ellul, Jacques. 1964. *The Technological Society*. New York: Vintage.

English, Jack. 1948. "Personalism and the Apostolate." *The Catholic Worker*, June.

Erdoes, Richard, and Alfonso Ortiz. 1984. *American Indian Myths and Legends*. New York: Pantheon.

Erikson, Kai. 1976. *Everything in Its Path*. New York: Simon and Shuster.

Filson, Floyd. 1939. "The Significance of the Early House Churches." *Journal of Biblical Literature* 58: 105–12.

Firth, Raymond. 1959. *Social Change in Tikopia*. London: George Allen and Unwin.

Forest, Jim. 1986. *Love is the Measure*. New York: Paulist.

Frazer, James. 1911. *The Golden Bough*. 3rd ed. Part 2: "Taboo and the Perils of the Soul." London: Macmillan.

Freidson, Eliot. 1970. *Professional Dominance*. Chicago: Aldine.

Furfey, Paul Hanley. 1969. *The Morality Gap*. New York: Macmillan.

Galper, Jeffrey. 1975. *The Politics of Social Services*. Englewood Cliffs, N.J.: Prentice-Hall.

Gandhi, Mohandas K. 1957. *An Autobiography: The Story of My Experiments with Truth*. Boston: Beacon.

Garfinkel, Harold. 1967. *Studies in Ethnomethodology*. Englewood Cliffs, N.J.: Prentice-Hall.

Garvey, Michael. 1978. *Confessions of a Catholic Worker*. Chicago: Thomas More Press.

Gerig, J. L. 1925. "Hospitality: Celtic." *Encyclopedia of Religion and Ethics.* Vol. 7. New York: Charles Scribner's Sons.

Glaser, Barney, and Anselm Strauss. 1967. *The Discovery of Grounded Theory: Strategies for Qualitative Research.* New York: Aldine.

Goffman, Erving. 1959. *The Presentation of Self in Everyday Life.* Garden City, N.Y.: Doubleday.

———. 1961. *Asylums.* Garden City, N.Y.: Anchor.

Golden, Remy, and Michael McConnell. 1986. *Sanctuary: The New Underground Railroad.* Maryknoll, N.Y.: Orbis.

Goodin, Robert. 1985. *Protecting the Vulnerable.* Chicago: University of Chicago Press.

Grant, Robert. 1977. *Early Christianity and Society.* San Francisco: Harper and Row.

Greer, Rowan A. 1974. "Hospitality in the First Five Centuries of the Church." *Monastic Studies.* No. 10: *On Hospitality and Other Matters.* Pine City, N.Y.: Mt. Saviour Monastery.

Greifer, Julian L. 1945. "Attitudes to the Stranger: A Study of the Attitudes of Primitive Society and Early Hebrew Culture." *American Sociological Review* 10: 739–45.

Gross, Leonard. 1982. *The Last Jews in Berlin.* Toronto: Bantam.

Gubrium, Jaber. 1975. *Living and Dying at Murray Manor.* New York: St. Martin's Press.

Guyot, Gilmore. 1947. *Scriptural References for the Baltimore Catechism: The Biblical Basis for Catholic Beliefs.* New York: Joseph F. Wagner.

Haarhoff, Theodore. 1948. *The Stranger at the Gate.* Oxford: Basil Blackwell.

Hallie, Philip. 1979. *Lest Innocent Blood Be Shed.* New York: Harper and Row.

Hamilton-Grierson, P. J. 1925. "Strangers." *Encyclopedia of Religion and Ethics.* Vol. 11. New York: Charles Scribner's Sons.

———. 1980 [1903]. "The Silent Trade." *Research in Economic Anthropology.* Vol. 3. George Dalton, ed. Greenwich, Conn.: JAI Press.

Harrington, Michael. 1963. *The Other America.* Baltimore: Penguin.

———. 1977. *The Vast Majority: A Journey to the World's Poor.* New York: Simon and Schuster.

———. 1984. *The New American Poverty.* New York: Penguin.

Hasenfeld, Yeheskel. 1977. "People Processing Organizations: An Exchange Approach." *Human Service Organizations.* Yeheskel Hasenfeld and Richard English, eds. Ann Arbor: University of Michigan Press.

Heal, Felicity. 1982. "The Archbishops of Canterbury and the Practice of Hospitality." *Journal of Ecclesiastical History* 33: 544–63.

Hellman, John. 1980–1981. "John Paul II and the Personalist Movement." *Cross Currents* (Winter): 409–19.

———. 1981. *Emmanuel Mounier and the New Catholic Left, 1930–1950.* Toronto: University of Toronto Press.

Hengel, Martin. 1974. *Property and Riches in the Early Church.* Philadelphia: Fortress.

Hennacy, Ammon. 1954. "Christianity and Maxism [sic]." *The Catholic Worker*, September.

———. 1965. *The Book of Ammon*. Salt Lake City: Hennacy.

———. 1970. *The One-Man Revolution in America*. Salt Lake City: Hennacy.

Henry, Jules. 1951. "The Economics of Pilaga Food Distribution." *American Anthropologist* 53: 187–219.

Hocart, Arthur Maurice. [1955?] "The Divinity of the Guest." *The Life-Giving Myth and Other Essays*. Ch. 8. New York: Grove Press.

Homans, George. 1961. *Social Behavior: Its Elementary Forms*. New York: Harcourt, Brace, and World.

Hope, Marjorie, and James Young. 1986. *The Faces of Homelessness*. Lexington, Mass.: Lexington.

Ignatieff, Michael. 1985. *The Needs of Strangers*. New York: Penguin.

Jehenson, Roger. 1973. "A Phenomenological Approach to the Study of the Formal Organization." *Phenomenological Sociology: Issues and Applications*. George Psathas, ed. New York: John Wiley and Sons.

Kaff, Albert. 1988. "Hotel School Course Tells How to Care for Homeless." *Cornell '88*.

Kelly, Delos. 1984. *Deviant Behavior*. 2nd ed. New York: St. Martin's.

Koenig, John. 1985. *New Testament Hospitality*. Philadelphia: Fortress.

———. 1987. "Hospitality." *The Encyclopedia of Religion*. Vol. 7. New York: MacMillan.

Kropotkin, Peter. 1914. *Mutual Aid: A Factor of Evolution*. Boston: Porter Sargent.

———. 1972. *The Conquest of Bread*. New York: New York University Press.

Lang, Claire. 1981. "Good Cases—Bad Cases: Client Selection and Professional Prerogative in a Community Mental Health Center." *Urban Life* 10: 289–309.

Larson, Magali. 1977. *The Rise of Professionalism*. Berkeley, Calif.: University of California Press.

LeBrun, John. 1973. *The Role of the Catholic Worker in American Pacifism, 1933–72*. Ann Arbor, Mich.: University Microfilms.

Levine, Donald. 1985. *The Flight from Ambiguity*. Chicago: University of Chicago Press.

Lifton, Norman. 1981. *Saintliness and Deviance: The Catholic Worker Movement*. Ann Arbor, Mich.: University Microfilms International.

Lindholm, Charles. 1982. *Generosity and Jealousy: The Swat Pukhtun of Northern Pakistan*. New York: Columbia University Press.

Lipsky, Michael. 1980. *Street-Level Bureaucracy: Dilemmas of the Individual in Public Services*. New York: Russell Sage.

Lofland, Lyn H. 1972. *A World of Strangers: Order and Action in Urban Public Space*. New York: Basic Books.

Lubove, Roy. 1977. *The Professional Altruist*. New York: Atheneum.

Lucian. 1962. *Selected Satires of Lucian*. Chicago: Aldine.

MacEoin, Gary, ed. 1985. *Sanctuary*. San Francisco: Harper and Row.

Malherbe, Abraham. 1983. *Social Aspects of Early Christianity*. Philadelphia: Fortress.

Malinowski, Bronislaw. 1961 [1922]. *Argonauts of the Western Pacific*. New York: Dutton.

Marcel, Gabriel. 1950. *The Mystery of Being*. Vols. 1 and 2. South Bend, Ind.: Gateway.

Margoliouth, D. S. 1925. "Hospitality: Arabian." *Encyclopedia of Religion and Ethics*. Vol. 7. New York: Charles Scribner's Sons.

Margolis, Howard. 1982. *Selfishness, Altruism and Rationality: A Theory of Social Choice*. Chicago: University of Chicago Press.

Maritain, Jacques. 1966. *The Person and the Common Good*. South Bend, Ind.: University of Notre Dame Press.

————. 1968. *Integral Humanism*. South Bend, Ind.: University of Notre Dame Press.

————. 1971. *Freedom in the Modern World*. New York: Gordian Press.

Marshall, Daniel. Undated. "Towards a Catholic Worker Vision: A Synopsis of the Easy Essays of Peter Maurin." Photocopy.

Marshall, Lorna. 1961. "Sharing, Talking, and Giving: Relief of Social Tensions among !Kung Bushmen." *Africa: Journal of the International African Institute* (July): 231–49.

Martin, David. 1978. *A General Theory of Secularization*. New York: Harper and Row.

Maurin, Peter. 1977. *Easy Essays*. Chicago: Franciscan Herald Press.

Mauss, Marcel. 1967. *The Gift*. New York: W. W. Norton.

Mayer, Fanny. 1984. *Ancient Tales in Modern Japan*. Bloomington: Indiana University Press.

McCall, Andrew. 1979. *The Medieval Underworld*. London: Hamish Hilton.

Mead, George Herbert. 1934. *Mind, Self, and Society*. Chicago: University of Chicago Press.

Mehan, Hugh, and Houston Wood. 1975. *The Reality of Ethnomethodology*. New York: Wiley.

Merton, Robert. 1968. *Social Theory and Social Structure*. New York: Free Press.

Michalowski, Raymond. 1985. *Order, Law, and Crime*. New York: Random House.

Miller, William. 1973. *A Harsh and Dreadful Love: Dorothy Day and the Catholic Worker Movement*. Garden City, N.Y.: Doubleday Image Books.

————. 1982. *Dorothy Day: A Biography*. San Francisco: Harper and Row.

Mirowsky, John, and Catherine Ross. 1989. "Psychiatric Diagnosis as Reified Measurement." *Journal of Health and Social Behavior* 30: 11–25.

Moore, Barrington, Jr. 1986. "Privacy." *Society* 22 (no. 4): 17–27.

Morgan, Lewis Henry. 1909. "Hospitality of the American Indians." *Source Book for Social Origins*. W. I. Thomas, ed. Chicago: University of Chicago Press.

————. 1922. *League of the Iroquois*. Secaucus, N.J.: Citadel Press.

Mounier, Emmanuel. 1938. *A Personalist Manifesto.* London: Longmans, Green, and Co.

———. 1952. *Personalism.* South Bend, Ind.: University of Notre Dame Press.

———. 1954. *Be Not Afraid: Studies in Personalist Sociology.* New York: Harper.

Moynihan, Kenneth. 1976. "The Door Is Always Open." *Worcester,* November: 21–24.

Murray, Alexander. 1962. *Manual of Mythology.* New York: Tudor Publishing Co.

Murray, Charles. 1984. *Losing Ground: American Social Policy, 1950–1980* New York: Basic.

Murray, Harry. 1986. "Time in the Streets." *Housing the Homeless.* Jon Erickson and Charles Wilhelm, eds. New Brunswick, N.J.: Rutgers Center for Urban Policy Research.

———. 1987. *Isaiah's Fast: The Practice of Hospitality in the Catholic Worker Movement.* Ann Arbor, Mich.: University Microfilms International.

Naughton, Irene. 1946. "Hospitality." *Catholic Worker,* October.

Newman, Katherine. 1980. "Incipient Bureaucracy: The Development of Hierarchies in Egalitarian Organizations." *Hierarchy and Society.* Gerald Britan and Ronald Cohen, eds. Philadelphia: Institute for the Study of Human Issues.

Nouwen, Henri. 1972. "Education to Ministry." *Theological Education* 9: 48–57.

———. 1975. *Reaching Out.* Garden City, N.Y.: Doubleday.

Novitsky, Anthony. 1976. *The Ideological Development of Peter Maurin's Green Revolution.* Ann Arbor, Mich.: University Microfilms.

Ogletree, Thomas W. 1985. *Hospitality to the Stranger.* Philadelphia: Fortress.

Ovid. 1958. *The Metamorphoses.* New York: New American Library.

Palmer, Parker. 1985. *The Company of Strangers.* New York: Crossroad.

Parsons, Talcott. 1951. *The Social System.* New York: Free Press.

Peyrot, Mark. 1982. "Caseload Management: Choosing Suitable Clients in a Community Health Clinic Agency." *Social Problems* 30: 157–67.

Piehl, Mel. 1982. *Breaking Bread: The Catholic Worker and the Origin of Catholic Radicalism in America.* Philadelphia: Temple University Press.

Polanyi, Karl, Conrad Arensberg, and Harry Pearson. 1957. *Trade and Market in the Early Empires.* New York: Free Press.

Price, John A. 1975. "Sharing: The Integration of Intimate Economies." *Anthropologica* 17: 3–27.

———. 1980. "On Silent Trade." *Research in Economic Anthropology.* Vol. 3. George Dalton, ed. Greenwich, Conn.: JAI Press.

Prottas, Jeffrey. 1979. *People-Processing: The Street-Level Bureaucrat in Public Service Bureaucracies.* Lexington, Mass.: D. C. Heath.

Pryor, Frederic L. 1977. *The Origins of the Economy.* New York: Academic Press.

Pryor, Frederic L., and Nelson H. Graburn. 1980. "The Myth of Reciprocity." *Social Exchange: Advances in Theory and Research.* Kenneth J. Gergen,

Martin S. Greenberg, and Richard H. Willis, eds. New York: Plenum Press.

Rader, Victoria. 1986. *Signal Through the Flame: Mitch Snyder and America's Homeless.* Kansas City, Mo.: Sheed and Ward.

Ramsey, Boniface, OP. 1982. "Almsgiving in the Latin Church: The Late Fourth and Early Fifth Centuries." *Theological Studies* 43: 226–59.

Richardson, Cyril, ed. 1970. *Early Christian Fathers.* New York: Macmillan.

Riddle, Donald. 1938. "Early Christian Hospitality: A Factor in the Gospel Transmission." *Journal of Biblical Literature* 57: 141–54.

Roberts, Nancy L. 1984. *Dorothy Day and the "Catholic Worker."* Albany: SUNY Albany Press.

Rosenhan, David. 1975. "On Being Sane in Insane Places." *Labeling Madness.* Thomas Scheff, ed. Englewood Cliffs, N.J.: Prentice-Hall.

Roth, Julius. 1977. "Some Contingencies of the Moral Evaluation and Control of Clientele: The Case of the Hospital Emergency Service." *Human Service Organizations.* Yeheskel Hasenfeld and Richard English, eds. Ann Arbor: University of Michigan Press.

Rothman, David. 1971. *The Discovery of the Asylum.* Boston: Little, Brown.

Rothschild-Whitt, Joyce. 1979. "The Collectivist Organization." *American Sociological Review* 44 (no. 4): 509–27.

Rouche, Michel. 1987. "The Early Middle Ages in the West." *A History of Private Life.* Vol. 1: *From Pagan Rome to Byzantium.* Paul Veyne, ed. Cambridge, Mass.: Belknap Press of Harvard University Press.

Rubenstein, Richard. 1975. *The Cunning of History: The Holocaust and the American Future.* New York: Harper.

Rubington, Earl, and Martin S. Weinberg. 1987. *Deviance: The Interactionist Perspective.* 5th ed. New York: Macmillan.

Ryan, John, SJ. 1972. *Irish Monasticism.* Ithaca, N.Y.: Cornell University Press.

Sahlins, Marshall. 1972. *Stone Age Economics.* New York: Aldine.

Sandberg, John. 1979. *The Eschatological Ethic of the Catholic Worker.* Ann Arbor, Mich.: University Microfilms.

Scheff, Thomas. 1965. "Typification in the Diagnostic Practices of Rehabilitation Agencies." *Sociology and Rehabilitation.* Marvin Sussman, ed. Washington, D.C.: American Sociological Association.

Scheler, Max. 1973. *Formalism in Ethics and Non-Formal Ethics of Values.* Evanston, Ill.: Northwestern University Press.

Schutz, Alfred. 1962. *Collected Papers.* Vol. 1: *The Problem of Social Reality.* Maurice Natanson, ed. The Hague: Martinus Nijhoff.

———. 1967. *The Phenomenology of the Social World.* Evanston, Ill.: Northwestern University Press.

———. 1970. *On Phenomenology and Social Relations.* Helmut R. Wagner, ed. Chicago: University of Chicago Press.

———. 1971. *Collected Papers. Vol. 2: Studies in Social Theory.* Arvid Broderson, ed. The Hague: Martinus Nijhoff.

Schutz, Alfred, and Thomas Luckmann. 1973. *The Structures of the Life-World.* Evanston, Ill.: Northwestern University Press.

Scott, Robert. 1981. *The Making of Blind Men.* New Brunswick, N.J.: Transaction Press.

Selznick, Philip. 1966. *TVA and the Grass Roots.* New York: Harper and Row.

Sennett, Richard. 1974. *The Fall of Public Man.* New York: Vintage.

Sharp, Gene. 1980. *Social Power and Political Freedom.* Boston: Porter Sargent.

Sheehan, Arthur. 1959. *Peter Maurin: Gay Believer.* Garden City, N.Y.: Hanover House.

Simmel, Georg. 1950. *The Sociology of Georg Simmel.* Kurt Wolff, ed. New York: Free Press.

———. 1955. *Conflict and the Web of Group-Affiliations.* Kurt Wolff and Reinhard Bendix, trans. New York: Free Press.

———. 1971. *On Individuality and Social Forms.* Donald Levine, ed. Chicago: University of Chicago Press.

Simon, Herbert. 1945. *Administrative Behavior.* New York: Free Press.

Spradley, James. 1972. *Guests Never Leave Hungry: The Autobiography of James Sewid, a Kwakiutal Indian.* Montreal: McGill-Queen's University Press.

Stack, Carol. 1974. *All Our Kin.* New York: Harper.

Stanley, Manfred. 1978. *The Technological Conscience: Survival and Dignity in an Age of Expertise.* Chicago: University of Chicago Press.

Stark, Werner. 1983. *The Social Bond: An Investigation into the Bases of Law-abidingness.* Vol. 4: *Ethos and Religion.* New York: Fordham University Press.

Starr, Paul. 1982. *The Social Transformation of American Medicine.* New York: Basic Books.

Stock, St. G. 1925. "Hospitality: Greek and Roman." *Encyclopedia of Religion and Ethics.* Vol. 7. New York: Charles Scribner's Sons.

Strauss, Anselm. 1978. *Negotiations.* San Francisco: Jossey-Bass.

Sudnow, David. 1973. "Normal Crimes." *Deviance: The Interactionist Approach.* Earl Rubington and Martin Weinberg, eds. 2nd ed. New York: Macmillan.

Szasz, Thomas. 1974. *The Myth of Mental Illness.* New York: Harper and Row.

Taylor, Steven, and Robert Bogdan. 1984. *Introduction to Qualitative Research Methods.* New York: Wiley.

Tec, Nechama. 1986. *When Light Pierced the Darkness: Christian Rescue of Jews in Nazi-Occupied Poland.* New York: Oxford University Press.

Theissen, Gerd. 1977. *Sociology of Early Palestinian Christianity.* Philadelphia: Fortress.

———. 1982. *The Social Setting of Pauline Christianity: Essays on Corinth.* Philadelphia: Fortress.

Thibaut, John, and Harold Kelley. 1959. *The Social Psychology of Groups.* New York: John Wiley and Sons.

Thiesen, Jerome. 1976. "Hospitality: A Model of Local Ecumenical Involvement." *Dialog* 15: 309–13.

Thomas, Elizabeth Marshall. 1959. *The Harmless People*. New York: Knopf.

Titmuss, Richard. 1971. *The Gift Relationship*. New York: Vintage.

Tolstoy, Leo. 1905. *The Kingdom of God Is Within You*. New York: Noonday Press of Farrar, Straus and Giroux.

————. 1970. *The Law of Love and the Law of Violence*. New York: Holt, Rinehart, and Winston.

Torrey, E. Fuller. 1988. *Nowhere to Go: The Tragic Odyssey of the Homeless Mentally Ill*. New York: Harper and Row.

Trattner, Walter. 1974. *From Poor Law to Welfare State*. New York: Free Press.

Trolander, Judith Ann. 1975. *Settlement Houses and the Great Depression*. Detroit: Wayne State University Press.

Turnbull, Colin M. 1972. *The Mountain People*. New York: Simon and Schuster.

Turner, Roy, ed. 1974. *Ethnomethodology*. Baltimore: Penguin.

Van Gennep, Arnold. 1960. *The Rites of Passage*. Chicago: University of Chicago Press.

Vishnewski, Stanley. 1984. *Wings of the Dawn*. New York: Catholic Worker.

Walsh, R. P., *et al.* 1937. "House of Hospitality." *Blackfriars* 18: 935–38.

Walsh, William, SJ, and John Langan, SJ. 1977. "Patristic Social Consciousness—The Church and the Poor." *The Faith That Does Justice*. John Haughey, ed. New York: Paulist Press.

Walzer, Michael. 1983. *Spheres of Justice*. New York: Basic Books.

Weber, Max. 1949. *The Methodology of the Social Sciences*. New York: Free Press.

————. 1978. *Economy and Society*. Berkeley: University of California Press.

————. 1985. *The Protestant Ethic and the Spirit of Capitalism*. London: Unwin.

White, Arthur. 1968. *Palaces of the People: A Social History of Commercial Hospitality*. London: Rap and Whiting.

Wiley, Juniper. 1988. "Role Blurring in a Holistic Therapeutic Community." *Journal of Contemporary Ethnography* 17: 3–39.

Winch, Peter. 1958. *The Idea of a Social Science and its Relation to Philosophy*. London: Routledge and Kegan Paul.

Wink, Walter. 1986. *Unmasking the Powers: The Invisible Forces That Determine Human Existence*. Philadelphia: Fortress.

Winnick, Charles. 1956. *Dictionary of Anthropology*. New York: Philosophical Library.

Winzen, Damasus. 1974. "Conference on the Reception of Guests." *Monastic Studies*. No. 10: *On Hospitality and Other Matters*. Pine City, N.Y.: Mt. Saviour Monastery.

Wiseman, Jacqueline. 1970. *Stations of the Lost: The Treatment of Skid Row Alcoholics*. Chicago: University of Chicago Press.

Wood, Margaret Mary. 1934. *The Stranger: A Study in Social Relationships*. Studies in History, Economics, and Public Law. No. 399. New York: Columbia University Press.

Wyman, David. 1984. *The Abandonment of the Jews*. New York: Pantheon.

Zablocki, Benjamin. 1971. *The Joyful Community*. Baltimore: Penguin.

Index

Addams, Jane, 23, 200. *See also* Hull House; Settlement House movement
Advocacy, 78–79, 107–108, 136, 200
Agrarianism, 5–6, 51, 77, 80–81, 166
Agronomic universities. *See* Agrarianism
Almsgiving, 31, 41
Altruism, 217, 258–259, 267
Ambassadors of God, 51–52, 54, 70, 128
Ambrose, Saint, 41
Anarchism, 5–6, 15, 68–69, 77–79, 91, 92, 95, 143, 162–163, 166, 178, 214, 250
Anderson, Robin, 261
Aronica, Michele, 91, 262, 264
Augustine, Saint, 43, 263
Avila, Charles, 42
Axes of variation, 207

Backstage behavior, 86, 91
Bahr, Howard, 250
Bailey, Roy, 82
Basil the Great, 42
Bau, Ignatius, 16
Bell, Inge Powell, 216
Bellah, Robert, 259
Bendix, Reinhard, 4
Benedict, Saint, 44
Berdyaev, Nikolai, 67, 68–69, 212, 258, 263
Berger, Bennett, 15
Bethany House (Rochester), 131, 138
Bishop, Jonathan, 130
Blau, Peter, 34
Blumer, Herbert, 83, 256, 265

Bodley, John, 29, 262
Bogdan, Robert, 83, 257, 264
Bonet-Maury, G., 44
Bornkamm, Gunther, 35
Brake, Mike, 82
Brothers Karamazov, 71–72
Brubaker, Rogers, 263
Bruderhoff community, 15
Buber, Martin, 5, 67, 224. *See also* I–Thou relation
Bureaucracy, 61, 71, 116, 128, 133, 211, 225, 230–236, 249, 250–252, 254, 257, 267
Bureaucratization, 21–24, 254

Campbell, Donald, 255
Canterbury, archbishops of, 47
Cantin, Eileen, 263
Carry It On (newsletter of House of Ammon), 164
Cassilly, Francis, 74
Categorization, 4, 109, 148, 212, 230–236, 240–243, 244, 245, 256, 264, 266–267
Catholic Worker, 6, 49, 50, 55, 56, 58, 59, 62, 63, 66, 71, 90, 113, 114
Catholic Worker farm (Tivoli), 90, 165
Catholic Worker Houses of Hospitality. *See* Houses of Hospitality
Catholic Worker movement: and agrarianism, 81; and anarchism, 77–79; and hospitality, 49–57, 62–66, 81–83, 212–215, 217–230, 243–249; and nonviolence, 80–81; and personal-

Catholic Worker movement (*cont.*)
ism, 67–74, 212–230, 248–249; and
voluntary poverty, 79–80; and Works
of Mercy, 74–77; history of, 5–6,
49–66; implications of, for homeless,
250–252; social implications of, 252–
259. *See also* Day, Dorothy; Maurin,
Peter; Mustard Seed; Personalism;
St. Joseph's House (New York City);
St. Joseph's House (Rochester)
Catholics Against Nuclear Arms (CANA),
158–160
Central Intelligence Agency, 18
Chamberlin, Judy, 251
Charity, 45, 55, 65, 76. *See also* Hospi-
tality; Works of Mercy
Chavez, Cesar, 6
Chicago, 59, 65. *See also* St. Francis's
House
Christ room, 42–43, 53, 72
Chrysologus, Peter, 41
Coalition for the Homeless, 250
Cochiti Indians, 26
Coffin, Lorane, 44
Coles, Robert, 76, 253, 255, 259,
262, 263
Collectivist organizations, 204
Commensality, 31, 35–36
Community, 154–156, 181–183, 186–
187, 202, 208–210, 243
Community for Creative Nonvio-
lence, 250
Connolly, Bob, 261
Conrad, Peter, 4, 21
Corinthians, First Letter to, 35, 36
Cornell University, 3, 7
Coser, Lewis, 178
Coy, Patrick, 262
Cure of Ars. *See* Vianney, Jean Baptiste

Daily Worker, 5
Davidson, H. R., 25
Day, Dorothy, 13, 55, 59, 87, 124, 178,
200, 253, 255, 259, 262–263; and
foundation of Catholic Worker, 5, 6,
49–51, 62–66; and House of Ammon,
163, 164, 165, 168; and personalism,
67, 69–73, 215, 223; and St. Joseph's
House (New York City), 8, 90, 91, 96,

98, 169, 224; and St. Joseph's House
(Rochester), 127–129; on Works of
Mercy, 75–77; on pacifism, 66, 75,
80–81, 129; on voluntary poverty,
79–80
"Death of Peregrinus," 39–40
Decision making: at House of Ammon,
163; at Mustard Seed, 170, 174–75,
177–183, 202–208; at St. Joseph's
House (New York City), 91–95; at
St. Joseph's House (Rochester), 132–
134
Dempsey, Father Timothy, 58–59
Depersonalization, 43, 223, 257
Didache, 30, 40–41
Doherty, Baroness Catherine de Hueck,
59, 171
Dostoevsky, Fyodor, 71–72
Drass, Kriss, 231, 235
DSM-III (Diagnostic and Statistical
Manual of the APA), 241, 267
Duby, Georges, 18, 46
Durkheim, Emile, 17, 263, 267

Egalitarianism, 88–90, 116–117, 118,
155, 163, 203, 208, 226–230, 246–
248
Elijah, 26
Ellis, Marc, 262, 263
Ellis Island, 57
Ellul, Jacques, 21, 22, 67
Emmaus, 27
Enchiridion, 263
Erdoes, Richard, 26
Erikson, Jon, 262
Erikson, Kai, 207
Esprit, 67
Eucharist, 35–36, 81, 164, 199
Eyster, James, 3

Filson, Floyd, 37
Forest, Jim, 263
*Formalism in Ethics and Non-formal Ethics
of Values*, 67
Fourth Lateran Council, 45–46
Frazer, James, 27
Freidson, Eliot, 4
"Friends of the house," 99, 228
Friendship House, 59–60

Functionary types, 239–242, 245. *See also* Typification, phenomenology of

Furfey, Paul Hanley, 262

Galper, Jeffrey, 82
Gandhi, Mohandas K., 79
Garvey, Michael, 117
Gerig, J. L., 46
Goal displacement and organizational maintenance, 254–255
Goffman, Erving, 91, 226, 233, 244–245
Golden, Remy, 16
Goodin, Robert, 14, 47
Graburn, Nelson, 29
Grant, Robert, 42
Gratitude, 35, 44, 76, 106
Greer, Rowan, 44
Greifer, Julian, 262
Griffin, John, 62
Gross, Leonard, 15
Gubrium, Jaber, 216–217
Guest: as Christ, 12, 42–43, 63, 70–71, 223; as supernatural, 18; social role of, 18–20, 71, 214, 246–248, 250. *See also* Poor, as Christ
Gumbleton, Bishop Thomas, 215
Gurswitch, Aaron, 67
Guyot, Gilmore, 263

Haarhoff, Theodore, 30
Habits of the Heart, 259
Hallie, Philip, 15
Hamilton-Grierson, P. J., 27, 262
Harrington, Michael, 6, 90, 223, 265
Hasenfeld, Yeheskel, 5, 231
Heal, Felicity, 45–47
Hebrews, Letter to the, 36
Hellman, John, 263
Hennacy, Ammon, 90
Henry, Jules, 29
Hergenhan, Herman, 60–62
Hocart, Arthur, 25
Holocaust, 15, 257
Homelessness: Catholic Worker response to, 3–6, 74–77, 78–83, 218–230, 243–252; during Great Depression, 57–62; professional response to, 3–5, 82–83, 232, 235, 236. *See also* Mustard Seed; St. Joseph's House (New York City);
St. Joseph's House (Rochester); Unity Kitchen
Hope, Marjorie, 250
Hospitality: ancient Greek, 29–30, 48, 51; ancient Roman, 30; commercial, 17, 30, 52; contrasted with rehabilitation, 20–21, 82–83; early Christian, 25, 30–41, 53; functions of, 14, 28–29; in foraging and horticultural societies, 28–29; in myth, 25–28; involuntary, 18; Irish, 46–47, 48; Islamic, 19, 45, 48, 51; personalist, 4, 9, 19, 49–57, 62–66, 81–83, 212–230, 241, 243–249, 250–252; temporal dimension of, 19, 45, 246; versus building community, 246–248
Host, 18–20, 71, 214, 246–248, 250
House of Ammon (Worcester), 162–169, 178, 185, 209
Houses of Hospitality, 49–57, 62–66. *See also* Bethany House; Martin de Porres Hospice; Matt Talbot House; Mustard Seed; St. Francis's House; St. Joseph's House (New York City); St. Joseph's House (Rochester)
Hull House, 56. *See also* Addams, Jane; Settlement House movement
Hunthausen, Bishop Raymond, 215

Ideal types, 109, 148, 211, 217, 230–231, 234–236, 240–243, 261, 264, 266–267
Ignatieff, Michael, 71
Ignatius, Saint, 7
I–Thou relation, 5, 69, 74, 214, 217, 223–225, 254

James, Letter of, 89
Jehenson, Roger, 236, 265
Jerome, Saint, 41
Jesus, 27, 31–35, 38, 39–40, 63, 66, 69, 70, 71, 75, 76, 77, 79, 80, 89, 123, 253, 262. *See also* Guest, as Christ; Poor, as Christ
John, Second Letter of, 39–40
John, Third Letter of, 38–39
John Chrysostom, Saint, 42
John Paul II, 263
Joseph, Saint, 60

Julian, Emperor, 42
Justice, 76, 255; distributive, 136, 143–144

Kaff, Albert, 3
Kelly, Delos, 231
Kings, First Book of, 26
Koenig, John, 20, 28, 45
Kropotkin, Peter, 255

Labeling theory, 60
Lang, Claire, 234, 265
Langan, John, 42–43
Larson, Magali, 22
Last Judgment, 33, 75–76, 262, 263
Law of imperfect selection, 251
LeBrun, John, 262
LeChambon, 15
Legion of Mary (Rochester), 129
Levine, Donald, 261
Lifton, Norman, 227–228, 262
Lindholm, Charles, 45
Lipsky, Michael, 5, 232–233
Lofland, Lyn, 47
Lubove, Roy, 23
Lucian, 39–40
Luckmann, Thomas, 239, 265, 266
Ludlow, Robert, 78–79
Luke, Gospel of, 31, 32, 33, 34

McCall, Andrew, 46
McConnell, Michael, 16
MacEoin, Gary, 16
Malherbe, Abraham, 37, 38
Malinowski, Bronislaw, 28
Marcel, Gabriel, 5, 67
Margoliouth, D. S., 45
Margolis, Howard, 258
Maritain, Jacques, 67, 263
Mark, Gospel of, 31, 32, 262
Martin, David, 21
Martin de Porres Hospice (D.C.), 128
Maryhouse (New York City), 8, 88, 90, 91, 100, 112–113
Mass. *See* Eucharist
Matt Talbot House (Worcester), 162, 164
Matthew, Gospel of, 31, 32, 33, 34, 75, 262. *See also* Last Judgment

Maurin, Peter, 5, 46, 49–51, 54, 64, 66, 67, 75, 81, 82, 90, 96, 163, 187, 258, 263; Easy Essays of, 51–54, 83, 259
Mauss, Marcel, 28–29
Mayer, Fanny, 27
Mead, George Herbert, 256, 263, 265
Meese, Edwin, 99
Mehan, Hugh, 86
Melita House (Rochester), 131
Merleau-Ponty, Maurice, 67
Merton, Robert, 250
Michalowski, Raymond, 258
Miller, William, 262, 263
Mirowsky, John, 267
Morgan, Lewis Henry, 28
Mounier, Emmanuel, 67–69, 212, 263
Moynihan, Kenneth, 175
Municipal Lodging House (New York City), 52, 59, 60–62, 88, 92
Murray, Alexander, 25
Murray, Charles, 251
Murray, Harry, 13, 87, 261, 262
Mustard Seed (Worcester), 84–85, 86, 160, 222, 229, 230; barring guests at, 218–219; community structure, 181–183, 186–187, 243, 247–248; clothing distribution at, 198–199; division of labor at, 183–184, 248; food distribution at, 188–194, 214; history of, 169–177; my arrival at, 161–162; organization of, 180–186; physical description of, 178–179; schism at, 162, 177–178, 192, 228; shelter at, 194–198; style of hospitality at, 199–201; typifications of people at, 186–188
Mystical Body of Christ, 6, 36

Naughton, Irene, 81
Negotiated order, 92
Negotiations: for shelter, 101–104, 137–141; of roles, 111–113, 134, 150–153, 247–248; of rules, 192, 222–223
Newman, Katherine, 203, 206
Nonviolence, 77, 80–81, 85, 174–175, 197–199, 201. *See also* Pacifism
Normal crimes, 234
Nouwen, Henri, 17, 18, 242, 252
Novitsky, Anthony, 263

Objectification, 22, 68, 69, 71, 225, 247. *See also* Depersonalization
Odysseus, 29
Ogletree, Thomas, 17
"On the house" system, 92–95, 103–104, 118–119, 133, 226, 184–185
Ortiz, Alfonso, 26
Other America, 6, 265
Ovid, 26
Oxford Inn (Syracuse), 13, 141

Pacifism, 5, 66, 75, 80–81, 129. *See also* Nonviolence; Peace movement
Palmer, Parker, 18
Parsons, Talcott, 20–21, 267
Participant observation, 83–87, 192
Paul, Saint, 35
Peace movement, 127, 177–179, 187. *See also* Nonviolence; Pacifism; Peace witness
Peace witness, 156–160. *See also* Nonviolence; Pacifism; Peace movement; Political activism
People-processing organizations, 5, 231, 249
Person as ultimate value, 68–71, 212–213, 217, 218–221. *See also* Personalism
Personal interaction, 69, 74, 214–215, 223–230, 256. *See also* I–Thou relation; Personalism
Personal responsibility, 72–74, 77–78, 95, 198, 201, 206, 213, 217, 221–223, 250. *See also* Personalism
Personal types, 239–245, 265–266. *See also* Typification
Personalism: as means of social change, 215, 265; Catholic Worker, 50, 67–74, 116, 212–230, 248–249; European, 5, 67–71, 73, 212, 263. *See also* Catholic Worker; Person as ultimate value; Personal responsibility
Peter, First Letter of, 36
Peter Claver, Saint, 70
Peyrot, Mark, 234, 265
Phenomenology. *See* Typification
Philemon and Baucis, myth of, 26
Piehl, Mel, 262

Pittsburgh, 65, 111
Political activism, 154. *See also* Nonviolence; Pacifism; Peace movement; Peace witness
Poor: as Christ, 41, 42–43, 70, 166, 223; deserving vs. undeserving, 69–70, 166, 235. *See also* Guest, as Christ; Homelessness
Price, John, 29
Professional service agencies. *See* Social service agencies
Professionalism, 116, 229, 251, 256–257, 259
Professionalization, 3, 21–24, 254
Prottas, Jeffrey, 231–236
Pryor, Frederic, 29

Qualitative methods. *See* Participant observation

Rader, Victoria, 250
Ramsey, Boniface, 41–44, 71
Rationalization, 3–5, 21–24, 254–257
Reciprocity, 29, 44, 48, 76, 86, 112, 130, 183, 199, 200–201, 221–222
Red Cross, 15
Rehabilitation: and typification, 231–236, 249, 265; contrasted with hospitality, 20–21, 82–83, 194, 211, 250–252
Richardson, Cyril, 40–41
Ricouer, Paul, 67
Riddle, Donald, 37
Roberts, Nancy, 6, 262
Rochester, New York, 65. *See also* Bethany House; St. Joseph's House (Rochester)
Romans, Letter to the, 36
Rosebaugh, Larry, 215
Rosenhan, David, 233
Ross, Catherine, 267
Roth, Julius, 235, 236
Rothman, David, 262
Rothschild-Whitt, Joyce, 204, 206
Rouche, Michel, 45
Rubenstein, Richard, 257
Rubington, Earl, 232
Ryan, John, 47

Sahlins, Marshall, 29, 262
St. Benedict's Farm (Rochester), 129
St. Benedict's Farm (Upton, Mass.), 162
St. Francis's House (Chicago), 12
St. Joseph's House (New York City), 88–
    126, 127, 128, 154, 156, 160, 168,
    169, 191, 221, 222, 223, 224, 226,
    229, 265; advocacy at, 107–108; bar-
    ring guests, 219; clothing distribution
    at, 104–106, 119, 198; food distribu-
    tion at, 96–100, 110, 125, 213, 214;
    founding of, 62–65; methods of re-
    stricting demand, 125–126, 211; my
    arrival at, 88–90; my first visit to,
    7–9; organization of, 90–95, 248;
    participant observation methods at,
    84; residents of, 110–111, 121–122;
    shelter at, 100–104, 220; status at,
    116–125; typifications of people at,
    108–116, 147–148
St. Joseph's House (Rochester), 86,
    127–160, 191, 201, 221, 222, 223,
    229, 265; advocacy at, 136, 145–146;
    barring guests at, 219; board of direc-
    tors of, 128, 132–133, 211; clothing
    distribution at, 141–144; food dis-
    tribution at, 134–137; funerals at,
    146; history of, 127–131; ideals of
    community vs. service at, 154–156;
    incorporation of, 128–129; my arrival
    at, 127; organization of, 132–133,
    248; physical description of, 131–132;
    picnics at, 144–145; shelter at, 134,
    137–141; typifications of people at,
    147–153; working vs. helping out at,
    148; workers contrasted with guests
    at, 148, 247–248
St. Peter Claver Society (Rochester), 127
Salvation Army, 55, 128, 172, 176,
    199, 242
Sanctuary movement, 15–16
Sandberg, John, 73–74, 263
Scheff, Thomas, 234–235
Scheler, Max, 67
Schneider, Joseph, 4, 21
Schutz, Alfred, 108, 116, 217, 236–241,
    257, 261, 265, 266, 267
Scott, Llewellyn, 128
Scott, Robert, 23

Selznick, Philip, 216
Seneca Army Depot, 158–159
Settlement House movement, 23
Sharp, Gene, 255
Sheehan, Arthur, 263
Simmel, Georg, 17, 43, 71, 178, 224, 261
Simon, Herbert, 256
Social exchange, 33–35
Social margin, 117, 124
Social-service agencies, 3–5, 11, 21–
    24, 60–62, 71, 82–83, 109, 216–217,
    230–236, 244, 251. *See also* Advocacy;
    Rehabilitation; Social work; Therapy
Social work, 23, 83, 128, 166, 212, 242.
    See also Social service agencies
Spencer, Howard, 231, 235
Spiritual Exercises, 6
Stack, Carol, 200
Stanley, Manfred, 4, 21, 257
Stark, Werner, 47
Starr, Paul, 4
Status, 116–125, 150
Stock, St. G., 29–30
Stranger, 4, 18–19, 25, 47, 194, 261; as
    supernatural, 27–28. *See also* Guest
Strauss, Anselm, 92
Street-level bureaucracy, 5, 231–243
Sudnow, David, 234
Summa Theologica, 74
Swat Pukhtun, 45
Syndicalism, 5
Syracuse, New York, 83, 135, 227, 230.
    See also Oxford Inn; Unity Kitchen
Szasz, Thomas, 4

Taylor, Steven, 83, 257, 264
Tec, Nechama, 17
Technique, 5, 22. *See also* Rationalization
Teresa, Saint, 60, 73
Teresa-Joseph Cooperative, 63, 90
Theissen, Gerd, 35–38, 262
Theory of office, 231
Therapy, 44, 259. *See also* Rehabilitation
They-relation, 237, 266
Thiesen, Jerome, 17
Thomas Aquinas, Saint, 74, 75
Timothy, First Letter to, 36
Titus, Letter to, 36
Torma, Joseph, 160

Torrey, E. Fuller, 251
Training: and hospitality, 72; Catholic Worker, 94–95, 264; professional, 4, 22, 256
Trattner, Walter, 262
Traveler's Aid, 15
Trocme, André, 15
Trolander, Judith, 23
True View Farm (Athol, Mass.), 162
Typification: phenomenology of, 237–243, 265; of persons, 212; in Catholic Worker, 243–246; in Mustard Seed, 186–188; in St. Joseph's House (New York City), 108–116, 147–148; in St. Joseph's House (Rochester), 142, 147–153; in social-service agencies, 230–236, 265. *See also* Functionary types; Personal types

Underground Railroad, 15
Unity Acres (Orwell, N.Y.), 9
Unity Kitchen (Syracuse, N.Y.), 9–14, 82, 83, 98, 134, 147, 218, 219, 220, 242, 265

Van Gennep, Arnold, 262
Vianney, Jean Baptiste, 60
Vietnam: War, 6, 66, 90, 169, 175; veterans, 10, 139, 196
Vincent de Paul, Saint, 76
Violence: in Mustard Seed, 186, 192, 197, 199, 219; in St. Joseph's House (New York City), 114, 223; in St. Joseph's House (Rochester), 147, 148, 265; in Unity Kitchen, 218, 265
Vishnewski, Stanley, 90, 262
Voluntary poverty, 5, 37, 41, 77, 79–80, 132, 163, 166

Walsh, R. O., 265
Walsh, William, 42–43
Walzer, Michael, 17
Weber, Max, 3, 4, 21, 263, 267
Weinberg, Martin, 232
We-relation, 237, 265, 266
White, Arthur, 30
Wiley, Juniper, 265
Winch, Peter, 84
Wink, Walter, 262
Winzen, Damasus, 44
Wiseman, Jacqueline, 117, 221, 233
Wood, Houston, 86
Worcester, Mass., 6–7. *See also* Mustard Seed
Works of Mercy, 6, 67, 74–77, 96, 130, 169, 211, 213, 215, 263
World War II, 6, 15, 66, 111, 129

Young, James, 250

Zablocki, Benjamin, 15
Zeus, 25